GCSE

DESIGN AND TECHNOLOGY

RESISTANT MATERIALS
Practice Papers

Edited by Waleed Aslam

Cambridge IGCSE

Cambridge International Examinations
Cambridge International General Certificate of Secondary Education

CANDIDATE NAME	

CENTRE NUMBER		CANDIDATE NUMBER	

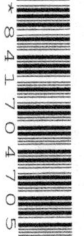

DESIGN AND TECHNOLOGY   0445/32

Paper 3 Resistant Materials   May/June 2014

     1 hour

Candidates answer on the Question Paper.

No Additional Materials are required.

To be taken together with Paper 1 in one session of 2 hours 15 minutes.

READ THESE INSTRUCTIONS FIRST

Write your Centre number, candidate number and name on all the work you hand in.

Write in dark blue or black pen.

You may use an HB pencil for any diagrams, graphs or rough working.

Do not use staples, paper clips, glue or correction fluid.

DO **NOT** WRITE IN ANY BARCODES.

Section A
Answer **all** questions in this section.

Section B
Answer **one** question in this section.

You may use a calculator.

The total of the marks for this paper is 50.
The number of marks is given in brackets [ ] at the end of each question or part question.

For Examiner's Use	
Section A	
Section B	
Total	

This document consists of **16** printed pages.

DC (NF/SW) 93007
© UCLES 2014

CAMBRIDGE International Examinations

[Turn over

Section A

Answer **all** questions in this section.

1 Fig. 1 shows a step ladder.

Fig. 1

(a) Name a suitable material for the step ladder.

.... [1]

(b) Give **one** reason for your choice.

.... [1]

2 Fig. 2 shows a coping saw being used to cut a curved shape in wood.

Fig. 2

Describe **two** checks that would need to be carried out before using the coping saw.

1 ....

2 .... [2]

3 (a) Complete the drawing below to show a hand file.

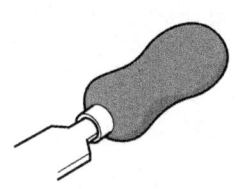

[2]

(b) Label the safe edge on the hand file you have drawn. [1]

4 Complete the table below by naming each tool and giving a specific use.

Tool	Name	Specific use

[4]

5 Fig. 3 shows a milk container made from a plastic.

Fig. 3

(a) State a suitable method of manufacture for the milk container.

....[1]

(b) Give **one** manufacturing reason for the tapered shape of the milk container.

....[1]

(c) Give **one** reason for the fluting on the milk container.

....[1]

6 Show on Fig. 4 **two** important anthropometric measurements that would be used to work out the size of a chair.

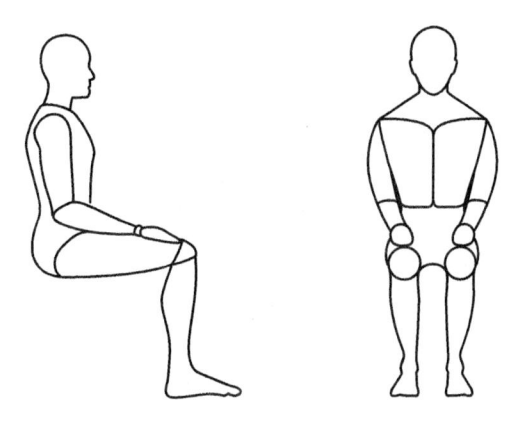

Fig. 4

[2]

7 Fig. 5 shows sheet material with centres for three holes marked out, ready to be drilled.

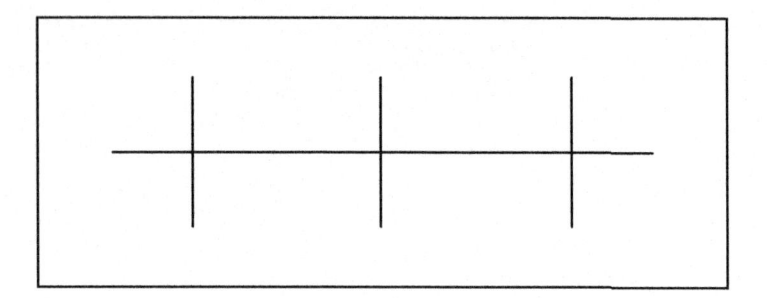

Fig. 5

Name the tool used to draw the lines on the sheet material when made from:

1 mm thick mild steel ....

3 mm thick acrylic ....[2]

8 Fig. 6 shows folding bars.

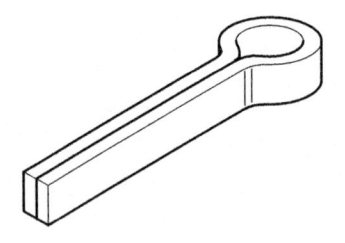

Fig. 6

Add to Fig. 6 to show a piece of sheet metal being bent to shape in the folding bars. [3]

9 Fig. 7 shows a student soldering electronic components.

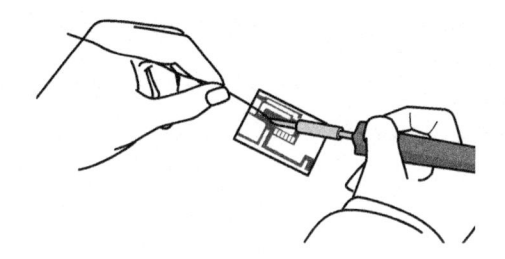

Fig. 7

(a) Name the type of solder being used.

....[1]

(b) Give **one** other example where this type of solder could be used.

....[1]

10 Fig. 8 shows two sun loungers used in a garden.

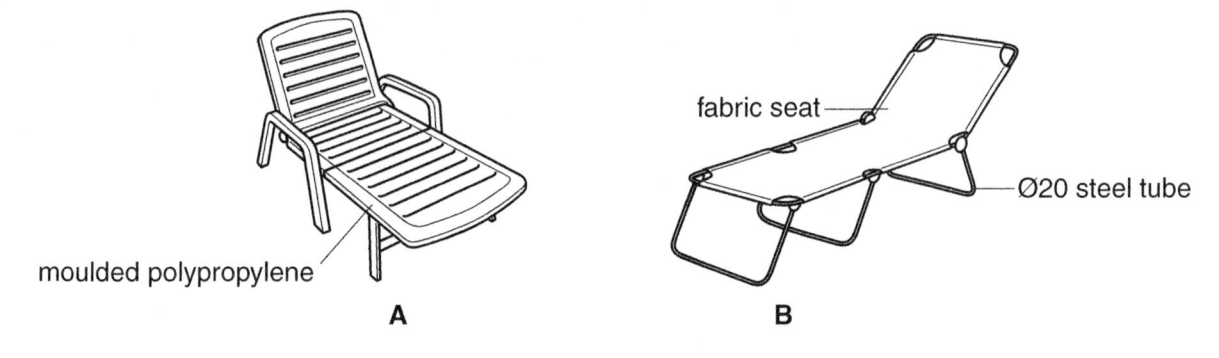

Fig. 8

Give **two** advantages of sun lounger **A** over sun lounger **B**.

1 ....

2 ....[2]

Section B

Answer **one** question from this section.

11 Fig. 9 shows views of a towel holder made from hardwood and non-ferrous metal.

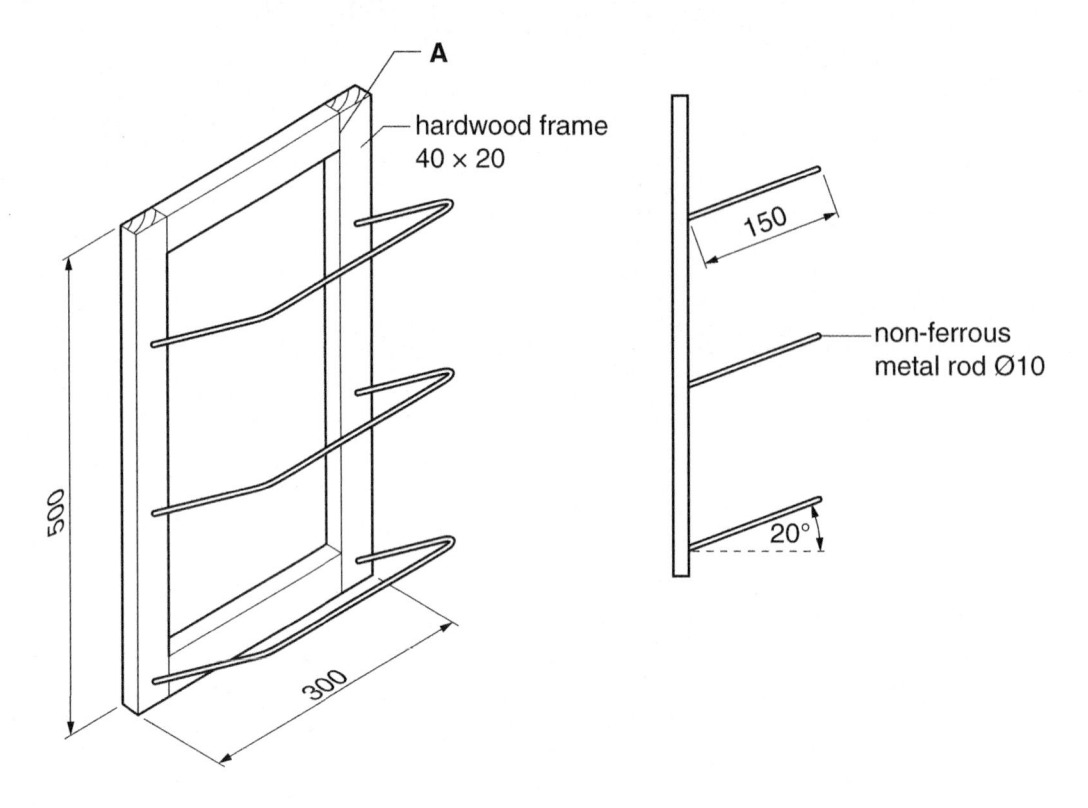

Fig. 9

(a) Sketch and name a suitable corner joint at **A**.

Name of joint..[4]

(b) The four sides of the hardwood frame will be glued and clamped together.

   (i) Name a suitable glue and state the time it will take to set.

   Glue..

   Time to set ....[2]

   (ii) Name the type of cramps used.

   ....[1]

   (iii) Describe **two** checks that would be made when clamping the frame.

   1 ....

   2 ....[2]

(c) Holes will be drilled into the sides of the frame to take the Ø10 metal rod.
The holes will need to be drilled at an angle of 20°.
Use sketches and notes to show how the holes could be drilled safely and accurately using a bench-mounted drill.

[3]

(d) Use sketches and notes to show a bending jig that could be used to make sure that the bends in all **three** metal rods are the same.

[4]

(e) Use sketches and notes to show how the towel holder could be fitted against a wall without screwing through the front of the frame. Include details of sizes and materials used.

[4]

(f) The towel holder could be sold as flat-pack for self-assembly.
Use sketches and notes to show how the design of the hardwood frame and Ø10 metal rods could be modified so that they would fit into the box shown below and sent to customers. Include **all** constructional details.

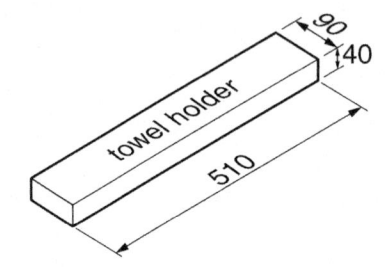

[5]

12 Fig. 10 shows details of a bird table.

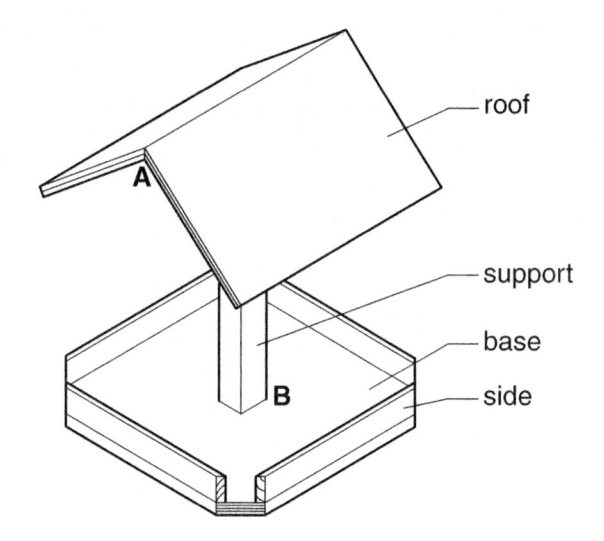

Part	Number required	Length × width × thickness	Material
Base	1	250 × 250 × 12	Plywood
Side	4	200 × 25 × 12	Pine
Support	1	300 × 30 × 30	Pine
Roof	2	250 × 200 × 9	Plywood

Fig. 10

(a) Give **two** benefits of making a card model of the bird table before making it from wood.

1 ....

2 ....[2]

(b) Sketch and name a suitable method of joining the support to the base at **B**.

Name of method ....[4]

(c) The roof is made in two halves that are joined together at **A** as shown in Fig. 10.
Fig. 11 shows details of one half of the roof marked out ready to be shaped to make the joint.

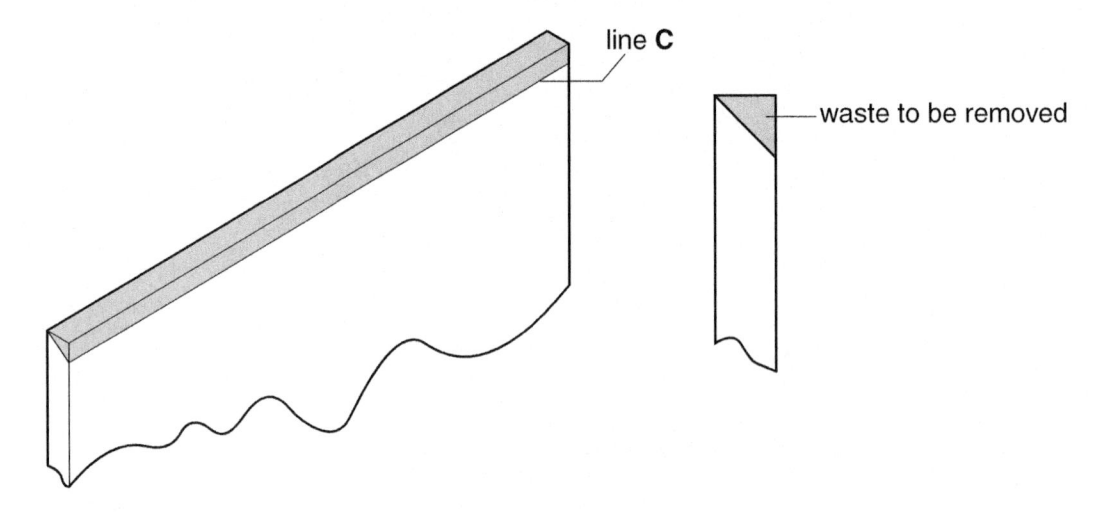

Fig. 11

(i) Give **two** advantages of using a cutting gauge rather than a pencil and try square to mark out line **C**.

1 ....

2 ....[2]

(ii) Use sketches and notes to describe how the waste could be removed.
Name all the tools and equipment used.

[3]

(d) Fig. 12 shows the base of the bird table marked out ready to be cut to shape.

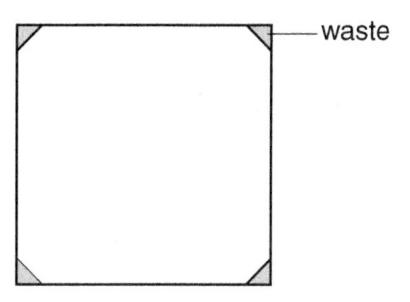

Fig. 12

Complete the table below by naming **one** tool that could be used for each process.

Process	Tools/equipment used
Mark out	
Saw off waste	
Make sawn edges smooth	

[3]

(e) The sides will be glued and nailed to the base.

(i) Name a suitable type of nail that could be used.

....[1]

(ii) Name a suitable glue to join the sides to the base.

....[1]

(iii) Give **one** reason why the sides fitted to the base have gaps in the corners.

....[1]

(f) Describe **two** problems when designing products for outdoor use and how each problem may be overcome.

Problem 1 ....

Overcome ....

Problem 2 ....

Overcome ....[4]

(g) Fig. 13 shows a length of pine used to make the support for the roof.

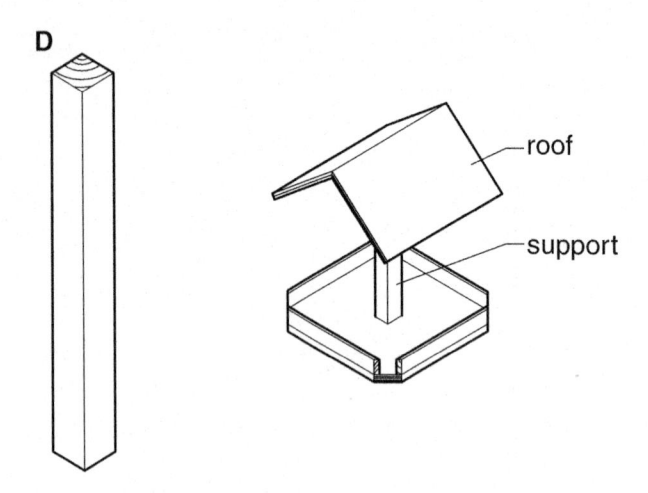

Fig. 13

Modifications will need to be made to the support at end **D** so that it can be joined securely to the roof.
Use sketches and notes to show how the support and roof could be joined permanently.
Include details of materials and constructions used.

[4]

14

13 Fig. 14 shows a combined photo frame and coat hook made from 4mm thick acrylic. It will be wall-mounted in a child's bedroom.

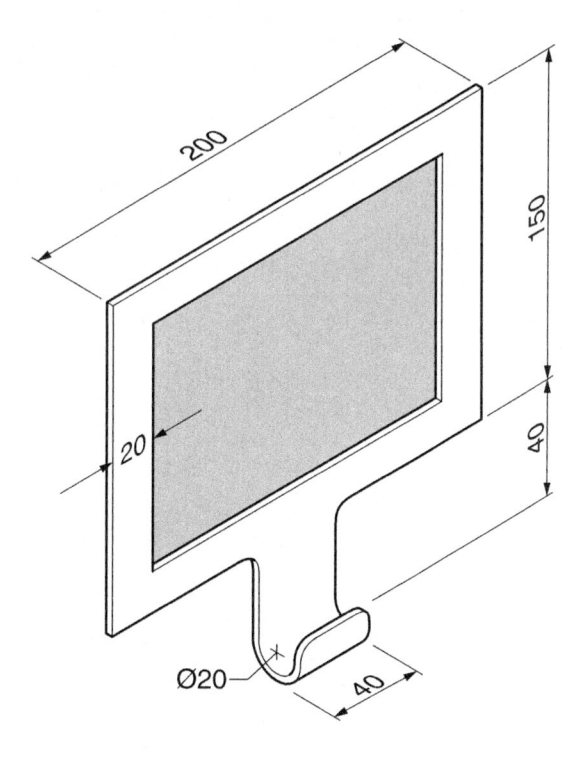

Fig. 14

(a) Fig. 15 shows the acrylic sheet from which the photo frame and coat hook will be cut.

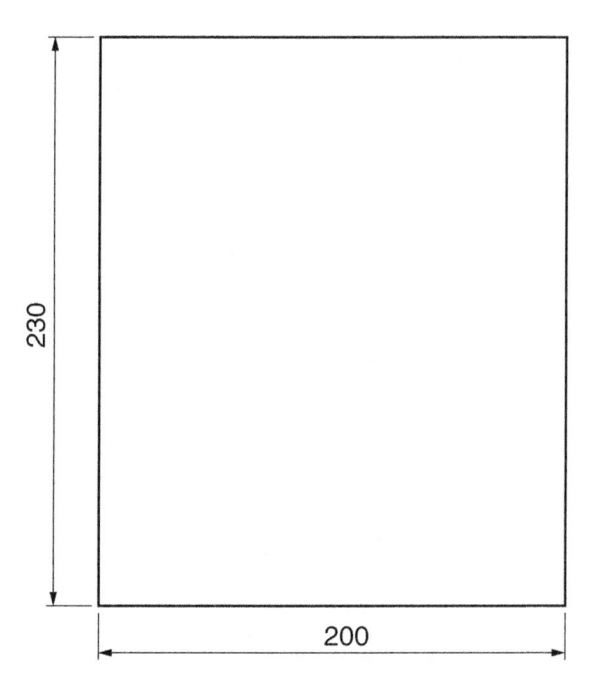

Fig. 15

(i) Draw on Fig. 15 the development (net) of the photo frame and coat hook. Include the cut out shape for the photo. [5]

(ii) Give **two** benefits of using a template to mark out the development (net).

1 ....

2 ....[2]

(b) When working with acrylic there is a danger that it could crack.
Use sketches and notes to show how this can be prevented when:

(i) sawing in a vice;

[3]

(ii) drilling on a bench-mounted drilling machine.

[3]

(c) When working with acrylic sheet, the surface can become easily scratched.
Describe how scratches can be removed from the surface of acrylic sheet.

....

....

....[2]

(d) Use sketches and notes to show how the coat hook would be heated and bent to shape.

[4]

(e) Use sketches and notes to show how a photograph could be supported behind the photo frame. Your design must allow the photo to be replaced quickly and easily.
Include details of sizes and constructions.

[6]

Cambridge IGCSE	**Cambridge International Examinations** Cambridge International General Certificate of Secondary Education

CANDIDATE NAME	

CENTRE NUMBER		CANDIDATE NUMBER	

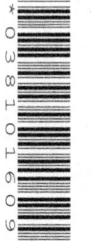

DESIGN AND TECHNOLOGY 0445/32

Paper 3 Resistant Materials October/November 2014

1 hour

Candidates answer on the Question Paper.

No Additional Materials are required.

To be taken together with Paper 1 in one session of 2 hours 15 minutes.

READ THESE INSTRUCTIONS FIRST

Write your Centre number, candidate number and name on all the work you hand in.
Write in blue or black pen.
You may use an HB pencil for any diagrams, graphs or rough working.
Do not use staples, paper clips, glue or correction fluid.
DO **NOT** WRITE IN ANY BARCODES.

Section A
Answer **all** questions in this section.
Section B
Answer **one** question in this section.

You may use a calculator.

The total of the marks for this paper is 50.
The number of marks is given in brackets [ ] at the end of each question or part question.

For Examiner's Use	
Section A	
Section B	
Total	

This document consists of **15** printed pages and **1** blank page.

DC (NF/CGW) 94729/1
© UCLES 2014

[Turn over

Section A

Answer **all** questions in this section.

1 Fig. 1 shows waste wood being cut out.

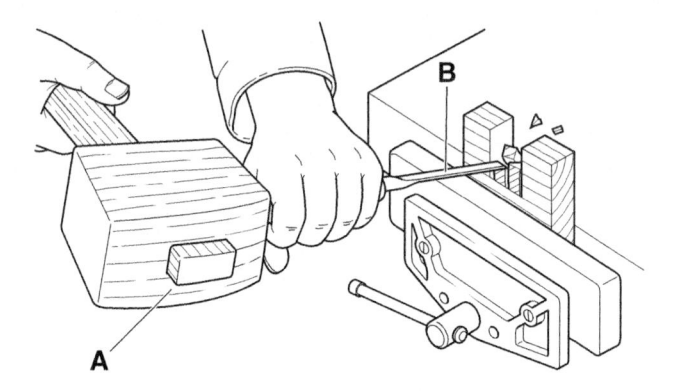

Fig. 1

Name each tool labelled **A** and **B** in Fig. 1.

A ....

B .... [2]

2 Fig. 2 shows a butt joint being glued and nailed.

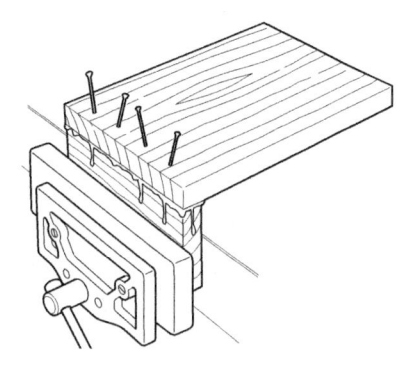

Fig. 2

(a) Name the method of nailing shown in Fig. 2.

.... [1]

(b) Give **one** reason why the nails are put in at an angle.

.... [1]

(c) Name a suitable adhesive.

.... [1]

3   Fig. 3 shows a small plastic dish.

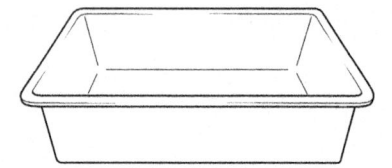

Fig. 3

(a) Name a process that could be used to produce the dish.

.... [1]

(b) Name a suitable plastic from which the dish could be made using the process named in (a).

.... [1]

4   A list of metals is given below.

        copper   cast iron   stainless steel   duralumin

From the list of metals select:

(a) a ferrous alloy;

.... [1]

(b) a non-ferrous alloy.

.... [1]

5   Fig. 4 shows the end grain of a piece of solid wood being planed.

Fig. 4

Describe how the planing should be completed without splitting the end grain.

....

....

.... [2]

6 Complete the drawing below to show a tee bridle joint.

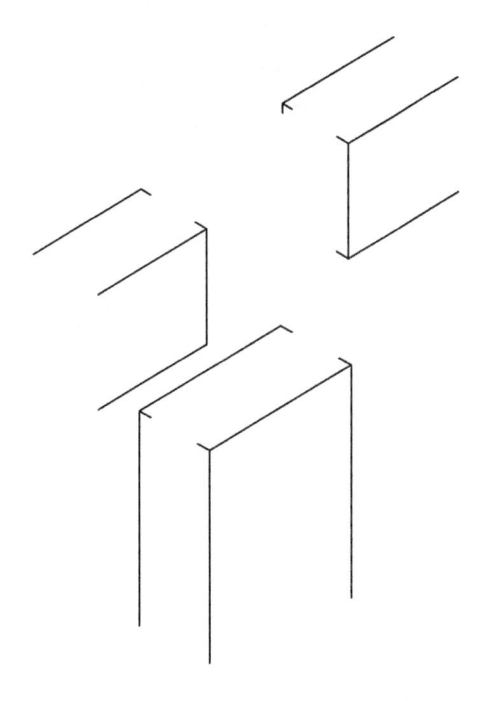

[3]

7 Complete the table below by giving a specific name and a specific use for each saw.

Tool	Specific name	Specific use

[4]

8 Fig. 5 shows a wheelbarrow. The body of the wheelbarrow is made from mild steel.

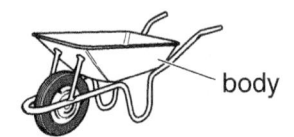

Fig. 5

(a) Give **one** reason why the body of the wheelbarrow would need a surface finish.

.... [1]

(b) Name a suitable surface finish for the body of the wheelbarrow.

.... [1]

9 (a) Complete the drawing below to show a back flap hinge.

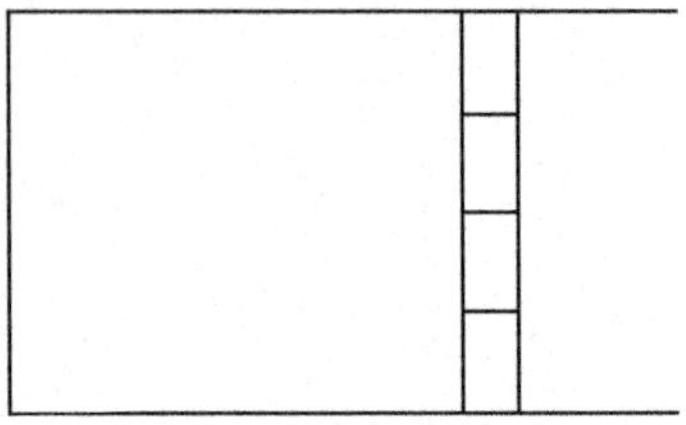

[2]

(b) Give **one** advantage of a back flap hinge over a butt hinge.

.... [1]

10 Fig. 6 shows a marking knife.

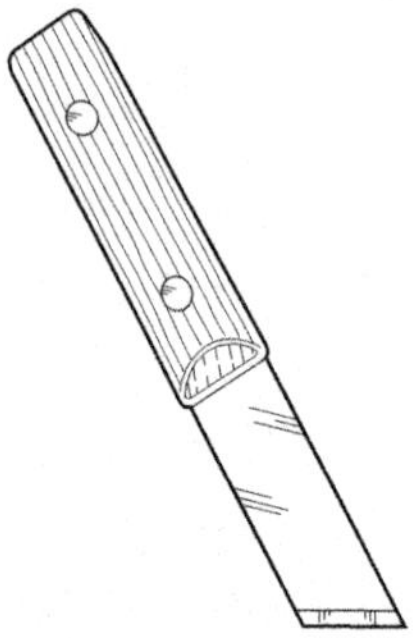

Fig. 6

(a) Describe **one** situation where a marking knife would be used to mark out wood rather than a pencil.

.... [1]

(b) Name **one** other marking out tool that scores/cuts the surface of the wood.

.... [1]

Section B

Answer **one** question from this section.

11 Fig. 7 shows a toy boat made mainly from wood.

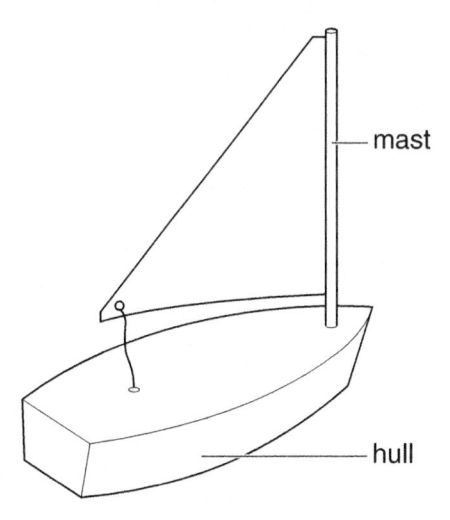

Fig. 7

(a) The mast is made from round section wood.

(i) Give the technical term for round section wood.

.... [1]

(ii) Name a waterproof adhesive that could be used to fix the mast into the hull.

.... [1]

(b) Give **two** reasons why a template would be useful to mark out the shape of the hull.

1 ....

2 .... [2]

(c) Fig. 8 shows the hull of the toy boat marked out on a block of wood.

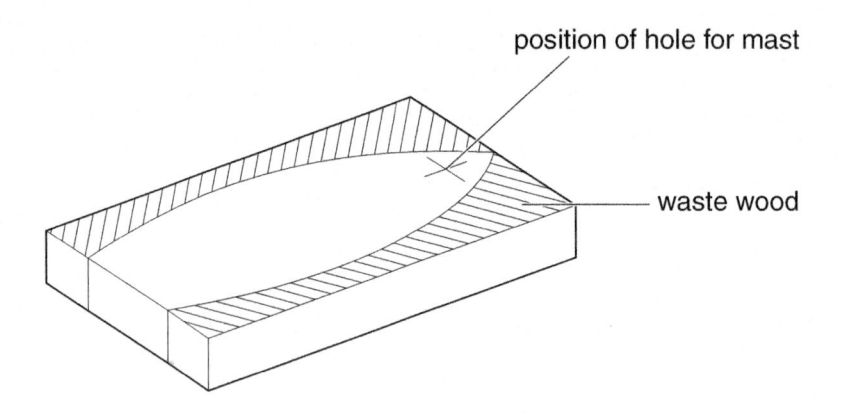

Fig. 8

Complete the table below by naming **one** tool or item of equipment used for each process.

Stage	Process	Tool or item of equipment
1	Cut off the waste	
2	Make the hole for the mast	
3	Make edges smooth	

[3]

(d) Fig. 9 shows part of the hull and rudder.

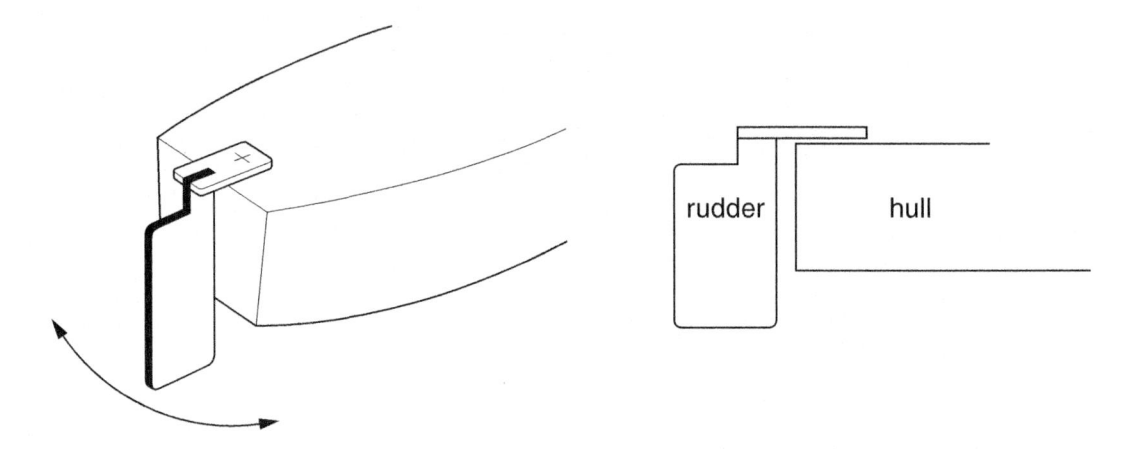

Fig. 9

Add sketches and notes to Fig. 9 to show how the rudder could be fitted to the hull and be able to move from side to side.

[2]

(e) Fig. 10 shows a different design for a toy boat.
The toy boat has a vacuum formed hull and a separate deck made from polystyrene.

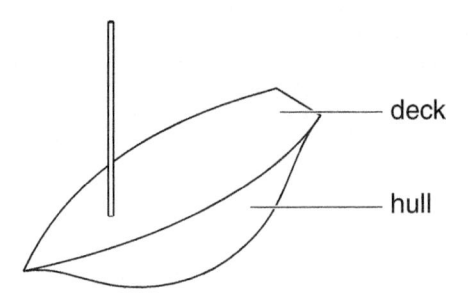

Fig. 10

Give **two** properties of polystyrene that makes it suitable for the toy boat.

1 ....

2 .... [2]

(f) Fig. 11 shows the separate parts of the hull and deck.

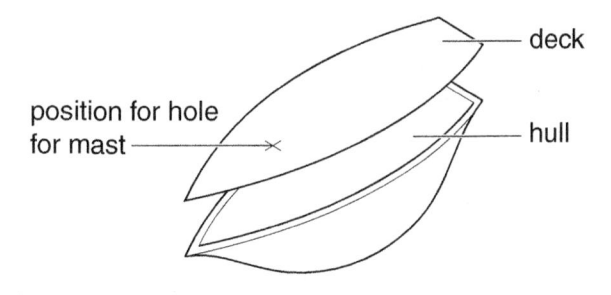

Fig. 11

Use sketches and notes to show how the hull would be vacuum formed.

[8]

(g) Use sketches and notes to show how the deck would be secured while drilling the hole for the mast.

[2]

(h) Give **two** safety precautions you must take when using polystyrene cement to join the deck to the hull.

1 ....

2 .... [2]

(i) Describe **two** ways by which designers make toys appealing to young children.

1 ....

2 .... [2]

12 Fig. 12 shows a tray table.
The tray is made from MDF and the stand could be made from **either** square section wood **or** square metal tube.

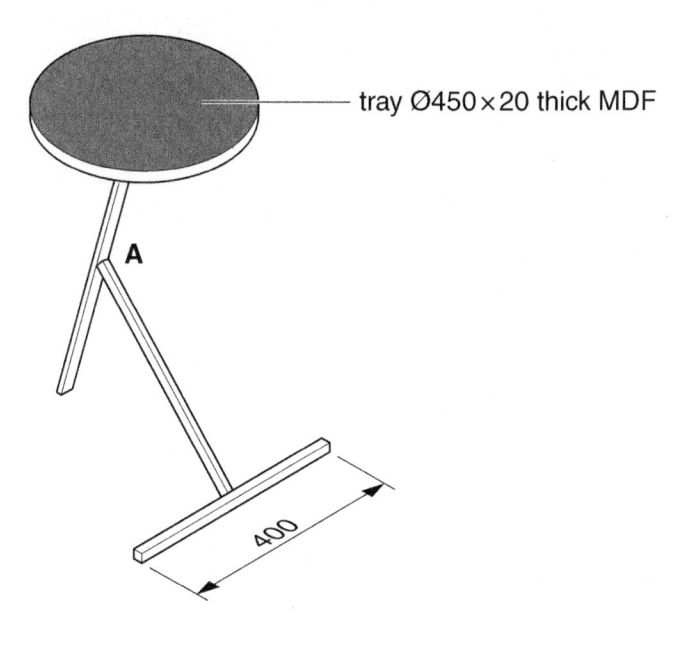

Fig. 12

(a) (i) Use sketches and notes to show a method of construction at **A** if the stand was made from square section wood.

[3]

(ii) Explain why a sliding bevel would be a useful tool to mark out part of the construction at **A**.

....

....

.... [2]

(b) (i) The stand could be made from square metal tube.
State a suitable standard size of square metal tube.

.... [1]

(ii) Use sketches and notes to describe how the construction at **A** would be brazed if the stand was made from square metal tube.

[6]

(c) Use sketches and notes to show how the stand could be fixed to the underside of the tray. You may choose to make the stand in square section wood **or** square metal tube.

[6]

(d) Starting with the MDF block shown below, use sketches and notes to show how the tray could be produced.

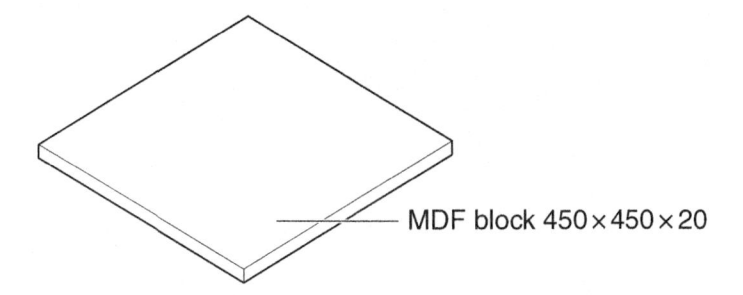

MDF block 450 × 450 × 20

[4]

(e) The surface of the tray is covered with a plastic laminate.

(i) Give **two** benefits of covering the MDF tray with a plastic laminate.

1 ....

2 .... [2]

(ii) Name a suitable adhesive to join the plastic laminate to the MDF.

.... [1]

13 Fig. 13 shows a desk tidy made from two parts, tray **A** and tray **B**. Both trays are made from 6 mm thick MDF.

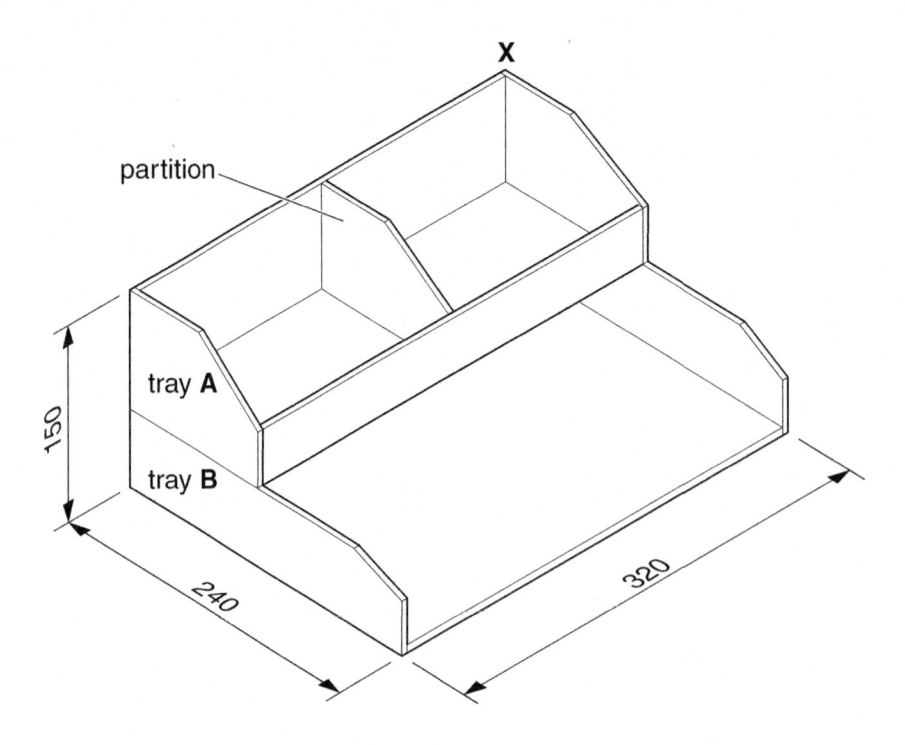

Fig. 13

(a) Give **two** advantages of MDF compared with other manufactured boards.

1 ....

2 .... [2]

(b) Give **two** items of research a designer would need to consider when designing the desk tidy.

1 ....

2 .... [2]

(c) (i) Use sketches and notes to show how a 6 mm thick MDF base could be fitted to tray **A**. The edges of the base must not be visible.

[3]

(ii) Use sketches and notes to show how the partition in tray **A** could be fixed to the sides and base.

[3]

(d) Use sketches and notes to show how tray **A** could be made to stack on top of tray **B** safely and securely. It must be easy to remove tray **A** from tray **B**.
Include constructional details and sizes.

[5]

(e) (i) Name a suitable finish for the desk tidy.

.... [1]

(ii) Describe how you would prepare the MDF to take your chosen finish.

....

....

.... [2]

(f) The MDF used for the desk tidy is only 6 mm thick.
Use sketches and notes to show a suitable corner joint at **X**.

[3]

(g) Describe **two** functional improvements to the desk tidy shown in Fig. 13.

1 ....

2 .... [2]

(h) Many desk tidies are made from plastic.
Give **two** advantages of making a desk tidy from plastic rather than MDF.

1 ....

2 .... [2]

/ Cambridge IGCSE

Cambridge International Examinations
Cambridge International General Certificate of Secondary Education

CANDIDATE NAME

CENTRE NUMBER

CANDIDATE NUMBER

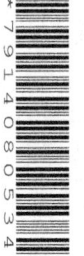

DESIGN AND TECHNOLOGY 0445/32

Paper 3 Resistant Materials May/June 2015

1 hour

Candidates answer on the Question Paper.
No Additional Materials are required.

READ THESE INSTRUCTIONS FIRST

Write your Centre number, candidate number and name on all the work you hand in.
Write in dark blue or black pen.
You may use an HB pencil for any diagrams, graphs or rough working.
Do not use staples, paper clips, glue or correction fluid.
DO **NOT** WRITE IN ANY BARCODES.

Section A
Answer **all** questions in this section.

Section B
Answer **one** question in this section.

You may use a calculator.

At the end of the examination, fasten all your work securely together.
The number of marks is given in brackets [ ] at the end of each question or part question.
The total of the marks for this paper is 50.

This document consists of **14** printed pages and **2** blank pages.

DC (NF/SG) 108053
© UCLES 2015

CAMBRIDGE
International Examinations

[Turn over

Section A

Answer **all** questions in this section.

1 Complete the table below by naming each tool.

Tool	Name
(mortise/marking gauge)	
(micrometer)	
(dividers/calipers)	

[3]

2 Fig. 1 shows a jigsaw. The jigsaw has a blade that can be replaced.

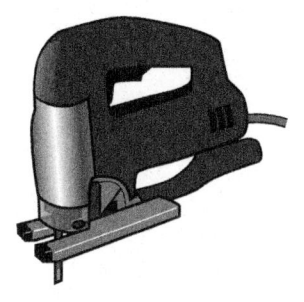

Fig. 1

Give **two** benefits of using a saw that has replaceable blades.

1 ....

2 ....[2]

3 From the list of materials shown below underline **two** composite materials.

    aluminium   Kevlar®   polystyrene   stainless steel   glass reinforced plastic

[2]

4 Fig. 2 shows a rod that will be joined permanently to a base.

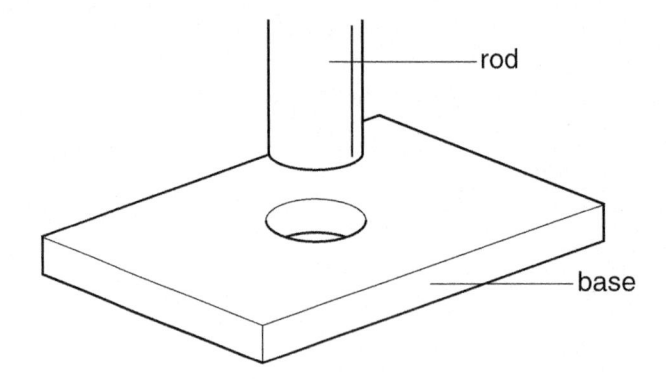

Fig. 2

State a method of joining the rod to the base permanently when both parts are made from:

(a) mild steel ....

(b) acrylic ....[2]

5 Fig. 3 shows two wood joints labelled **A** and **B**.

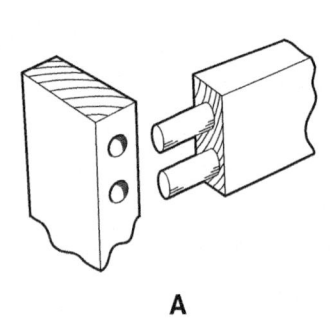

A   **B**

Fig. 3

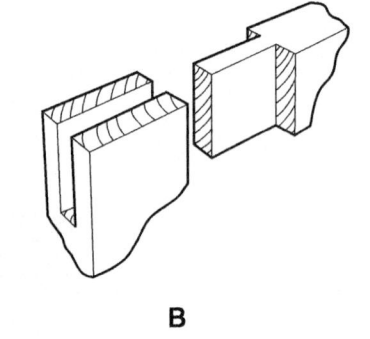

(a) Name each of the wood joints labelled **A** and **B**.

A ....

B ....[2]

(b) Give **one** reason why joint **B** is stronger than joint **A** when they are glued.

....[1]

6 (a) Name each of the tools labelled **A** and **B** shown below.

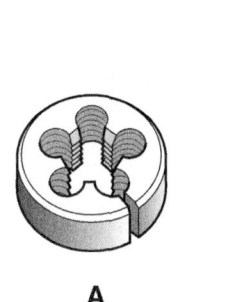

A ....

B ....[2]

(b) State the purpose of tool **A**.

....[1]

(c) State the purpose of tool **B**.

....[1]

7 Complete the drawing below to show a tee halving joint.

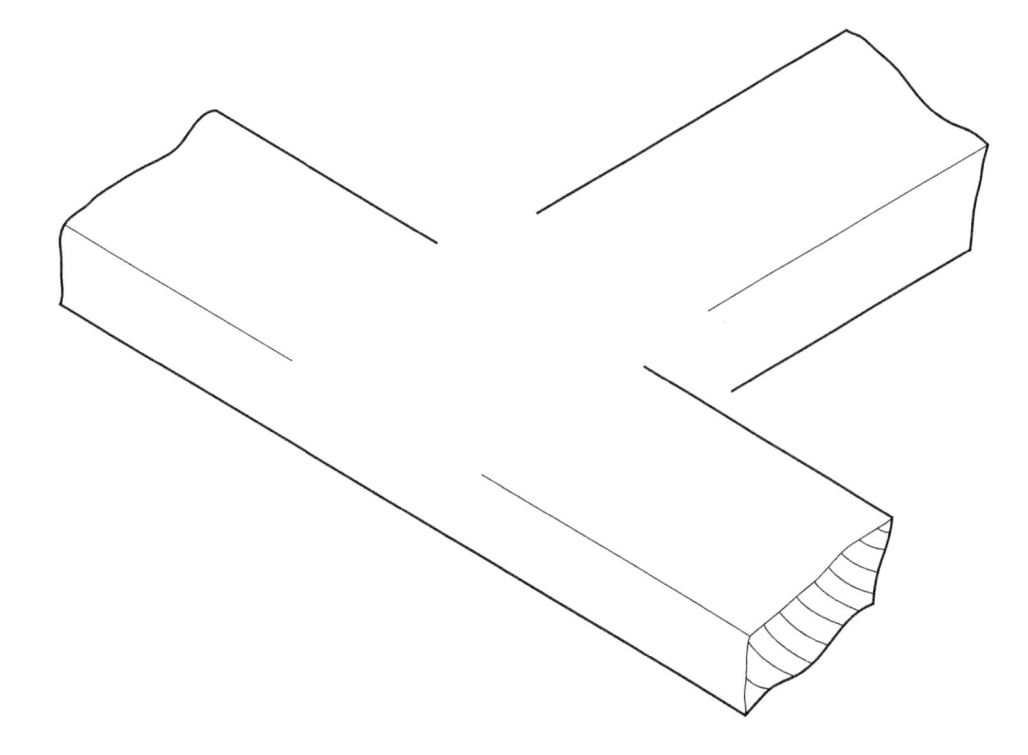

[3]

8 Fig. 4 shows a small table made from hardwood.

Fig. 4

Give **two** possible reasons why the table top has split.

1 ....

2 ....[2]

9 Fig. 5 shows a palm sander to be used on wood.

Fig. 5

Describe **two** ways by which the designer has considered ergonomics in the design of the palm sander.

1 ....

2 ....[2]

10 Fig. 6 shows a symbol found on a product made from a plastic.

HDPE

Fig. 6

(a) Name the plastic.

.... [1]

(b) State what is meant by the arrowed lines around the number 2.

.... [1]

Section B

Answer **one** question in this section.

11 Fig. 7 shows details of a variety of wooden shapes and pegs that are part of a child's construction kit. The construction kit will be made in a school workshop.

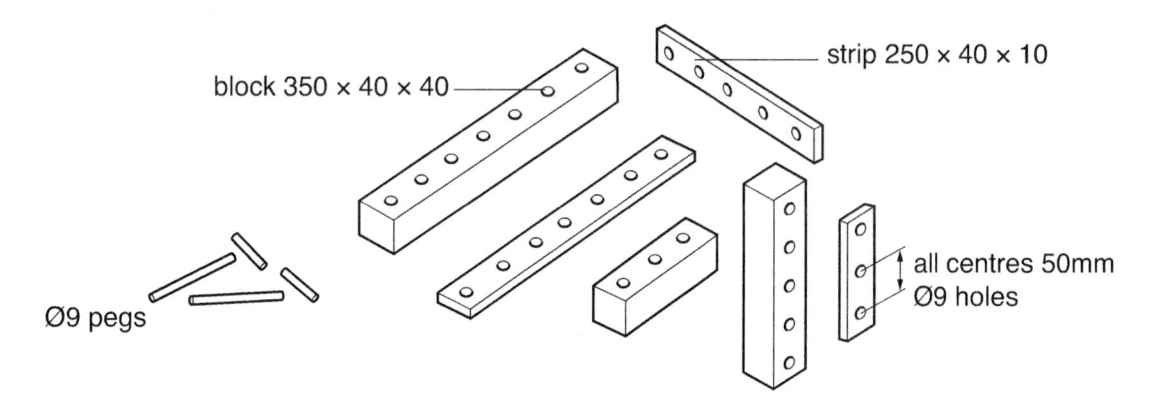

Fig. 7

(a) Fig. 8 shows a length of wood from which the strips are made.

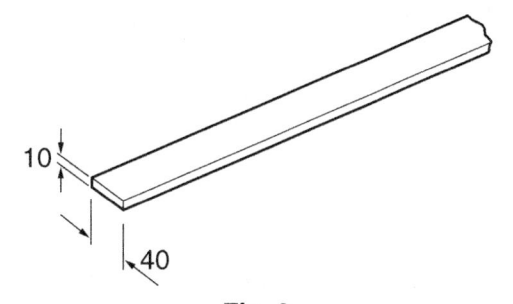

Fig. 8

Use sketches and notes to show the stages in producing a **one-off** strip 250 mm long complete with 9 mm diameter holes drilled. Name all the tools and equipment used.

[5]

(b) A drilling jig would be used to speed up batch production of the strips and blocks. Use sketches and notes to show a design for a jig used in the drilling of 9 mm holes. Name the materials used to make the jig.

[7]

(c) The wooden strips and blocks will have a finish applied to them.

(i) Give **one** advantage of applying a finish to the strips and blocks.

....

(ii) Give **one** disadvantage of applying a finish to the strips and blocks.

....[2]

(d) The construction kit needs a set of six identical wheels.
Use sketches and notes to show how **six** wheels could be produced.
Include the following details:
- specific materials;
- processes used;
- two important sizes.

[8]

(e) The wooden pegs, used to connect the strips and blocks, are made from round section wood.
Give the correct name for round section wood.

....[1]

(f) Many children's toys are made from plastic.
Give **two** advantages of making children's toys from plastic rather than from wood.

1 ....

2 ....[2]

12 Fig. 9 shows a desk tidy made from 4 mm thick acrylic.

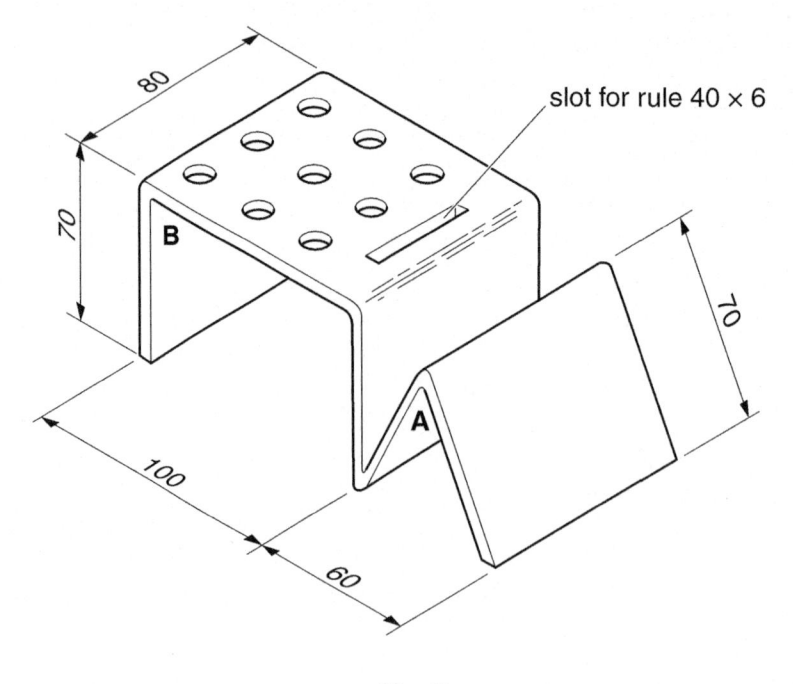

Fig. 9

(a) Complete the development (net) of the desk tidy below to show the bend lines. Do **not** include the holes or slot.

[4]

(b) Complete the table below by giving details of the stages involved in finishing the sawn edges of the acrylic to a high quality.

Stage	Process
1	Draw file edges, holding the acrylic in a vice.
2	
3	
4	

[3]

(c) (i) Use sketches and notes to show how the slot could be cut out and the edges made smooth.

[3]

(ii) State **two** precautions you would take to prevent the acrylic from cracking when drilling the holes.

1 ....

2 ....[2]

(d) Use sketches and notes to show how the bend at **A** in Fig. 9 could be produced.
Include:
- the method of softening the acrylic;
- the use of a former;
- the method of retaining the shape while the acrylic cools.

[4]

(e) When the desk tidy shown in Fig. 9 is picked up and moved around, the pens, pencils and rule fall out.
Use sketches and notes to show a modification to the desk tidy to overcome this problem.
Include details of materials and constructions used.

[4]

(f) The desk tidy shown in Fig. 9 could be made from 1 mm thick aluminium sheet.
Use sketches and notes to show how the bend at **B** could be produced when the desk tidy is made from 1 mm thick aluminium sheet.
Name the tools and equipment used.

[3]

(g) Both the acrylic and aluminium desk tidies will be self-finished.
Explain what is meant by the term 'self-finished'.

....

....

....[2]

13 Fig. 10 shows details of a child's puzzle and the tray in which the puzzle is placed. The puzzle is made from six pieces of MDF and the tray is made from plywood.

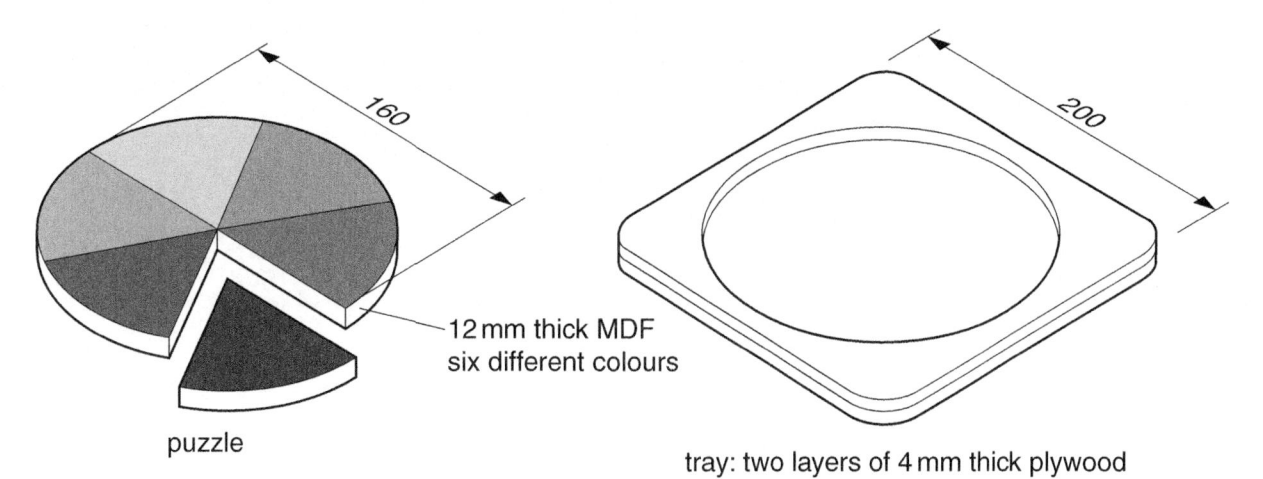

12 mm thick MDF
six different colours

puzzle

tray: two layers of 4 mm thick plywood

Fig. 10

(a) Give **two** advantages of using MDF rather than plywood for the puzzle.

1 ....

2 ....[2]

(b) Describe **three** ways in which the designer has made the puzzle suitable for young children.

1 ....

2 ....

3 ....[3]

(c) The tray shown in Fig. 10 is made from two pieces of 4 mm plywood glued together.

(i) Use sketches and notes to explain why the construction of plywood makes it more suitable for the tray than solid wood.

[3]

(ii) Use sketches and notes to show how the hole in the top piece of plywood could be cut out and the sides of the hole made smooth.

[5]

(iii) Use sketches and notes to show how the top and bottom pieces of plywood could be glued and clamped together.
Name a suitable adhesive and the type of cramps used.

[4]

(iv) The tray could be made from vacuum formed plastic.
Give **two** advantages of producing the tray from vacuum formed plastic rather than from plywood.

1 ....

2 .... [2]

(d) The puzzle could be produced using CAD/CAM.
Complete the abbreviations CAD/CAM below.

Computer Aided D ....

Computer Aided M .... [2]

(e) Describe **two** quality control checks that would be carried out **during** the manufacture of the puzzle and/or the tray.

1 ....

2 ....[2]

(f) Give **two** reasons why the use of manufactured boards such as MDF and plywood, rather than plastics, could be considered good for the environment.

1 ....

....

2 ....

....[2]

Cambridge IGCSE	**Cambridge International Examinations** Cambridge International General Certificate of Secondary Education	

CANDIDATE NAME		

CENTRE NUMBER		CANDIDATE NUMBER	

DESIGN AND TECHNOLOGY 0445/32

Paper 3 Resistant Materials October/November 2015

1 hour

Candidates answer on the Question Paper.

No Additional Materials are required.

READ THESE INSTRUCTIONS FIRST

Write your Centre number, candidate number and name on all the work you hand in.
Write in blue or black pen.
You may use an HB pencil for any diagrams, graphs or rough working.
Do not use staples, paper clips, glue or correction fluid.
DO **NOT** WRITE IN ANY BARCODES.

Section A
Answer **all** questions in this section.

Section B
Answer **one** question in this section.

You may use a calculator.

At the end of the examination, fasten all your work securely together.
The number of marks is given in brackets [ ] at the end of each question or part question.
The total of the marks for this paper is 50.

This document consists of **15** printed pages and **1** blank page.

[Turn over

Section A

Answer **all** questions in this section.

1   Give **three** pieces of information needed when ordering nuts and bolts.

1 ....

2 ....

3 .... [3]

2   Complete the drawing below to show a coping saw.

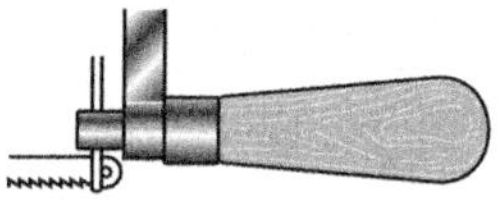

[2]

3   Fig. 1 shows a wooden frame construction glued and clamped.

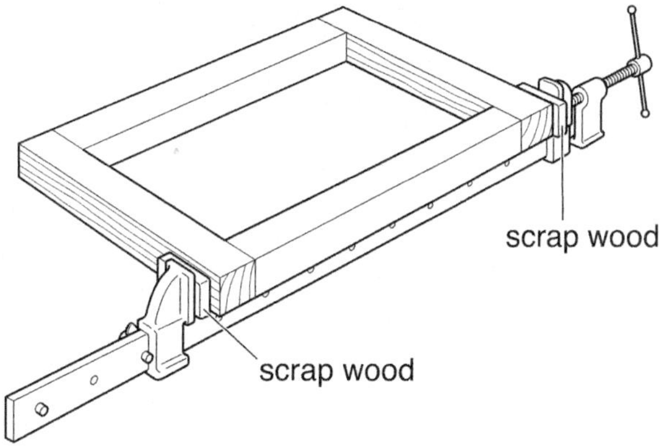

scrap wood

scrap wood

Fig. 1

(a) Name the type of cramp used.

....

(b) Give **one** reason why pieces of scrap wood are used.

.... [2]

4 Underline the **two** 'smart' materials in the list below.

aluminium   polymorph   nitinol   fibreglass   nylon   [2]

5 Complete the table below by naming each tool and giving a specific use.

Tool	Specific name	Specific use
(calipers)		
(brace)		

[4]

6 Fig. 2 shows a veneer being cut from a log.

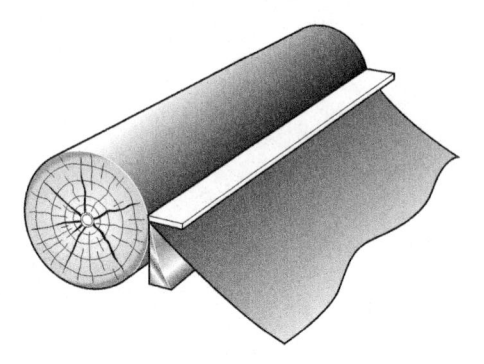

Fig. 2

(a) Give **one** advantage of using veneers when making furniture.

....

(b) Give **one** disadvantage of using veneers when making furniture.

.... [2]

7 Fig. 3 shows part of a wooden frame.
Add to Fig. 3 to show how the corner joint could be strengthened.

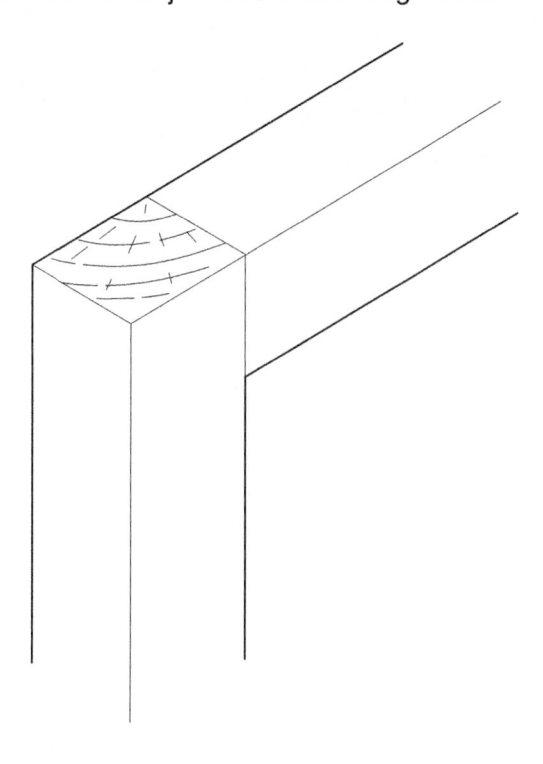

Fig. 3 [2]

8 Fig. 4 shows a handle made from aluminium alloy.

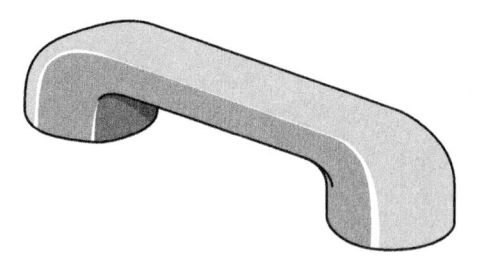

Fig. 4

(a) Name the process used to make the handle.

....

(b) Give **one** suitable finish for the handle.

.... [2]

9 Fig. 5 shows a block of wood with a shape marked out ready to be removed.

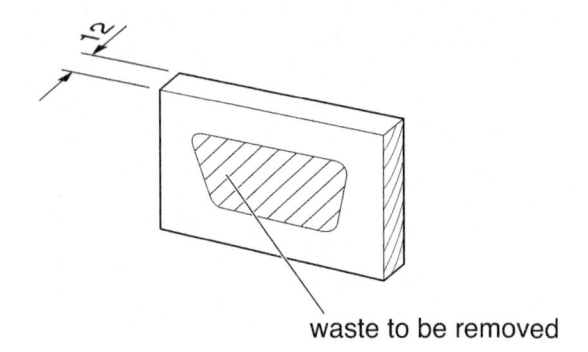

Fig. 5

Describe **three** main stages in removing the waste wood and producing clean, smooth edges.

1 ....

2 ....

3 .... [3]

10 Fig. 6 shows two different wooden chairs.

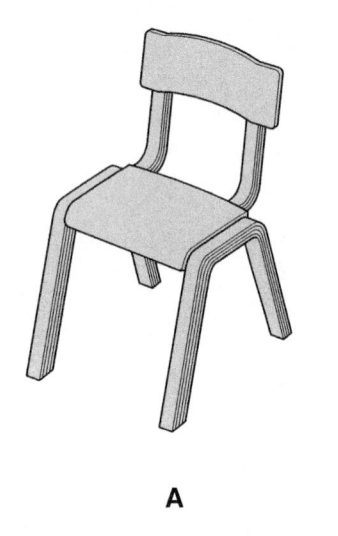

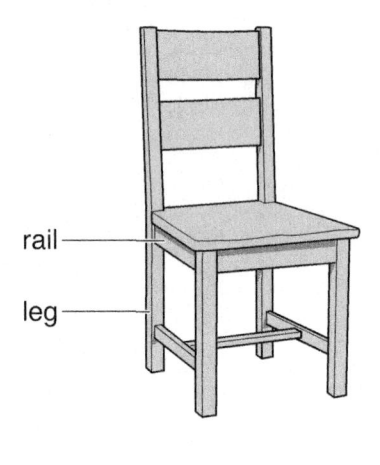

A   B

Fig. 6

(a) Name the process used to produce the legs in chair **A**.

....

(b) Name **one** construction that could be used to join the legs and rails in chair **B**.

....

(c) Give **one** advantage of the construction of chair **A** over chair **B**.

.... [3]

Section B

Answer **one** question in this section.

11 Fig. 7 shows views of a computer desk made from 15 mm thick manufactured board. The computer desk will be sold as flat-pack furniture for self-assembly.

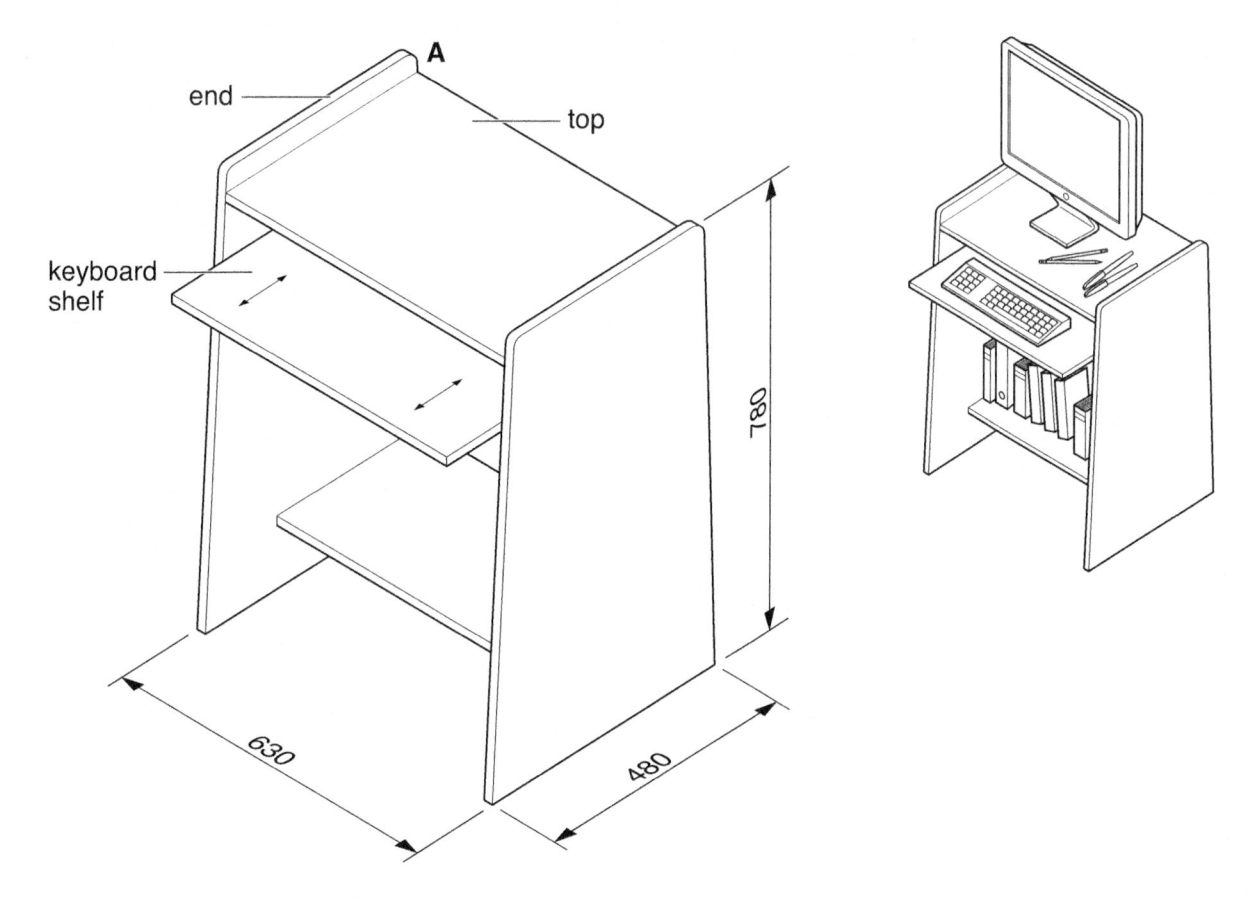

Fig. 7

(a) Give **two** benefits of flat-pack furniture for:

 (i) the consumer;

 1 ....

 2 .... [2]

 (ii) the manufacturer.

 1 ....

 2 .... [2]

(b) Use sketches and notes to show how knock-down (KD) fittings could be used to join the top to one end at **A**.

[4]

(c) Use sketches and notes to show how the keyboard shelf could be made to move in and out as shown in Fig. 7. Include details of materials and constructions used.

[4]

(d) The ends and shelves will be spray painted.

    (i) Give **two** advantages of spray painting rather than applying paint with a brush.

        1 ....

        2 .... [2]

    (ii) Describe **two** safety precautions you would take when spray painting.

        1 ....

        2 .... [2]

(e) Evaluate the design of the computer desk shown in Fig. 7 in terms of:

    (i) safety;

        ....

        .... [2]

    (ii) appearance;

        ....

        .... [2]

    (iii) costs.

        ....

        .... [2]

(f) Explain why the computer desk could be considered to have a limited lifetime.

    ....

    ....

    ....

    .... [3]

Question 12 is printed on the next page.

12 Fig. 8 shows an incomplete design for a freestanding barbecue.
The barbecue body is made from 1 mm thick mild steel sheet.

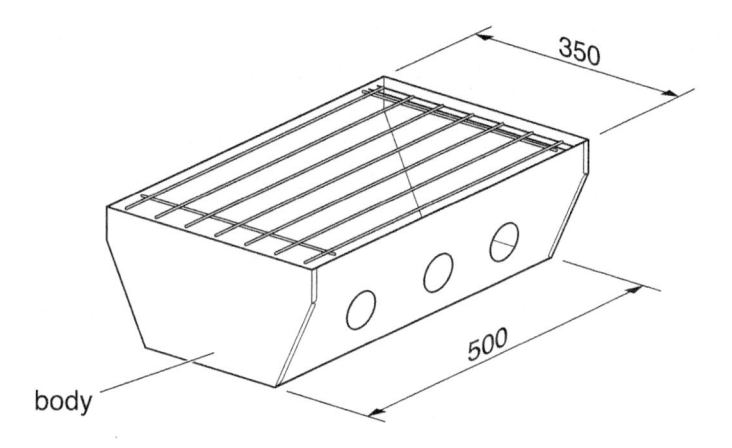

Fig. 8

(a) Give **two** reasons why mild steel is suitable for the barbecue body.

1 ....

2 .... [2]

(b) Give **one** reason why the mild steel sheet would need an applied finish.

.... [1]

(c) Fig. 9 shows one end of the barbecue body marked out, ready to be cut to shape.

flaps 10 mm wide

1 mm thick mild steel sheet

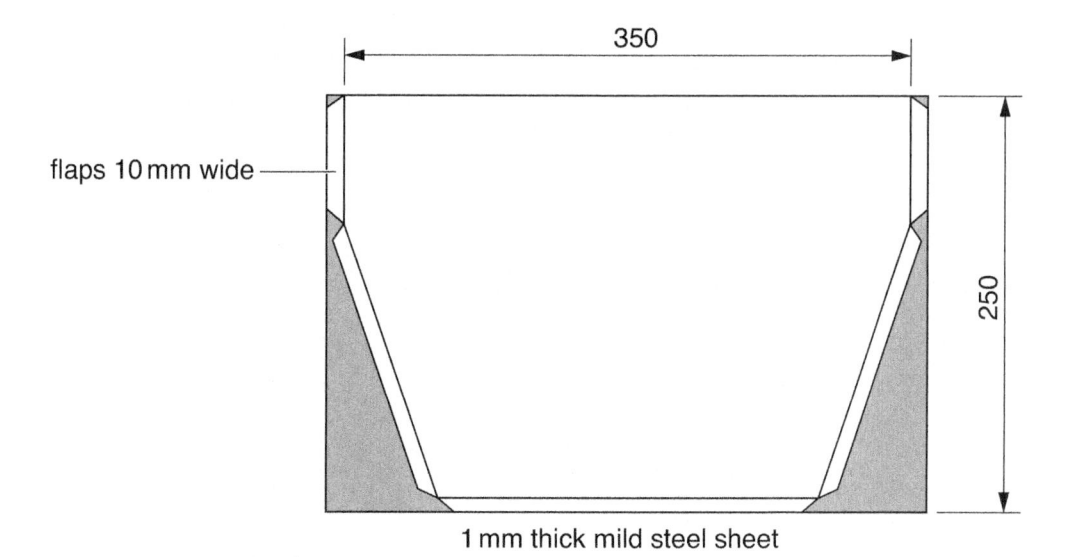

Fig. 9

Use sketches and notes to show how the shape could be cut out.
Name all the tools and equipment.

[4]

(d) Fig. 10 shows one end of the barbecue body with flaps bent to 90°.

flaps bent to 90°

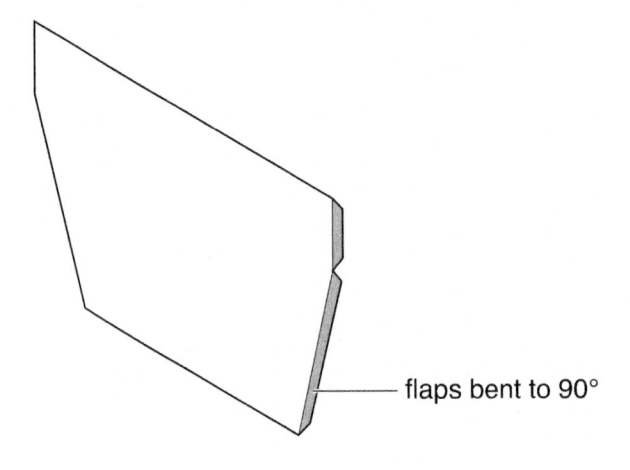

Fig. 10

Use sketches and notes to show how the flaps could be bent to 90°.

[3]

(e) Sketch **one** permanent method of joining the ends to the sides of the barbecue body.

[2]

(f) Use sketches and notes to show how the barbecue body could be supported at a height of 500 mm above the ground.

Your design must include:
- named materials;
- two important sizes;
- a temporary method of joining the support to the barbecue body.

[8]

(g) Fig. 11 shows three tools commonly used with the barbecue.

Fig. 11

Use sketches and notes to design a rack for the three tools that could be fixed to the barbecue body.
Include details of materials and constructions used.

[5]

13 Fig. 12 shows a palette used to mix paints. The palette is vacuum formed.

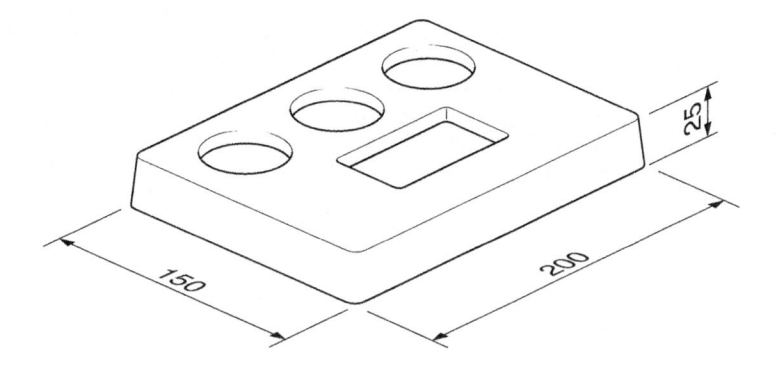

Fig. 12

(a) (i) Name a suitable plastic for the palette.

.... [1]

(ii) A former made from MDF is used to vacuum form the palette.
Give **two** advantages of using MDF rather than solid wood for the former.

1 ....

2 .... [2]

(iii) Describe **two** considerations you would take into account when making a former used to vacuum form the palette.

1 ....

2 .... [2]

(b) Use detailed sketches and notes to show how the palette would be vacuum formed.

[8]

(c) Fig. 13 shows a holder used when mixing paints.

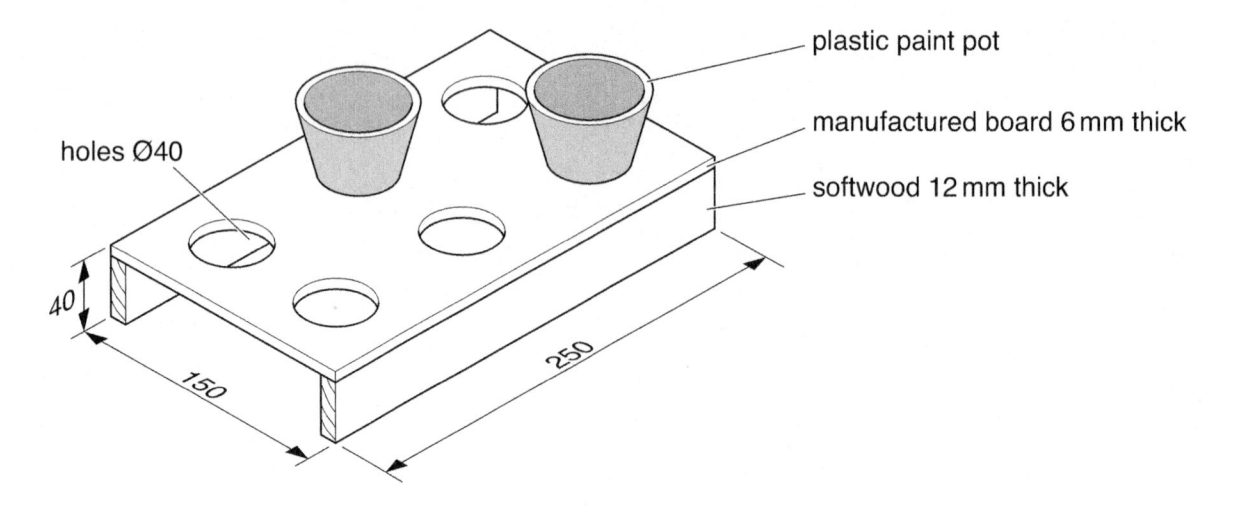

Fig. 13

(i) Name a manufacturing process, other than vacuum forming, used to produce the plastic paint pots.

.... [1]

(ii) Use sketches and notes to show how the manufactured board top would be held securely while the holes for the paint pots are drilled.

[3]

Question 13 continues on the following page.

(iii) Use sketches and notes to show how the manufactured board top could be joined permanently to the softwood sides.

[3]

(d) Fig. 14 shows three paintbrushes that will be stored with the holder shown in Fig. 13.

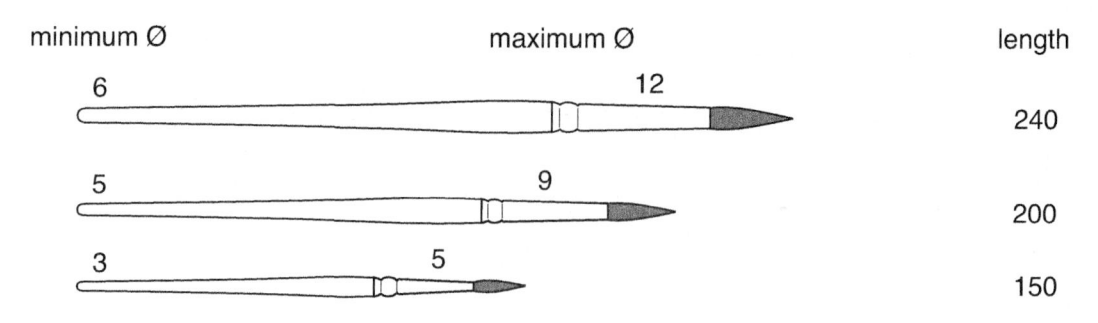

minimum Ø	maximum Ø	length
6	12	240
5	9	200
3	5	150

Fig. 14

Use sketches and notes to show a modification to the holder so that the three paintbrushes could be stored safely. Include details of materials, constructions and sizes.

[5]

Cambridge IGCSE

Cambridge International Examinations
Cambridge International General Certificate of Secondary Education

CANDIDATE NAME		
CENTRE NUMBER		CANDIDATE NUMBER

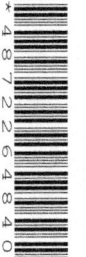

DESIGN AND TECHNOLOGY 0445/32

Paper 3 Resistant Materials May/June 2016

1 hour

Candidates answer on the Question Paper.
No Additional Materials are required.

READ THESE INSTRUCTIONS FIRST

Write your Centre number, candidate number and name on all the work you hand in.
Write in dark blue or black pen.
You may use an HB pencil for any diagrams, graphs or rough working.
Do not use staples, paper clips, glue or correction fluid.
DO **NOT** WRITE IN ANY BARCODES.

Section A
Answer **all** questions in this section.

Section B
Answer **one** question in this section.

You may use a calculator.

At the end of the examination, fasten all your work securely together.
The number of marks is given in brackets [ ] at the end of each question or part question.
The total of the marks for this paper is 50.

This document consists of **17** printed pages and **3** blank pages.

DC (KN/FD) 116914/1
© UCLES 2016

[Turn over

Section A

Answer **all** questions in this section.

1   Name **three** different tools that would be used to tighten each of the fastenings **A**, **B** and **C** shown below.

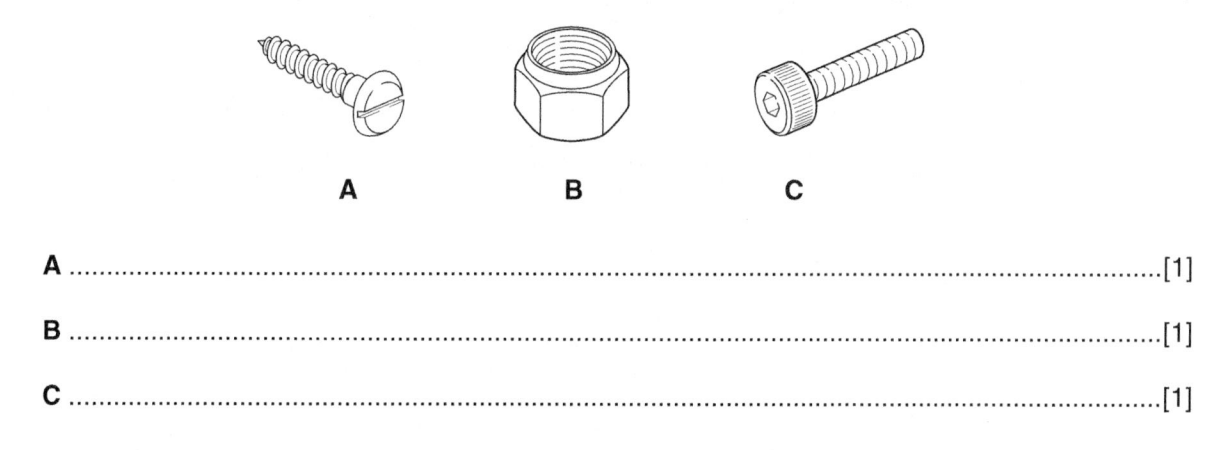

A ....[1]

B ....[1]

C ....[1]

2   Add to the drawing below to show how a bevel edge chisel would be used to cut out corner **A**.

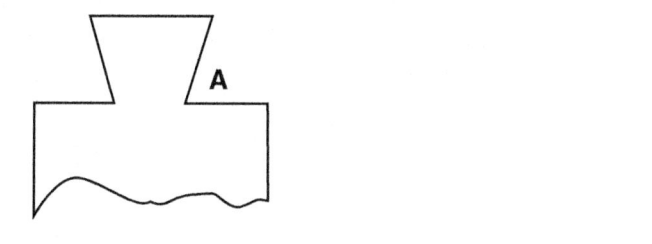

[2]

3   Fig. 1 shows two wood joints.

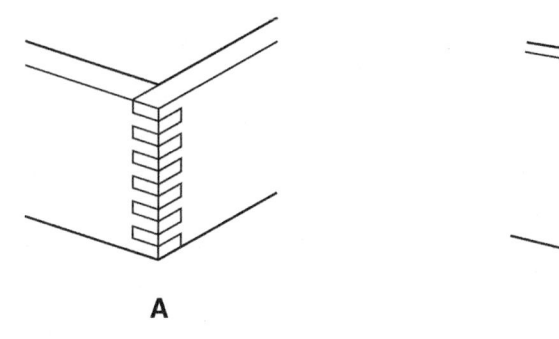

Fig. 1

(a) Name the joints **A** and **B** shown in Fig. 1.

A ....

B ....[2]

(b) Give **one** reason why joint **B** is stronger than joint **A**.

....[1]

4 Name the **two** standard metal sections shown below.

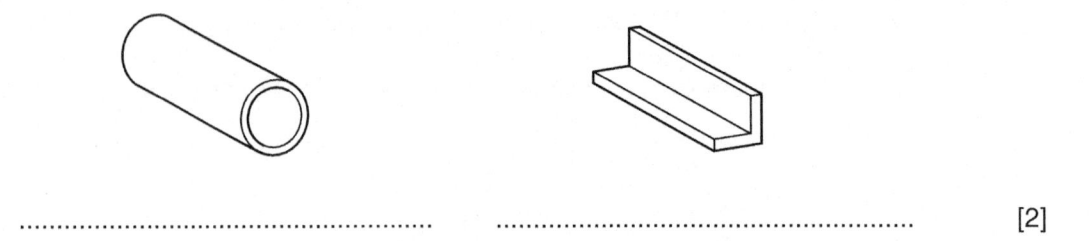

.... [2]

5 Fig. 2 shows a metal handle with a textured finish on its edge.

Fig. 2

(a) Give the correct name for the textured finish.

....[1]

(b) State the purpose of the textured finish.

....[1]

(c) Name the machine used to produce the textured finish.

....[1]

6 Fig. 3 shows a lap joint marked out.
Lines **A** and **B** have been marked out using two different gauges.

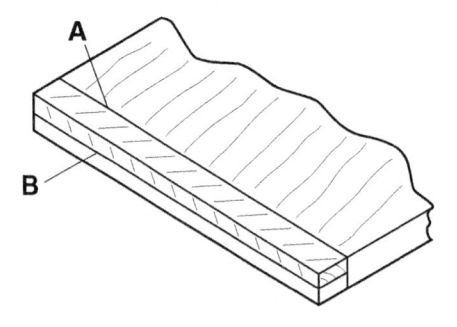

Fig. 3

Name the gauge used to mark out each line.

A ....

B ....[2]

7 Fig. 4 shows a car shell made from carbon fibre reinforced plastic (CFRP).

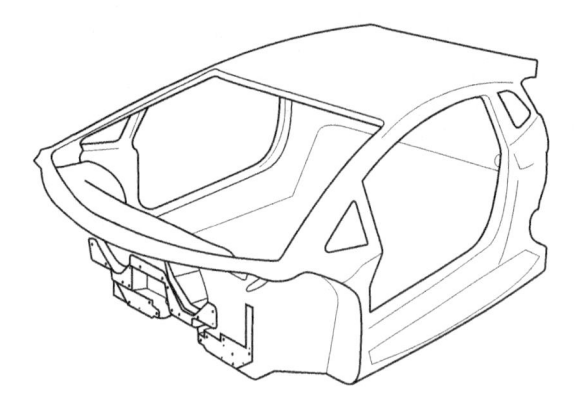

Fig. 4

Give **two** advantages of using carbon fibre reinforced plastic (CFRP) rather than steel for the car shell.

1 ....

2 ....[2]

8 Fig. 5 shows a child's sit-on toy made from wood.

Fig. 5

Describe **three** ways in which the designer has made the sit-on toy suitable for children.

1 ....

2 ....

3 ....[3]

9 State what is meant by each safety symbol shown below.

....[1]

....[1]

10 Complete the table below by naming a different metal that matches each of the properties given.

Name of metal	Property
	malleable
	corrosion resistant
	electrical conductivity

[3]

Section B

Answer **one** question in this section.

11 Fig. 6 shows an incomplete design for a book stand made from hardwood.
The book stand has two main parts: the frame and the ledge.

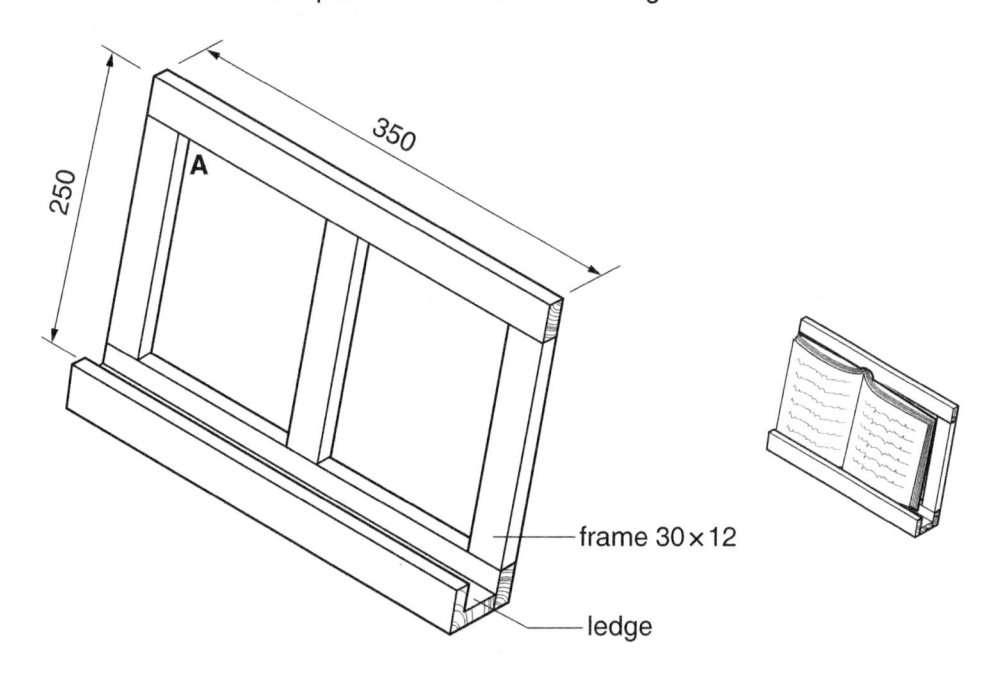

Fig. 6

(a) Give **two** advantages of using a frame made from separate pieces of hardwood for the book stand rather than one solid piece of wood.

1 ....

2 ....[2]

(b) Sketch and name a suitable joint at **A** in Fig. 6.

[4]

(c) Fig. 7 shows the frame ready to be clamped and glued together.

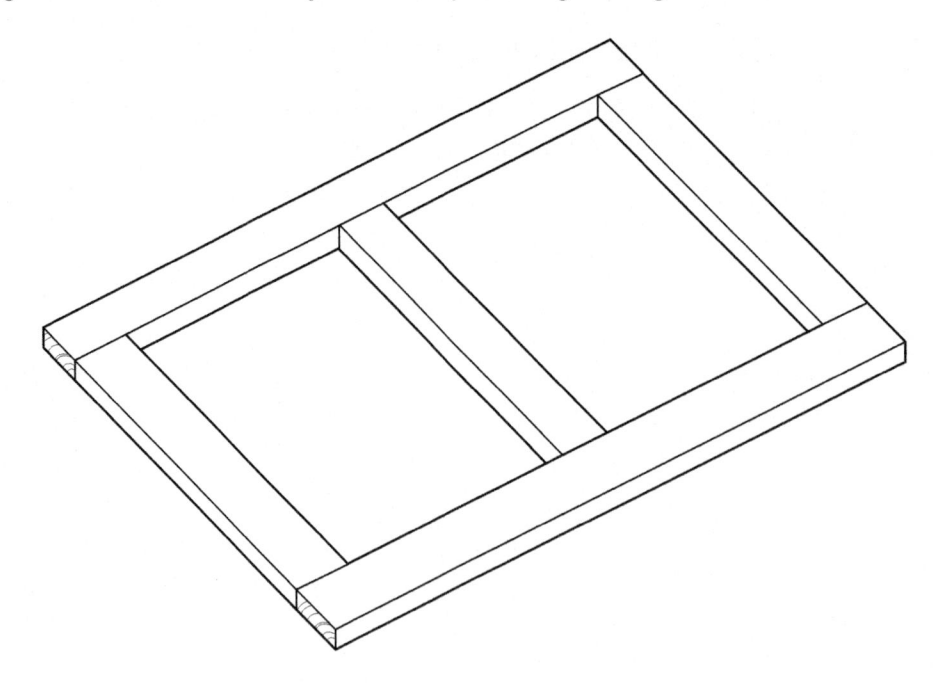

Fig. 7

(i) Add sketches and notes to Fig. 7 to show how the frame would be clamped while the glue sets. Name the type of cramps used. [3]

(ii) Use sketches and notes to show how the outside edges would be planed and the surfaces prepared to take a clear varnish finish.

[4]

(d) Fig. 8 shows details of the ledge.

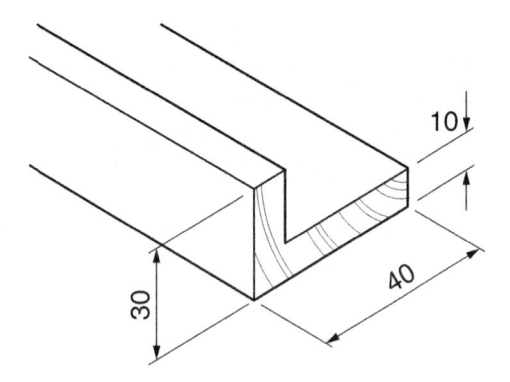

Fig. 8

Use sketches and notes to show how the ledge could be attached to the frame as shown in Fig. 6.

[2]

(e) When a book is placed on the book stand the book does not always stay open at the required page.
Use sketches and notes to show a modification to the design so that the book stays open.
Include details of materials and/or fittings used.

[4]

(f) Fig. 9 shows a side view of the book stand.

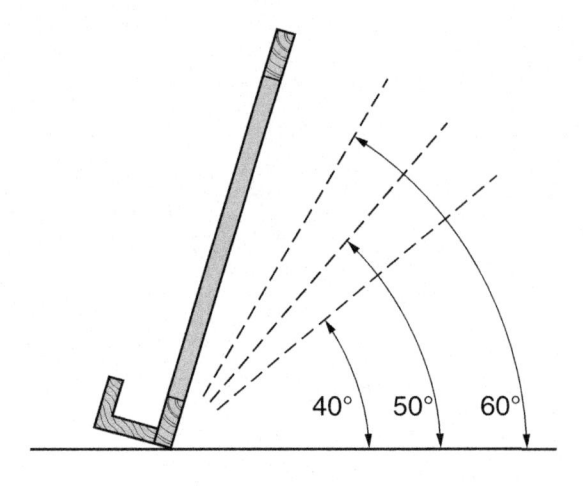

Fig. 9

Use sketches and notes to show how the book stand could be adjusted to **three** different positions as shown above.
Include details of materials, constructions and fittings used.

[6]

12 Fig. 10 shows a child's shape sorting toy. The box and shapes are made from beech. The top is made from acrylic.

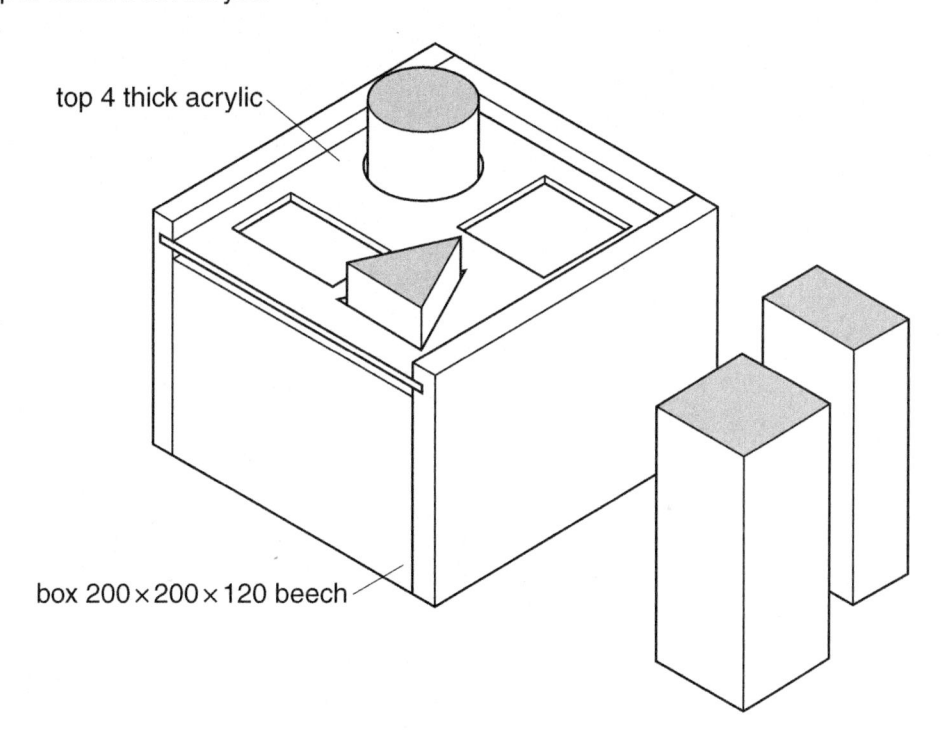

Fig. 10

(a) Give **two** reasons why beech is often used to make children's toys.

1 ....

2 ....[2]

(b) Fig. 11 shows the acrylic top with the shapes marked out.

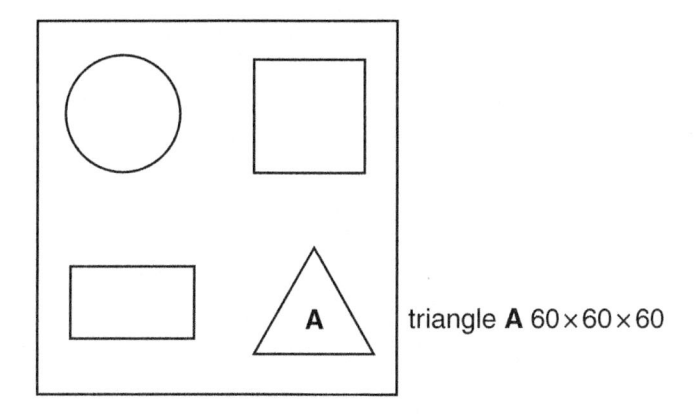

triangle **A** 60 × 60 × 60

Fig. 11

(i) Name a tool that would be used to mark the shapes on the surface of the acrylic.

....[1]

(ii) Use sketches and notes to show how triangle shape **A** could be cut out from the acrylic top and the edges made flat and smooth.

[4]

(iii) When working with acrylic there is a possibility that it could crack.
Describe **two** processes where this could occur and how the problem can be solved.

Process ....

Solution ....

Process ....

Solution ....[4]

(c) Fig. 12 shows part of the groove that allows the acrylic top to be removed.

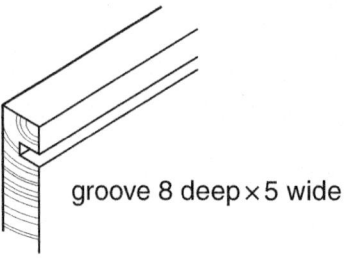

groove 8 deep × 5 wide

Fig. 12

Use sketches and notes to show how the groove could be produced.

[3]

[Turn over

(d) Fig. 13 shows the triangular shape **A** marked out on a length of beech.

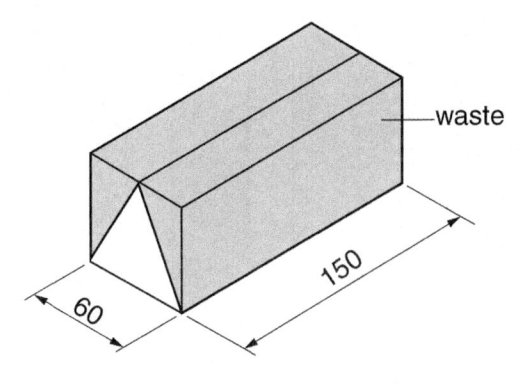

Fig. 13

Use sketches and notes to show how the triangular shape could be produced.
Name all the tools and equipment used.

[4]

(e) Fig. 14 shows a length of beech that will be used to make the round shape.
The round shape will be produced by turning between-centres on a wood turning lathe.

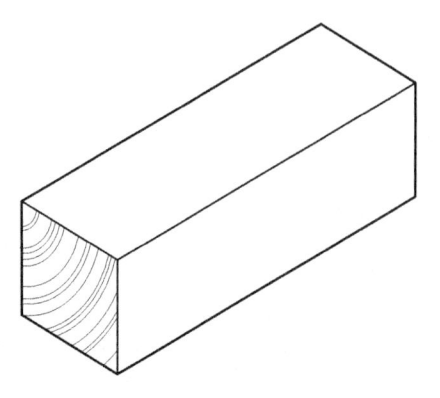

Fig. 14

Add sketches and notes to Fig. 14 to show how the beech would be prepared **before** it is set up on a wood turning lathe. [3]

(f) Fig. 15 shows hollow section plastic shapes that could also be used in the shape sorting toy.

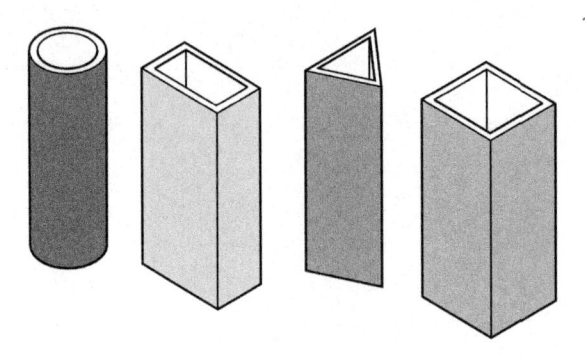

Fig. 15

(i) Give **three** advantages of using plastic rather than beech for the shapes.

1 ....

2 ....

3 ....[3]

(ii) Name a process that could be used to produce the hollow plastic shapes in quantity.

....[1]

13 Fig. 16 shows a wall-mounted key rack.
The front of the key rack and the key fob are made from 1.5 thick aluminium sheet.
The back is made from 12 thick MDF.

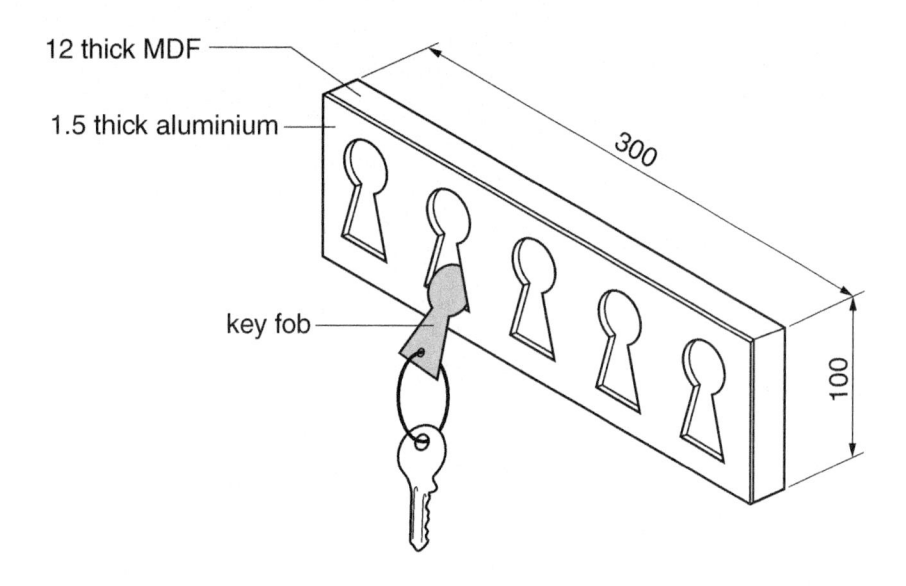

Fig. 16

(a) (i) Fig. 17 shows the keyhole shapes marked out on aluminium sheet.

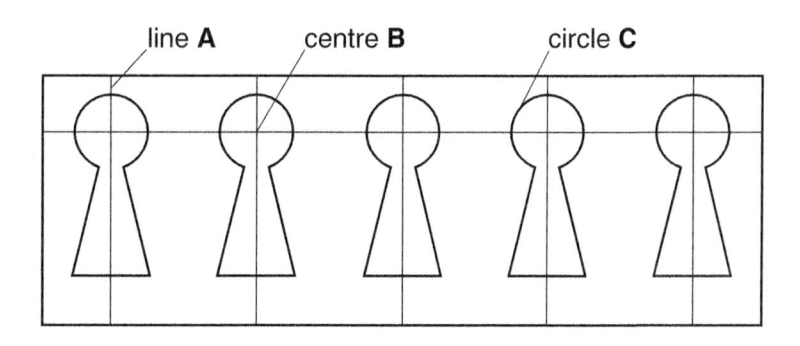

Fig. 17

Name a marking out tool that would be used to mark out:

line **A** ....

centre **B** ....

circle **C** ....[3]

(ii) Name a product that can be painted onto the surface of metal to make the marking out stand out more clearly.

....[1]

(b) Fig. 18 shows details of one of the keyhole shapes.

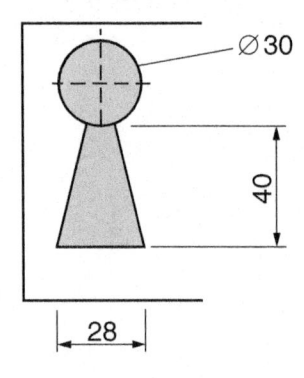

Fig. 18

Use sketches and notes to show how **one** of the keyhole shapes could be cut out and the edges made smooth. Name all the tools and equipment used.

[4]

(c) (i) Describe the process of self-finishing the aluminium to produce a polished surface.

....

....

....

....[3]

(ii) Aluminium can be anodised.
Give **one** reason for anodising the surface of aluminium.

....[1]

(d) Fig. 19 shows an exploded view of the key rack.

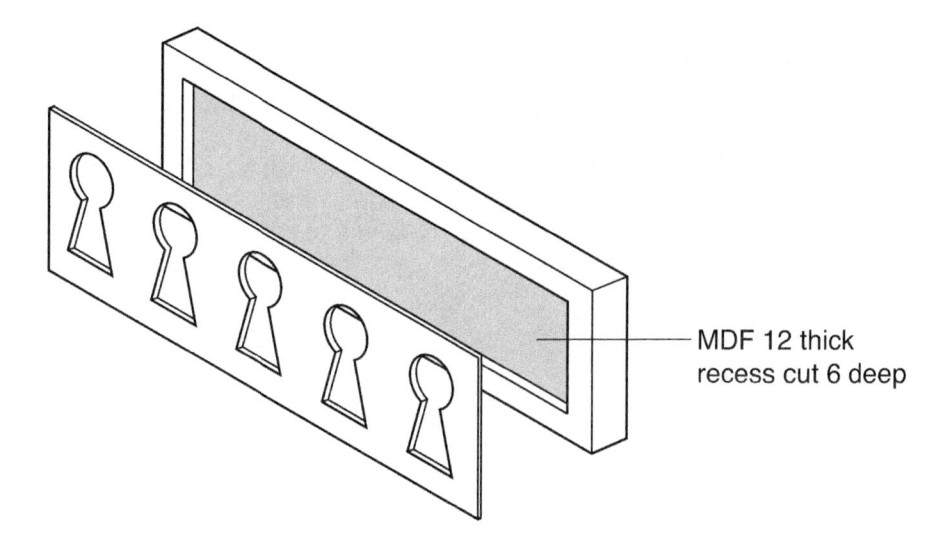

Fig. 19

MDF 12 thick
recess cut 6 deep

(i) Name **two** tools or items of equipment that could be used to cut out the recess shown in Fig. 19.

1 ....

2 ....[2]

(ii) Use sketches and notes to show how the front and back could be joined using an adhesive.
Name a suitable adhesive and show how the parts are held together while the adhesive sets.

[3]

(e) Give **two** benefits of using CAM (Computer Aided Manufacture) to make the key rack.

1 ....

2 ....[2]

(f) Use sketches and notes to show how the key rack could be fitted to a wall.
Screw holes must not be visible in the front of the key rack.
Include details of materials, constructions and fittings used.

[4]

(g) Describe **one** environmental impact of using aluminium in products.

....

....[2]

//// Cambridge IGCSE

Cambridge International Examinations
Cambridge International General Certificate of Secondary Education

CANDIDATE NAME

CENTRE NUMBER

CANDIDATE NUMBER

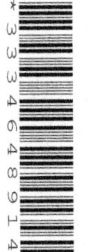

DESIGN AND TECHNOLOGY 0445/32

Paper 3 Resistant Materials October/November 2016

1 hour

Candidates answer on the Question Paper.
No Additional Materials are required.

READ THESE INSTRUCTIONS FIRST

Write your Centre number, candidate number and name on all the work you hand in.
Write in blue or black pen.
You may use an HB pencil for any diagrams, graphs or rough working.
Do not use staples, paper clips, glue or correction fluid.
DO **NOT** WRITE IN ANY BARCODES.

Section A
Answer **all** questions in this section.

Section B
Answer **one** question in this section.

You may use a calculator.

At the end of the examination, fasten all your work securely together.
The number of marks is given in brackets [ ] at the end of each question or part question.
The total of the marks for this paper is 50.

This document consists of **18** printed pages and **2** blank pages.

DC (NF/FD) 117567/1
© UCLES 2016

[Turn over

Section A

Answer **all** questions in this section.

1 Fig. 1 shows three saws used to cut wood.

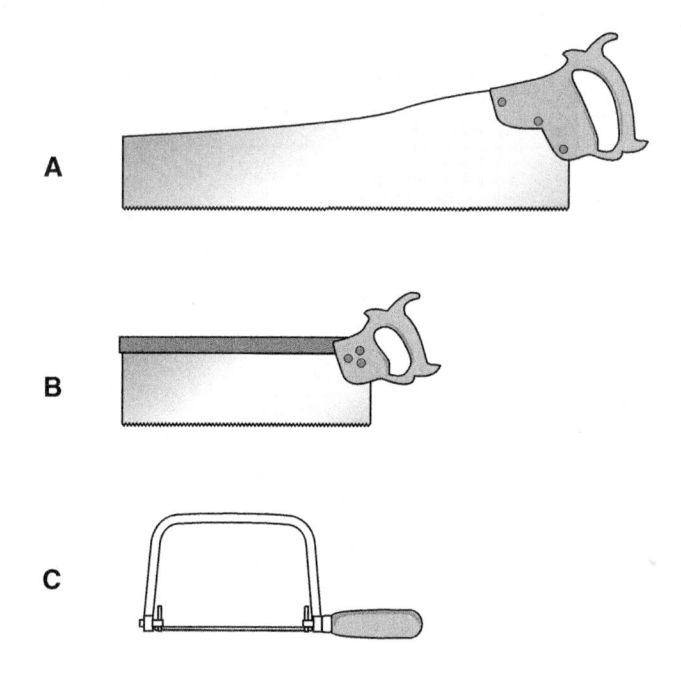

Fig. 1

Name each of the saws **A**, **B** and **C**.

A ....

B ....

C .... [3]

2 Complete the table below by naming a specific material for each product.

Product	Specific material
metal spoon	
metal wire	
plastic bowl	

[3]

3 Complete the drawing below to show a half lap joint.

[2]

4 Complete the table below by naming each of the marking out tools.

Marking out tool	Name

[3]

5 Fig. 2 shows a length of wood with three slots marked out.

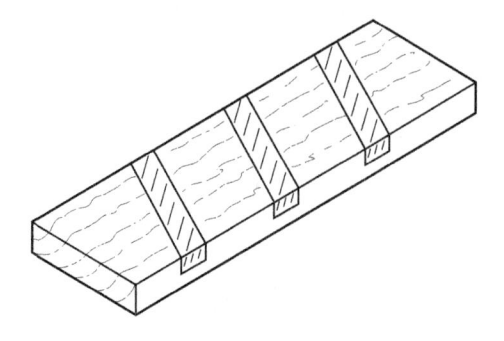

Fig. 2

(a) Give **one** reason why the lines would be marked out using a marking knife rather than a pencil.

.... [1]

(b) Name a tool that could be used with a marking knife to mark all the lines at the same angle across the grain of the wood.

.... [1]

6 Fig. 3 shows two products made from plastic.

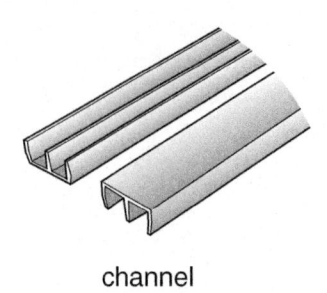

channel   container

Fig. 3

Name the moulding process used to make each product.

channel .... [1]

container .... [1]

7 Fig. 4 shows a mortise with a square haunch.

square haunch

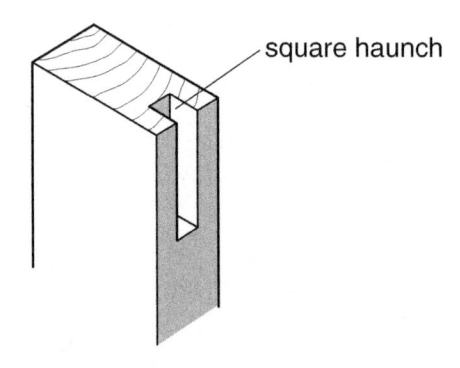

Fig. 4

(a) Draw a square haunch tenon that would fit into the square haunch mortise shown in Fig. 4.

[2]

(b) Describe the purpose of the square haunch.

.... [1]

8 Fig. 5 shows two different types of drill bit.

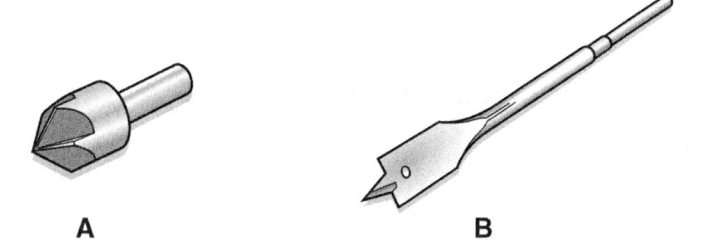

A   **B**

Fig. 5

Name the drill bits **A** and **B** shown in Fig. 5.

A ....

B .... [2]

9 Complete the table by naming each tool or item of equipment used to cut sheet metal.

Tool or item of equipment	Name

[3]

10 Fig. 6 shows two pieces of resistant material.

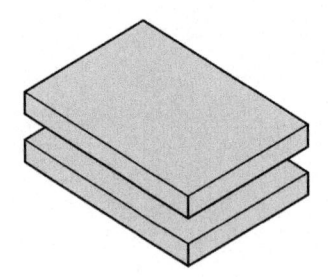

Fig. 6

Name a suitable adhesive that could be used to join the two pieces of material shown above when made from:

(a) pine ....

(b) steel .... [2]

Section B

Answer **one** question in this section.

11 Fig. 7 shows views of a clock used to teach children how to tell the time.
The clock face is made from plywood and the clock hands are made from acrylic.
The clock hands will be moved by the teacher.

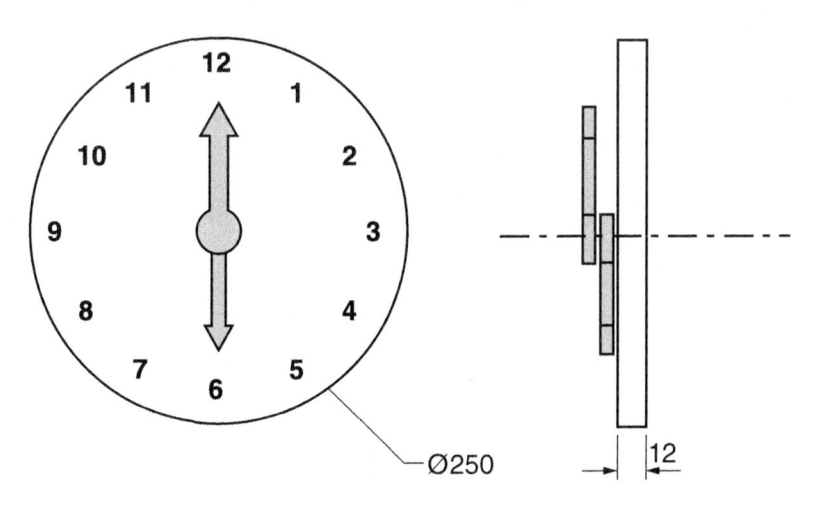

Fig. 7

(a) Give **two** specification points for the clock.

1 ....

2 .... [2]

(b) (i) Fig. 8 shows the clock face marked out on a sheet of 12 thick plywood.
The shape will be cut out using a jigsaw.

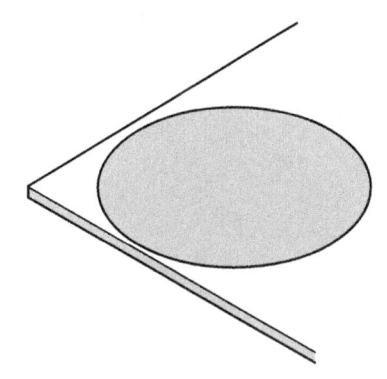

Fig. 8

Give **two** safety precautions that must be taken when using a jigsaw.

1 ....

2 .... [2]

(ii) Describe how the shape could be made round and the edges made smooth after it has been cut out with a jigsaw.

....

....

.... [2]

(c) Fig. 9 shows one clock hand marked out on 5 thick acrylic.

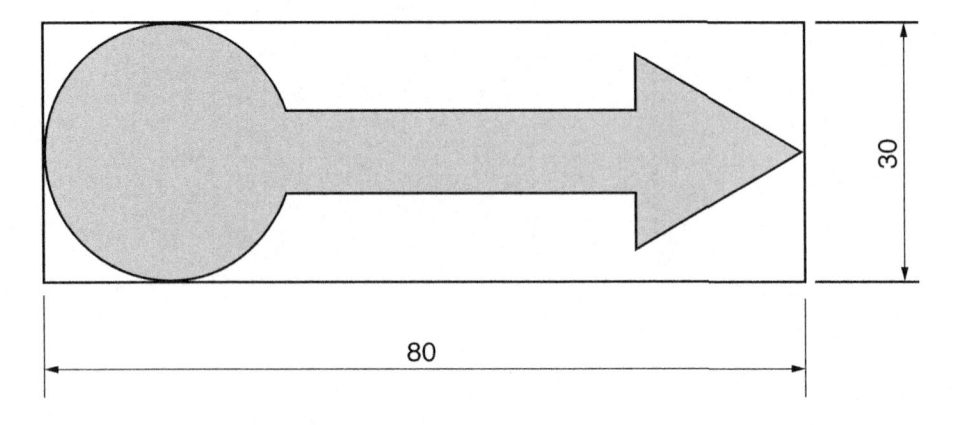

Fig. 9

Use sketches and notes to show how the clock hand could be cut out and the edges finished to a high quality.

[4]

(d) Give **one** benefit of using acrylic for the clock hands.

.... [1]

(e) Add sketches and notes to the drawing below to show how the clock hands could be fitted to the clock face.
The teacher must be able to move the clock hands.

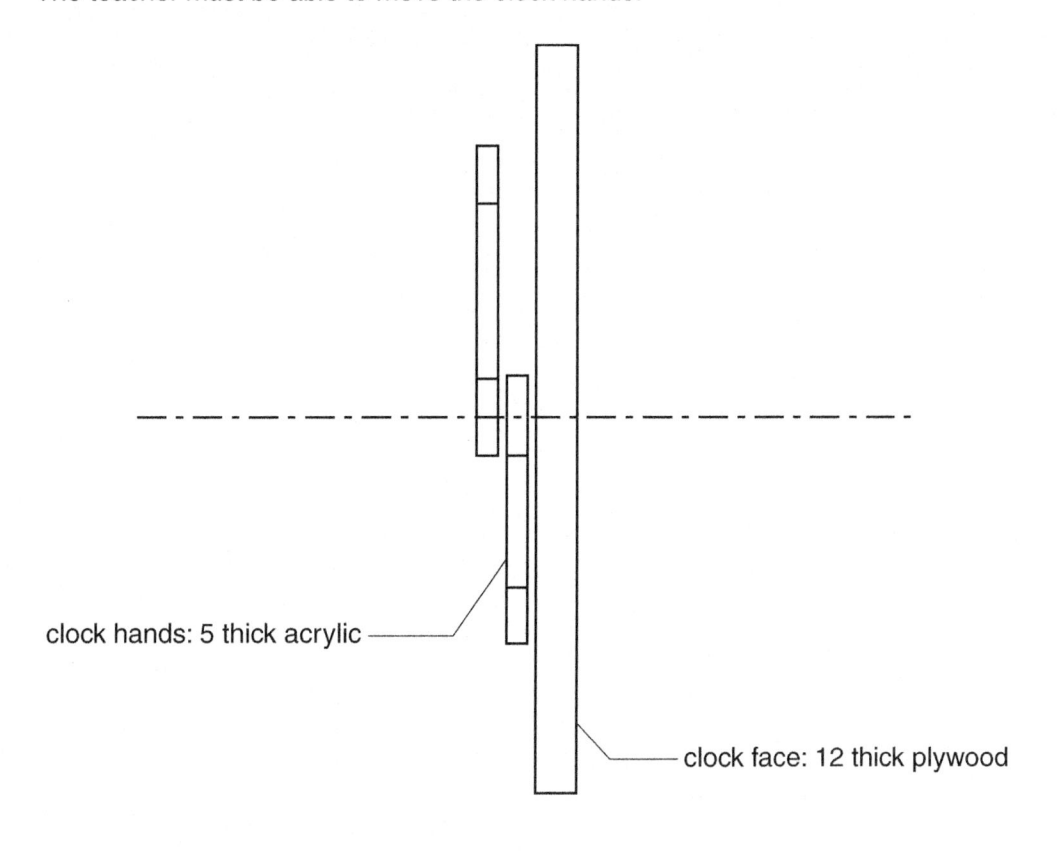

clock hands: 5 thick acrylic

clock face: 12 thick plywood

[3]

(f) The numbers on the clock face could be designed by CAD (Computer Aided Design) and made using CAM (Computer Aided Manufacture).
Give **one** benefit of using:

CAD to design the numbers;

.... [1]

CAM to make the numbers.

.... [1]

(g) Use sketches and notes to show how the clock could be made to stand on its own. Include details of materials, constructions and fittings used.

[5]

(h) Use sketches and notes to show how the clock could be made to fit to a wall instead of standing on its own. Include details of materials, constructions and fittings used.

[4]

12 Fig. 10 shows a wall-mounted shelf unit.

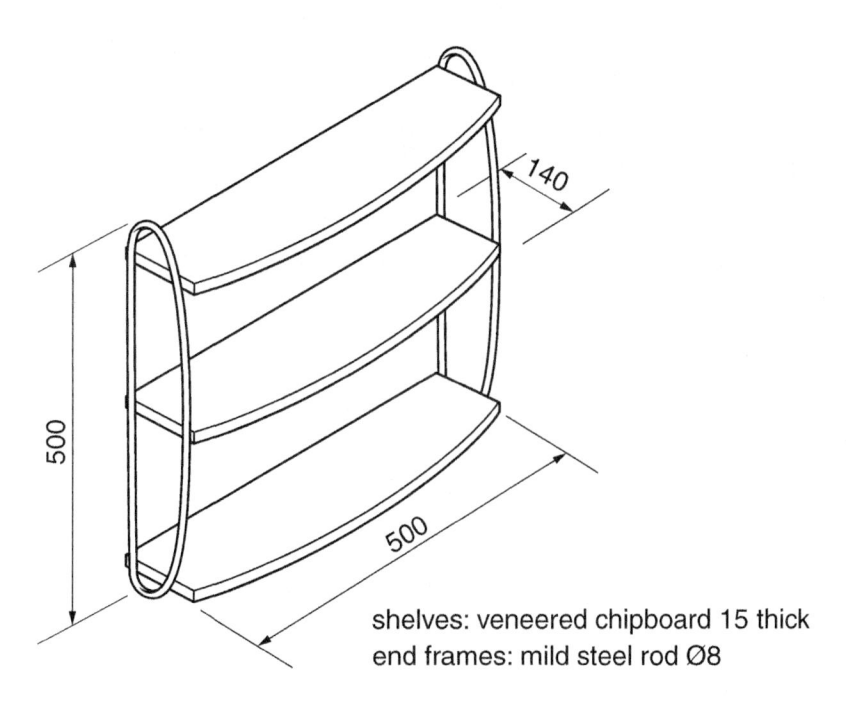

shelves: veneered chipboard 15 thick
end frames: mild steel rod Ø8

Fig. 10

(a) Give **two** advantages of using veneered chipboard rather than solid wood for the shelves of the wall-mounted shelf unit.

1 ....

2 .... [2]

(b) Fig. 11 shows a wooden former around which the mild steel rod will be bent to the shape of the end frame.

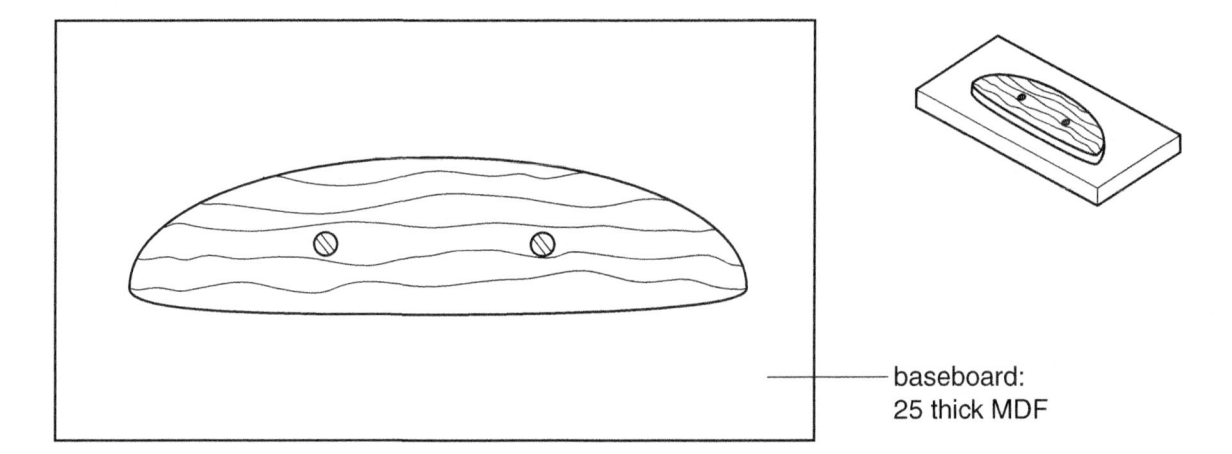

baseboard:
25 thick MDF

Fig. 11

(i) Add sketches and notes to Fig. 11 to show how the mild steel rod could be held against the former while it is bent to shape. [3]

(ii) When shaping the mild steel rod it can become work hardened. Explain what is meant by the term 'work hardened'.

....

....

.... [2]

(c) Fig. 12 shows the two ends of a length of Ø8 mild steel rod. The mild steel rod has been bent to the shape of the end frame. The ends will be brazed together.

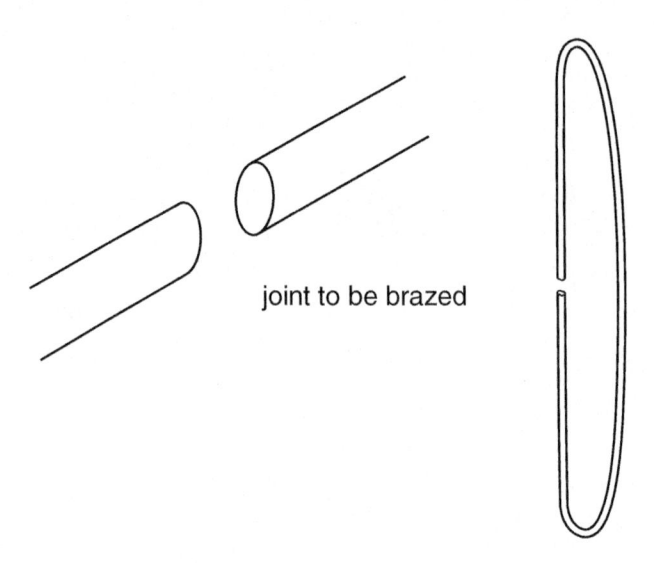

joint to be brazed

Fig. 12

Use sketches and notes to show how the ends of the mild steel rod could be brazed together. Include details of how the ends would be prepared before they are brazed.

[8]

(d) Use sketches and notes to show how the veneered chipboard shelves could be fixed to the end frames made from mild steel rod. Additional materials, fittings and fixings may be used.

[6]

(e) Give **one** reason why each of the materials used to make the wall-mounted shelf unit shown in Fig. 10 could be considered to be environmentally friendly.

Mild steel .... [1]

Veneered chipboard .... [1]

(f) Fig. 13 shows a wall-mounted shelf unit with veneered chipboard sides rather than mild steel end frames.

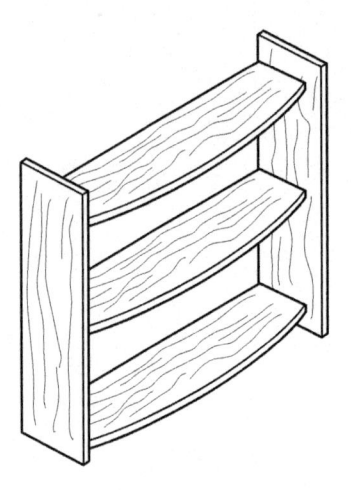

Fig. 13

Give **two** reasons why the designer has decided to use veneered chipboard sides rather than mild steel end frames.

1 ....

2 .... [2]

13 Fig. 14 shows views of an incomplete design for a towel holder made mainly from oak.

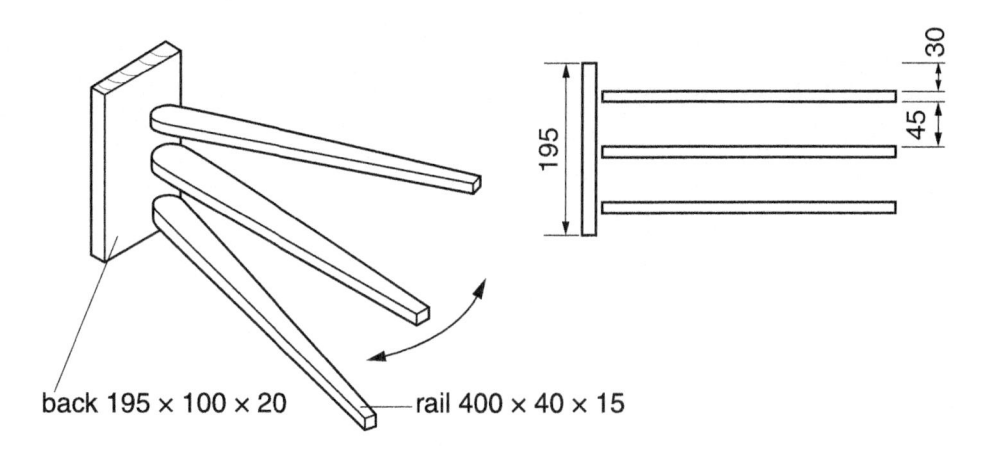

back 195 × 100 × 20   rail 400 × 40 × 15

Fig. 14

(a) Give **two** properties of oak that make it suitable for the towel holder.

1 ....

2 .... [2]

(b) Fig. 15 shows details of one rail marked out, ready to be shaped.

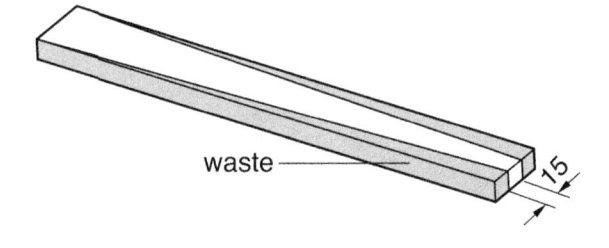

waste

Fig. 15

Use sketches and notes to show how the waste wood could be removed and the surfaces made flat and smooth. Include details of how the rail would be supported while it is shaped.

[5]

(c) Use sketches and notes to show how **all** the rails could be:
- connected to the back of the towel holder;
- allowed to swing as shown in Fig. 14;
- spaced apart.

Include details of materials, constructions and fittings used.

[8]

(d) Use sketches and notes to show how the towel holder could be fitted to a wall.
Holes must not be drilled in the front of the towel holder.
Include details of materials, constructions and fittings used.

[5]

(e) (i) Give **two** reasons why a clear polyurethane varnish would be a suitable finish for the towel holder.

1 ....

2 .... [2]

(ii) Describe **three** stages to prepare the parts of the towel holder to take a clear polyurethane varnish finish.

1 ....

2 ....

3 .... [3]

Cambridge IGCSE

Cambridge International Examinations
Cambridge International General Certificate of Secondary Education

CANDIDATE NAME

CENTRE NUMBER

CANDIDATE NUMBER

DESIGN AND TECHNOLOGY 0445/32

Paper 3 Resistant Materials

May/June 2017

1 hour

Candidates answer on the Question Paper.
No Additional Materials are required.

READ THESE INSTRUCTIONS FIRST

Write your Centre number, candidate number and name on all the work you hand in.
Write in dark blue or black pen.
You may use an HB pencil for any diagrams, graphs or rough working.
Do not use staples, paper clips, glue or correction fluid.
DO **NOT** WRITE IN ANY BARCODES.

Section A
Answer **all** questions in this section.

Section B
Answer **one** question in this section.

You may use a calculator.

At the end of the examination, fasten all your work securely together.
The number of marks is given in brackets [ ] at the end of each question or part question.
The total of the marks for this paper is 50.

This document consists of **15** printed pages and **1** blank page.

DC (NH/CGW) 136197/1
© UCLES 2017

[Turn over

Section A

Answer **all** questions in this section.

1 Fig. 1 shows two pieces of hardwood that have been glued together.

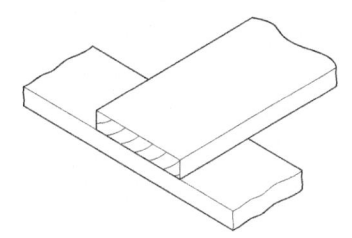

Fig. 1

From the list below (circle) the type of glue that would provide the strongest joint.

contact adhesive   **hot melt glue gun**   **PVA** [1]

2 Complete the drawing below to show odd leg calipers.

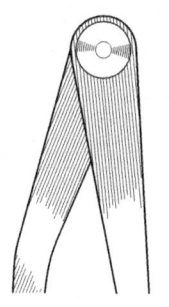

[2]

3 Complete the statement by adding the correct term from the list below.

lightweight   **recycled**   **smart**   **dense**

A thermochromic material changes colour with changes in temperature.

This is an example of a .... material. [1]

4 Fig. 2 shows the end of a length of wood.
Draw on Fig. 2 to show a groove and a rebate.

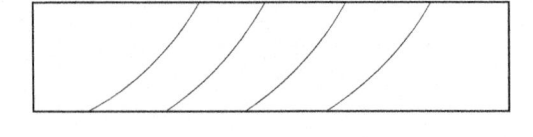

Fig. 2 [2]

5 Fig. 3 shows four items used to fasten materials together.

A   **B**   **C**   **D**

Fig. 3

Name each of the items **A**, **B**, **C** and **D** shown in Fig. 3.

A ....

B ....

C ....

D ....[4]

6 Fig. 4 shows three layers of a sheet of plywood.

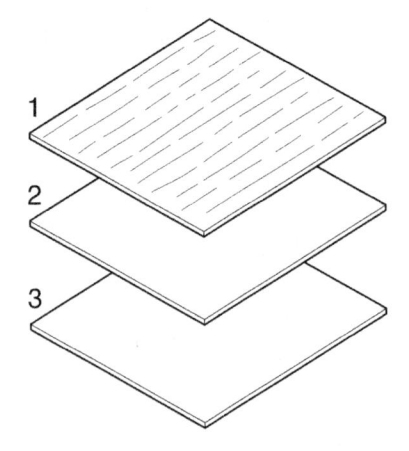

Fig. 4

Complete Fig. 4 by drawing the grain direction on layers 2 and 3 to show how plywood is constructed. [1]

7 The table below shows products made mainly from plastic.
Complete the table by naming a suitable plastic for each product.

Product	Name of plastic
electric plug body	
plastic blister packaging	
knife handle	

[3]

8 Fig. 5 shows a manufactured board.

Fig. 5

(a) Name the manufactured board.

....[1]

(b) Describe briefly how the manufactured board shown in Fig. 5 is made.

....

....

....[2]

(c) The manufactured board shown in Fig. 5 is widely used in the production of mass-produced furniture.
From the list below circle the most important benefit of using this manufactured board.

weight   **appearance**   **cost**   **strength**   [1]

9 Fig. 6 shows a mild steel bracket for a hanging basket.

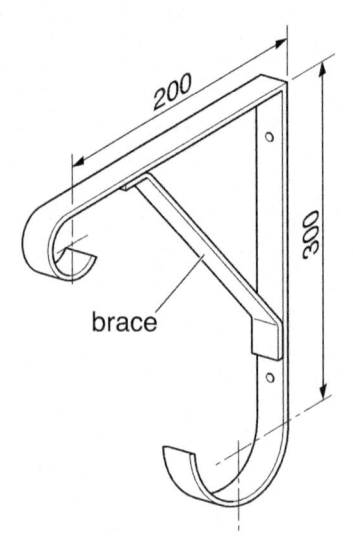

Fig. 6

(a) State a suitable thickness of mild steel strip for the bracket.

....[1]

(b) Give **two** methods of joining the brace to the bracket permanently.

1 ....

2 ....[2]

10 Fig. 7 shows a toast rack made from metal.

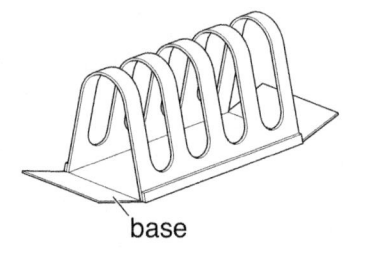

Fig. 7

(a) (i) Name a suitable ferrous metal for the toast rack.

....

(ii) Name a suitable non-ferrous metal for the toast rack.

....[2]

(b) Give **two** reasons why a base has been fitted to the toast rack.

1 ....

2 ....[2]

Section B

Answer **one** question from this section.

11 Fig. 8 shows views of an artist's drawing board.

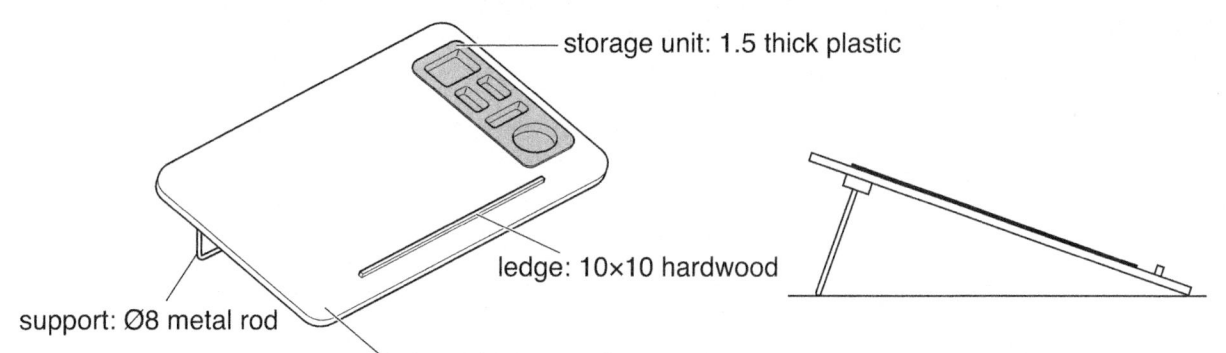

storage unit: 1.5 thick plastic
ledge: 10×10 hardwood
support: Ø8 metal rod
board: 15 thick manufactured board

Fig. 8

(a) Describe **two** good design features of the artist's drawing board.

1 ....

2 ....[2]

(b) Complete the parts list below by naming a specific material for each of the parts of the drawing board.

Part	Number Required	Length × Width × Thickness	Specific material
board	1	650 × 450 × 15	
storage unit	1	300 × 100 × 1.5	
ledge	1	400 × 10 × 10	
support	1	750 × Ø8	

[4]

(c) (i) Name a portable power saw that could be used to cut out the shape of the drawing board from a large sheet of manufactured board.

....[1]

(ii) Give **one** safety precaution, other than wearing eye protection, that must be taken when using portable power tools.

....[1]

(d) The storage unit that will fit into the drawing board is produced by vacuum forming.

   (i) Describe **two** important features of the design of the former used to vacuum form the storage unit.

   1 ....

   2 ....[2]

   (ii) Explain why it is important to heat the plastic to the correct temperature when vacuum forming.

   ....

   ....[2]

(e) Fig. 9 shows the ends of the support fixed into hardwood blocks.

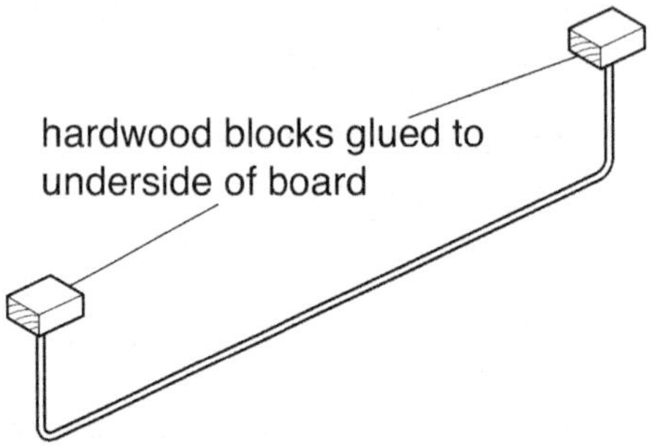

hardwood blocks glued to underside of board

Fig. 9

   (i) Explain why the designer has used hardwood blocks for the ends of the support to fit into rather than drilling holes directly into the drawing board.

   ....

   ....

   ....[2]

   (ii) The support will be made by bending one length of Ø8 metal rod to shape.
   Use sketches and notes to show how the Ø8 metal rod could be bent to shape.
   Name the tools and equipment used.

[3]

(f) Use sketches and notes to show a different method of supporting the drawing board to that shown in Fig. 8.
Include details of all materials and constructions used.

[6]

(g) Give **two** benefits of using a portable power sander to prepare the surface of the drawing board before a finish is applied.

1 ....

2 ....[2]

12 Fig. 10 shows a bird feeder made from wood and plastic.

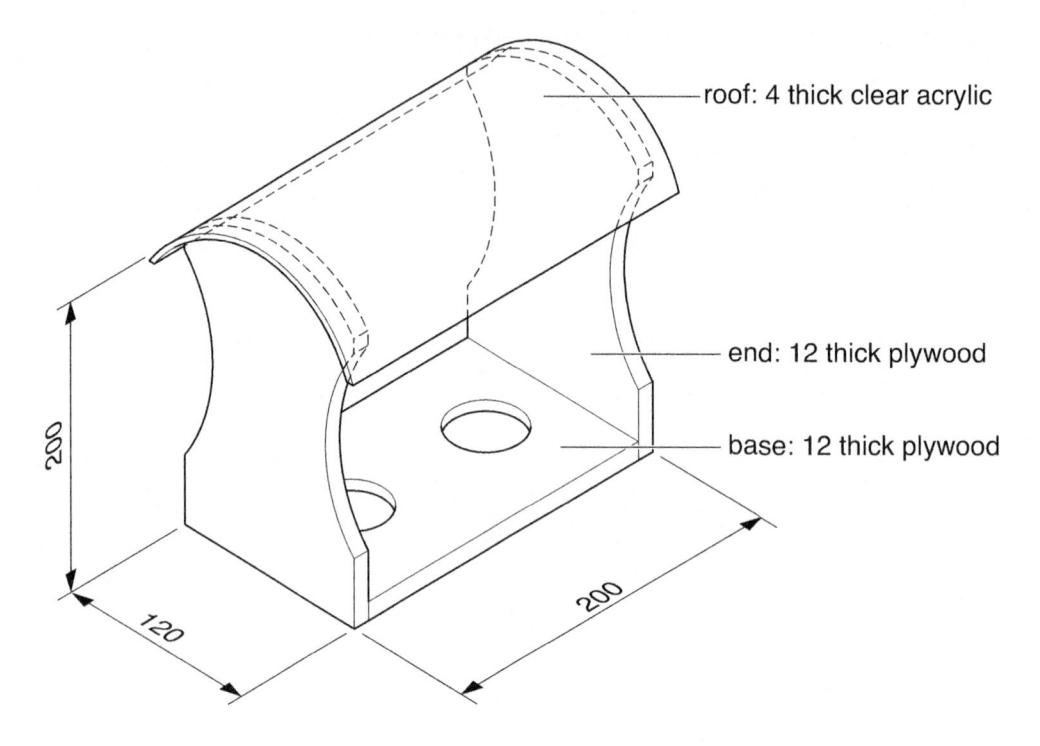

roof: 4 thick clear acrylic
end: 12 thick plywood
base: 12 thick plywood

Fig. 10

(a) Give **two** reasons why acrylic is a good choice of material for the roof of the bird feeder.

1 ....

2 ....[2]

(b) Fig. 11 shows a tool that could be used to produce the Ø50 holes in the base of the bird feeder.

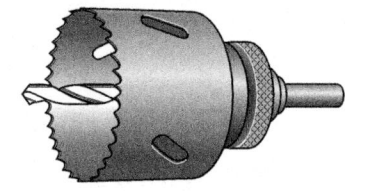

Fig. 11

Name the tool shown in Fig. 11.

....[1]

(c) Fig. 12 shows one end of the bird feeder marked out ready to be cut to shape.

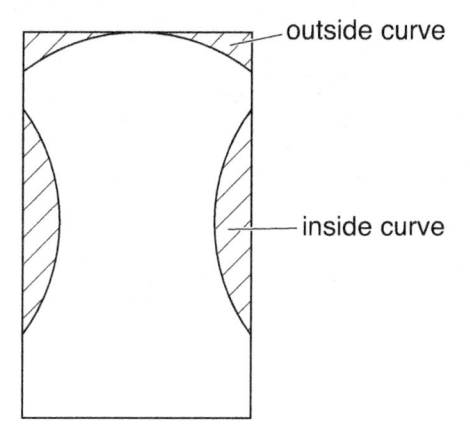

Fig. 12

(i) Name a machine saw that could be used to cut out the shape.

....[1]

(ii) Name a tool that could be used to finish the inside curve.

....[1]

(iii) Give **one** safety precaution you would take when using a disc sander to finish the outside curve.

....[1]

(d) Use sketches and notes to show how the base and ends could be joined together permanently.

[3]

(e) Fig. 13 shows the roof of the bird feeder marked out on a sheet of acrylic.

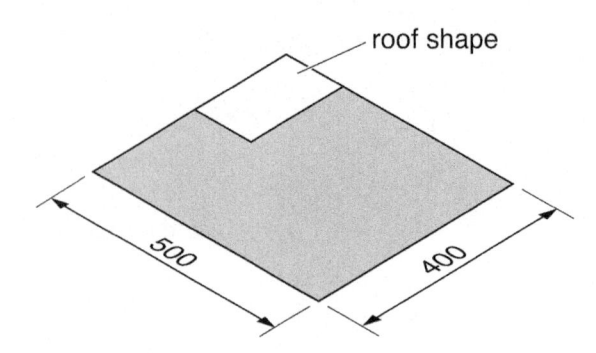

Fig. 13

(i) Name **two** ways of marking lines on the surface of acrylic.

1 ....

2 ....[2]

(ii) When sawing acrylic there is a possibility that it could crack.
Describe how this could be prevented.

....

....

....[2]

(f) Use sketches and notes to show how the curved shape of the roof could be produced.

[4]

(g) Two plastic bowls are needed to fit into the holes in the base of the bird feeder. Fig. 14 shows the former that will be used to vacuum form the plastic bowls.

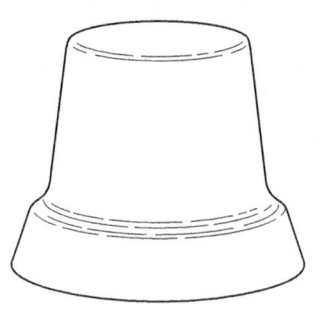

Fig. 14

(i) Describe **two** features of the design of the former that will allow the plastic bowls to be released from the former when vacuum formed.

1 ....

2 ....[2]

(ii) Use sketches and notes to show how **one** plastic bowl could be produced by vacuum forming.

[6]

13 Fig. 15 shows views of a computer desk manufactured as flat-pack for self-assembly. The end frames, back rail and supports are made from hardwood.

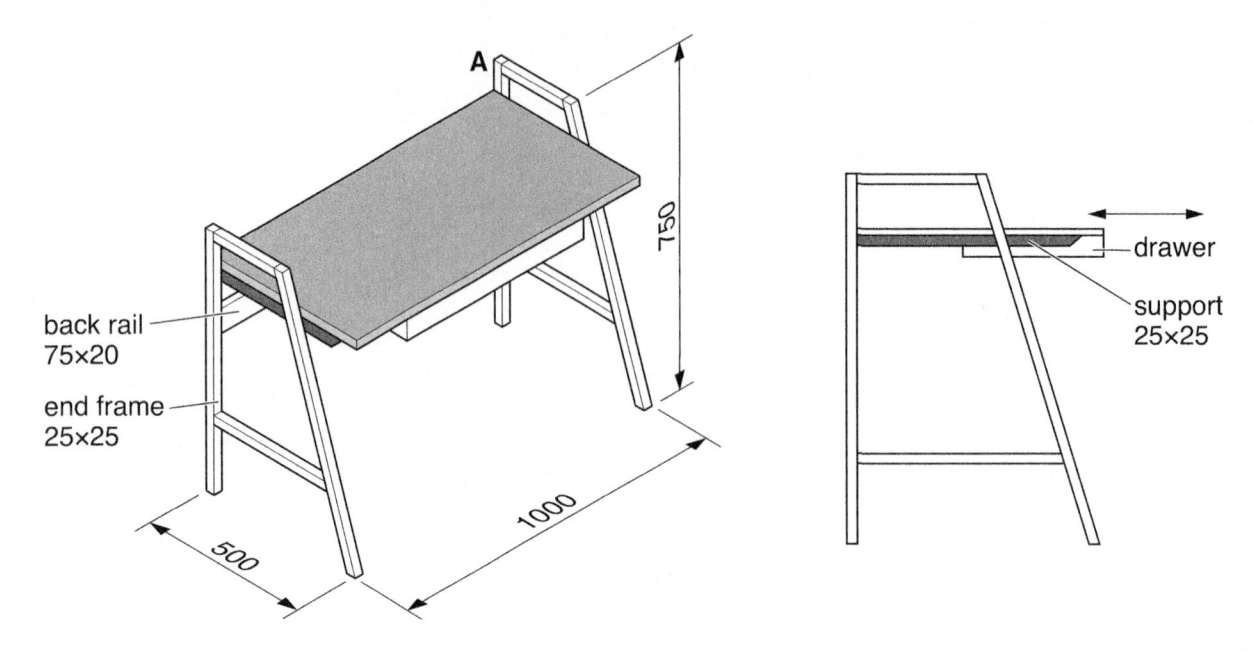

Fig. 15

(a) The computer desk top will be made from manufactured board.

   (i) Name a suitable manufactured board for the desk top.

   ....[1]

   (ii) Give a reason for your choice of manufactured board.

   ....[1]

(b) (i) Sketch and name a permanent joint that could be used at corner **A** in Fig. 15.

[4]

(ii) Fig. 16 shows an exploded view of a support and an end frame.
Use sketches and notes to show how the support could be joined to the end frame using a temporary fixing in the space below.

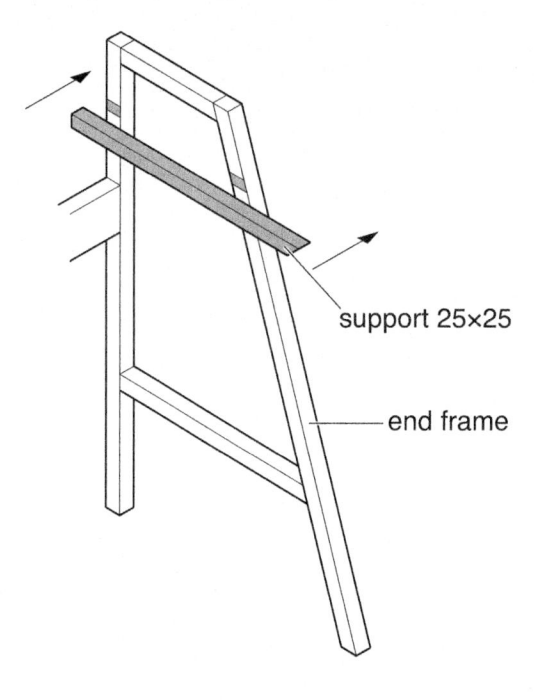

Fig. 16

[3]

(c) The hardwood parts of the computer desk will be finished with polyurethane varnish.

(i) Describe how each of the items listed below could be used to prepare the surfaces of the hardwood parts before a polyurethane varnish finish is applied.

Medium grade glasspaper

....

Fine grade glasspaper

....

Damp cloth

....

Cork block

....[4]

(ii) Give **two** reasons why polyurethane varnish is a suitable finish for the computer desk.

1 ....

2 ....[2]

(d) Explain how the designer has decided on the measurements of:

   (i) the length and width of the computer desktop;

   ....

   (ii) the height of the computer desk top above the ground.

   ....[2]

(e) Fig. 17 shows details of a drawer that will be supported below the computer desk top.

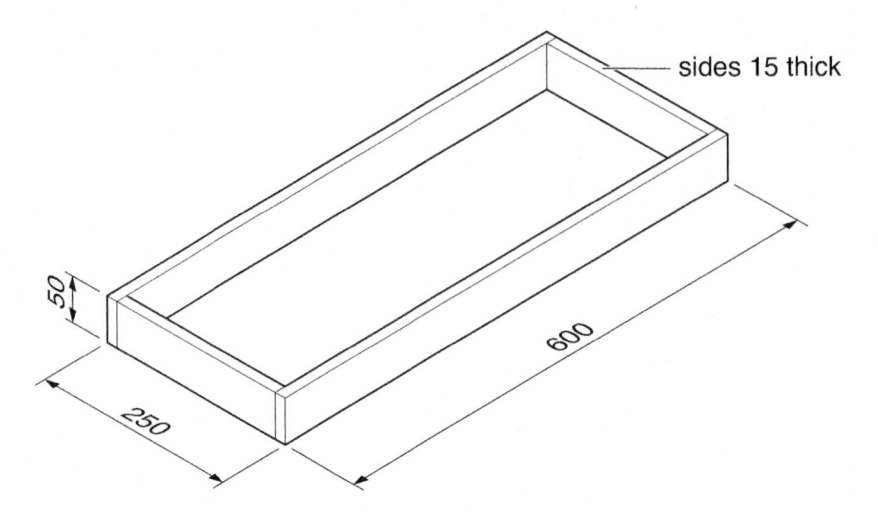

sides 15 thick

50
600
250

Fig. 17

Use sketches and notes to show how the drawer could be supported below the computer desk top and made to slide in and out as shown in Fig. 15.
Include details of materials, constructions and **two** important sizes.

[6]

(f) Many items of furniture are designed for self-assembly.
Give **two** drawbacks of self-assembly furniture.

1 ....

2 ....[2]

Cambridge IGCSE

Cambridge International Examinations
Cambridge International General Certificate of Secondary Education

CANDIDATE NAME

CENTRE NUMBER

CANDIDATE NUMBER

DESIGN AND TECHNOLOGY 0445/32

Paper 3 Resistant Materials October/November 2017

1 hour

Candidates answer on the Question Paper.
No Additional Materials are required.

READ THESE INSTRUCTIONS FIRST

Write your Centre number, candidate number and name on all the work you hand in.
Write in blue or black pen.
You may use an HB pencil for any diagrams, graphs or rough working.
Do not use staples, paper clips, glue or correction fluid.
DO **NOT** WRITE IN ANY BARCODES.

Section A
Answer **all** questions in this section.

Section B
Answer **one** question in this section.

You may use a calculator.

At the end of the examination, fasten all your work securely together.
The number of marks is given in brackets [ ] at the end of each question or part question.
The total of the marks for this paper is 50.

This document consists of **17** printed pages and **3** blank pages.

DC (AL/FC) 136179/2
© UCLES 2017

[Turn over

Section A

Answer **all** questions in this section.

1 Complete the drawing below to show the construction of blockboard.

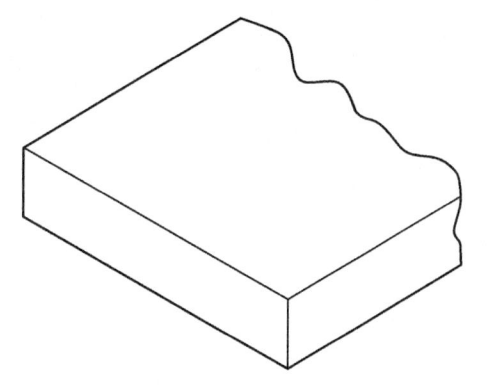

[2]

2 Fig. 1 shows a metalwork vice **A** and a woodwork vice **B**.

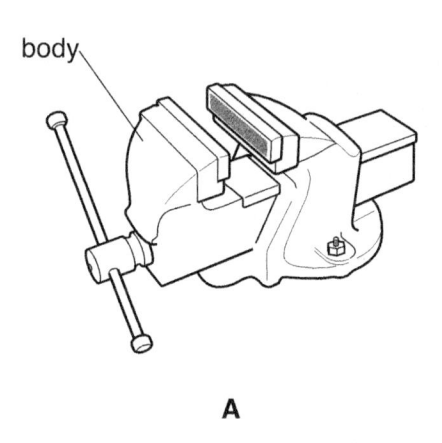

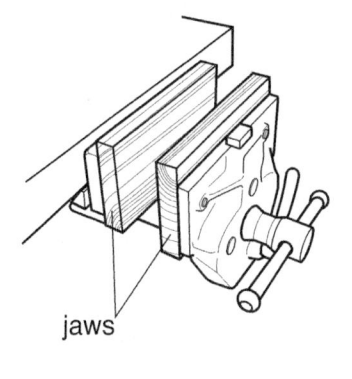

Fig. 1

(a) Name the metal from which the body of the metalwork vice is made.

....[1]

(b) Give **one** property of beech that makes it suitable for the jaws of the woodwork vice.

....[1]

3 Thermochromic materials are an example of 'smart' materials.
Complete the statement by adding the correct term from the list below.

weight　　　　　**temperature**　　　　　**hardness**　　　　　**light**

Thermochromic materials change colour with changes in ....
[1]

4 Fig. 2 shows two watering cans.

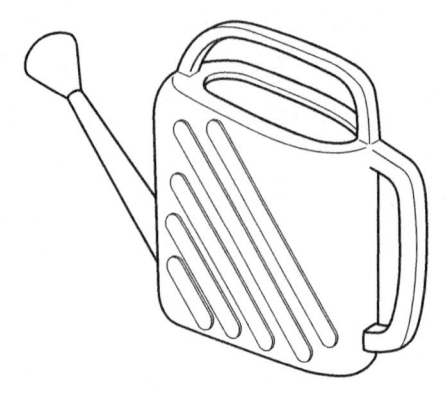

watering can **A**
polypropylene

watering can **B**
mild steel

Fig. 2

(a) Name a process used to manufacture the body of watering can **A**.

....[1]

(b) Explain why watering can **B** would be galvanised.

....

....[2]

(c) (i) State which of the two watering cans, **A** or **B**, would be cheaper to mass produce.

.... [1]

(ii) Give **one** reason for your choice.

....[1]

5 Complete the drawing below to show outside calipers.

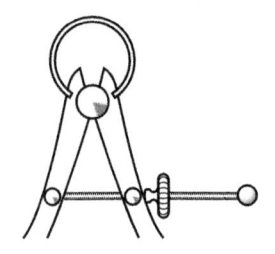

[2]

6 Two workshop processes that could be dangerous are listed in the table below.
Complete the table by describing each danger and how it can be prevented.

Process	Danger	How it can be prevented
Joining pieces of acrylic with acrylic cement		
Pouring molten aluminium when casting		

[4]

7 Fig. 3 shows a label on a box of screws.

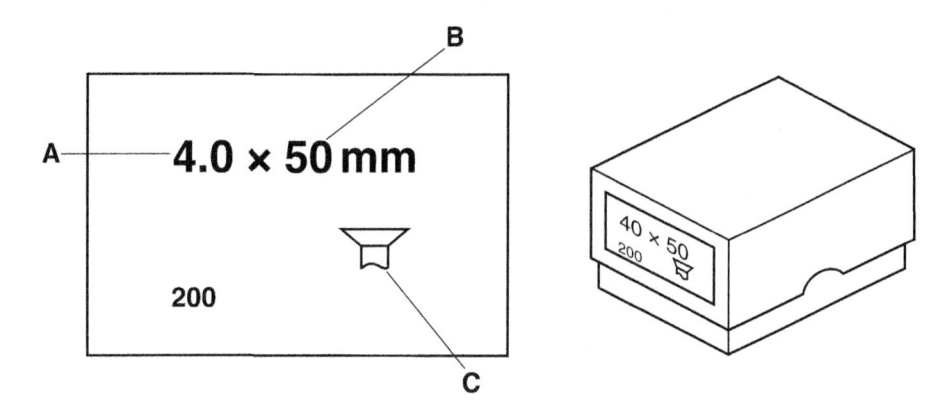

Fig. 3

State what each item of information means.

A...

B...

C...[3]

8 Complete the drawing below to show a tongue and groove joint.

[2]

9 Fig. 4 shows solid wood boards being seasoned outdoors in the open air.

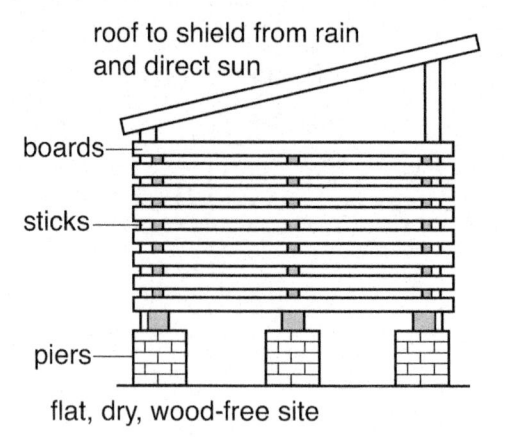

Fig. 4

(a) Give **one** reason why solid wood has to be seasoned.

....[1]

(b) Name a different method of seasoning solid wood boards.

....[1]

10 Complete the table by naming the correct plastic from the list below to match each description.

nylon   phenol formaldehyde   ABS   polypropylene   melamine formaldehyde

Plastic	Description
	hard, durable, used to make saucepan handles and dark electrical fittings
	self-lubricating, used to make gear wheels, clothing, combs, curtain rails

[2]

Section B

Answer **one** question from this section.

11 Fig. 5 shows a picnic table that can be folded flat to fit in the back of a car.

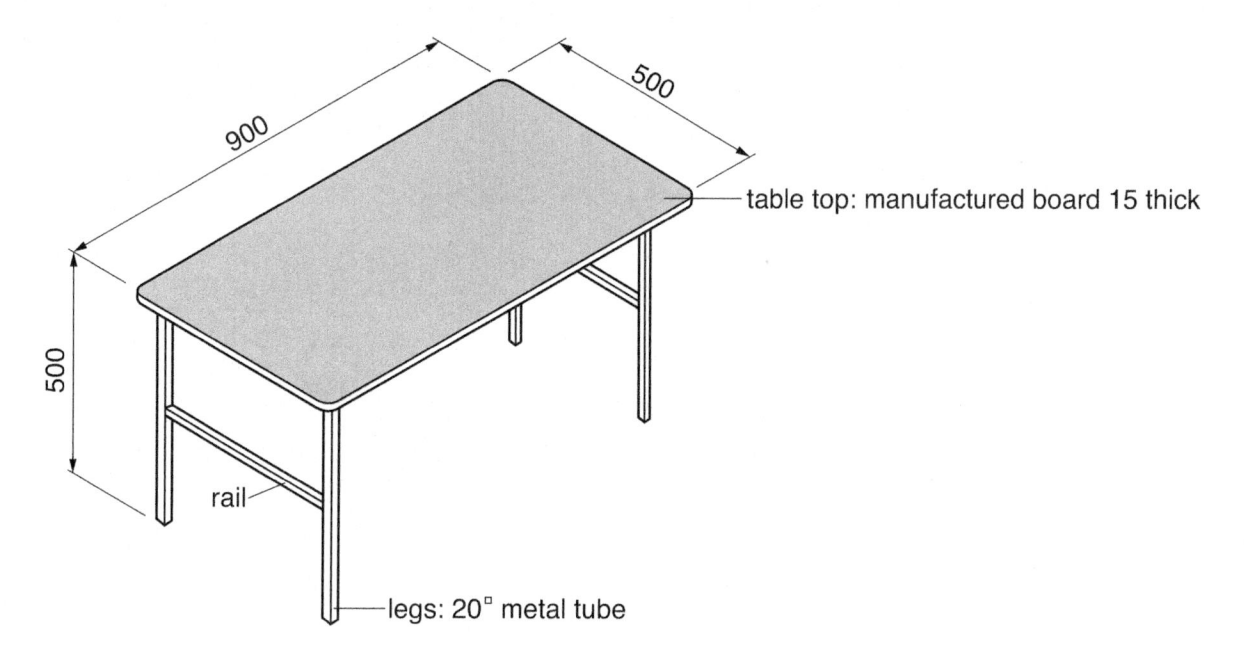

Fig. 5

(a) Give **three** items of research the designer would need to consider when designing the picnic table.

1 ....

2 ....

3 ....[3]

(b) (i) Name a suitable metal for the legs and rails.

....[1]

(ii) Name **two** heat processes that could be used to join the legs and rails.

1 ....

2 ....[2]

(c) Give **two** benefits of covering the table top with a plastic laminate.

1 ....

2 ....[2]

(d) Fig. 6 shows the underside of the table top and the two end frames.

end frame **A**

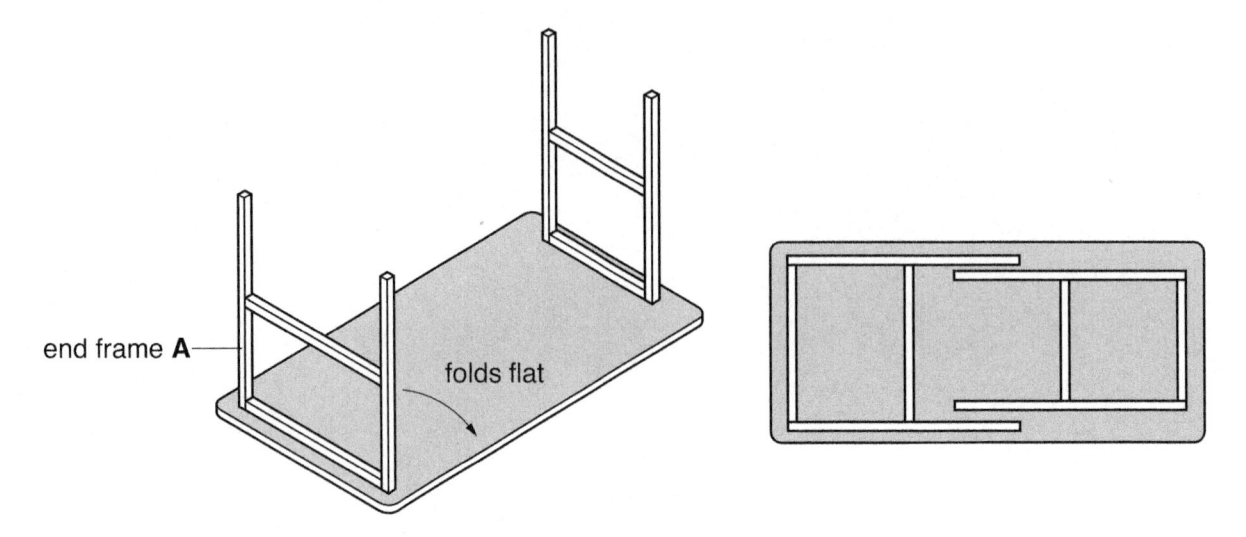

folds flat

Fig. 6

Include details of materials, fittings and constructions when answering parts **(i)**, **(ii)** and **(iii)**.

(i) Use sketches and notes to show how end frame **A** could be made to fold against the underside of the table top.

[4]

(ii) Use sketches and notes to show how both end frames could be held flat against the underside of the table top when carried.

[4]

(iii) Use sketches and notes to show how both end frames could be locked against the table top to prevent them from folding inwards when in use.

[4]

(e) Use sketches and notes to show a modification to the end frames so that the picnic table could remain level when positioned on uneven ground.
Include details of materials, fittings and constructions.

[5]

12 Fig. 7 shows a bird feeder and a parts list.

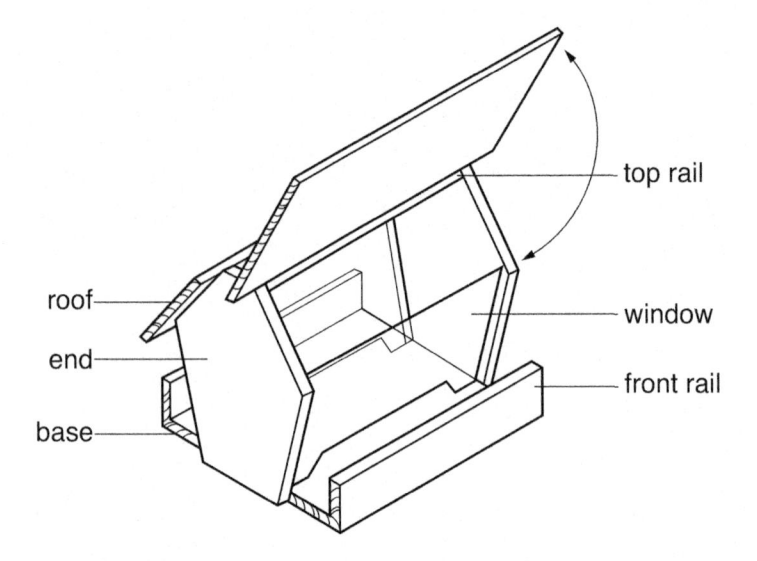

Part	Number Required	Length × Width × Thickness	Material
end	2	200 × 150 × 12	Pine
roof	2	300 × 140 × 12	Pine
base	1	225 × 200 × 12	Pine
top rail	1	225 × 50 × 12	Pine
front rail	2	225 × 50 × 12	Pine
window	2	235 × 120 × 4	Clear acrylic

Fig. 7

(a) Fig. 8 shows one end of the bird feeder marked out, ready to be cut to shape.

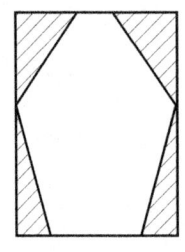

Fig. 8

(i) Use sketches and notes to show how a sliding bevel could be used to mark out the shape.

[2]

(ii) Name a saw that could be used to cut out the shape.

.... [1]

(iii) Name a plane that could be used to make the sawn edges flat and smooth.

.... [1]

(b) The ends will be glued and nailed to the base.

(i) Name a specific type of nail that could be used to join the ends to the base.

.... [1]

(ii) Name an adhesive suitable for outdoor use and state approximately how long it takes to set.

Suitable adhesive .... [1]

Time to set .... [1]

(c) The roof is made in two parts. Each part is hinged to the top rail as shown in Fig. 7. Sketch and name a suitable hinge.

[3]

Name of hinge .... [1]

(d) Fig. 9 shows details of the 4 thick clear acrylic window.

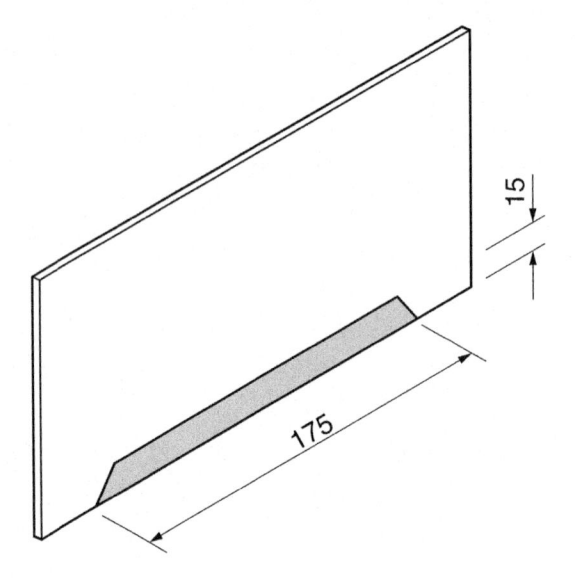

Fig. 9

(i) Use sketches and notes to show how the shaded area could be removed and the edges made flat and smooth.

[3]

(ii) Use sketches and notes to show how the 4 thick clear acrylic window could be fitted securely inside the bird feeder.
Include all constructional details.

[4]

(e) Fig. 10 shows a sectional view of part of the bird feeder with a Ø5 aluminium rod that will hook over the branch of a tree.

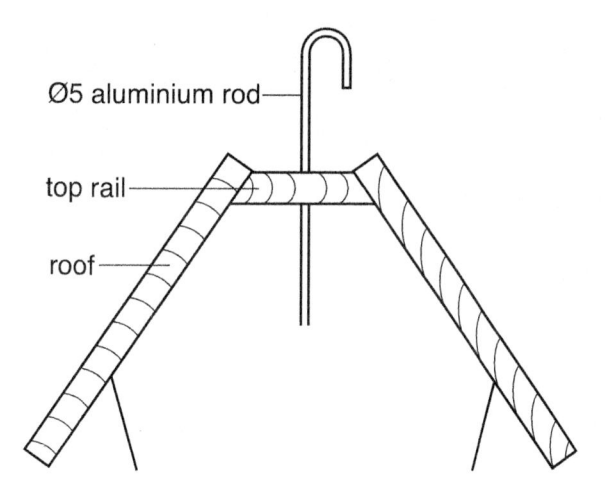

Fig. 10

Add sketches to Fig. 10 to show how the Ø5 aluminium rod could be attached to the top rail of the bird feeder. [3]

(f) Describe **two** problems that designers face when designing products for outdoor use and how they may be solved.

Problem 1 ....

....[1]

Solution ....

....[1]

Problem 2 ....

....[1]

Solution ....

....[1]

13 Fig. 11 shows views of a shelf unit made from 15 thick MDF in a school workshop. The shelf unit will be made as flat-pack for self-assembly.

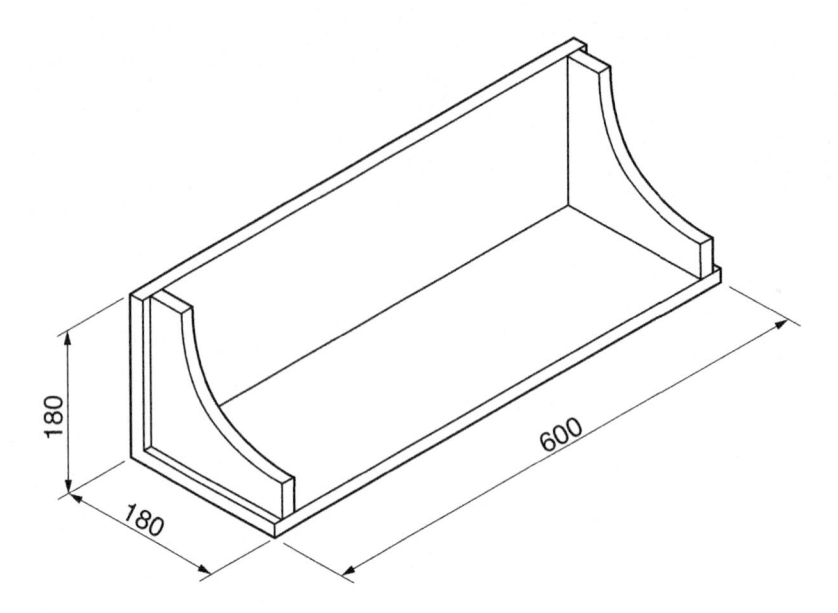

Fig. 11

(a) Give **two** advantages of making the shelf unit from MDF rather than solid wood.

1 ....

2 ....[2]

(b) Fig. 12 shows one end of the shelf unit with a template that will be used when drawing the shape onto the MDF.

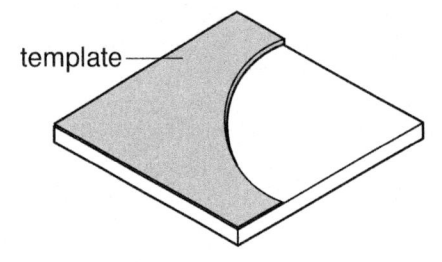

Fig. 12

(i) Give **one** advantage of using a template rather than marking out the shape by hand.

....[1]

(ii) Name **one** saw that could be used to cut out the shape.

....[1]

(iii) Name a tool that could be used to finish the inside curve.

....[1]

(c) The ends are joined to the shelf and back with dowels.
Fig. 13 shows one end of the shelf unit ready for the positions of dowels to be marked out.

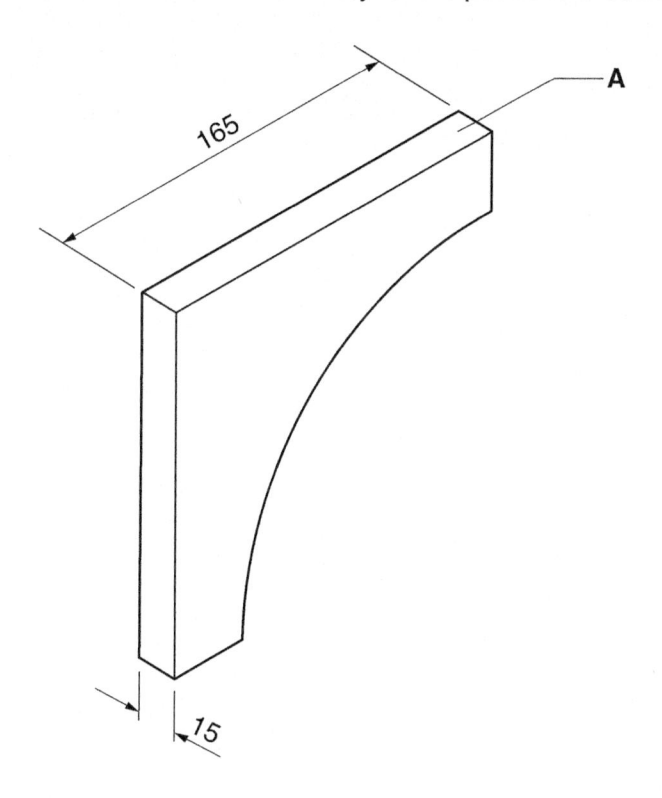

Fig. 13

(i) Draw accurately on end **A** shown in Fig. 13 the positions for **two** dowels.
Show clearly **all** dimensions. [3]

(ii) (Circle) the most appropriate diameter of dowel that could be used.

Ø4　　　　　　Ø6　　　　　　Ø9　　　　　　Ø12

[1]

(iii) State the purpose of the chamfer and the grooves on the dowel peg shown below.

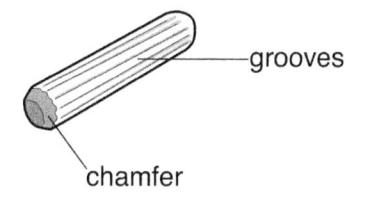

chamfer ....

grooves ....[2]

(iv) A batch of twenty identical shelf units will be made in a school workshop.
Use sketches and notes to show a design for a drilling jig that could be used when drilling the holes for the dowels in the ends of the shelf unit shown in Fig. 13.

[4]

(v) Explain how the drilling jig you have designed in part **(iv)** would be used.

....

....

....[2]

(d) Fig. 14 shows the back of the shelf unit.
Two brass plates 1.5 thick are set into the back so that the shelf unit can be fitted to a wall.

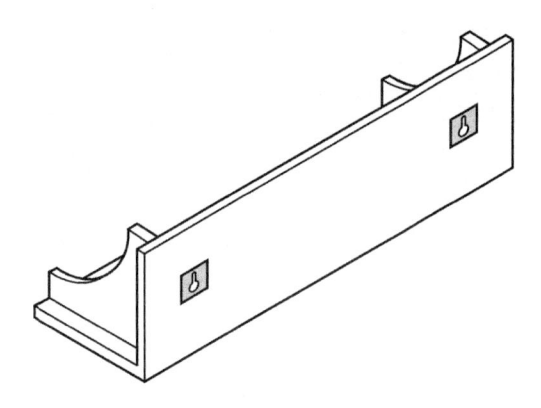

Fig. 14

Fig. 15 shows details of the brass plates.

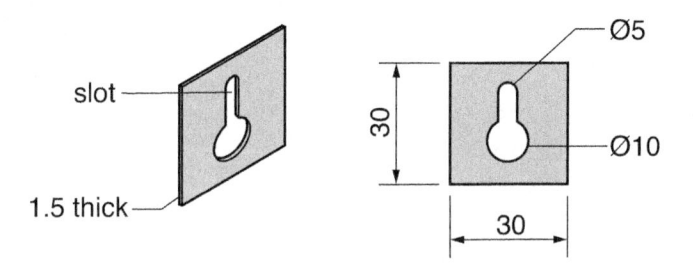

Fig. 15

Use sketches and notes to show how the slot could be cut out in the brass plate.
Name all the tools used. Do not include details of marking out.

[4]

(e) Give **two** reasons why the shelf unit would be given a painted finish rather than a clear varnished finish.

1..

2..[2]

(f) Give **two** reasons why self-assembly products are popular with consumers.

1..

2..[2]

BLANK PAGE

CANDIDATE NAME			

CENTRE NUMBER		CANDIDATE NUMBER	

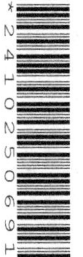

Cambridge International Examinations
Cambridge International General Certificate of Secondary Education

DESIGN AND TECHNOLOGY 0445/32
Paper 3 Resistant Materials May/June 2018
1 hour

Candidates answer on the Question Paper.
No Additional Materials are required.

READ THESE INSTRUCTIONS FIRST

Write your Centre number, candidate number and name on all the work you hand in.
Write in dark blue or black pen.
You may use an HB pencil for any diagrams, graphs or rough working.
Do not use staples, paper clips, glue or correction fluid.
DO **NOT** WRITE IN ANY BARCODES.

Section A
Answer **all** questions in this section.

Section B
Answer **one** question in this section.

You may use a calculator.

At the end of the examination, fasten all your work securely together.
The number of marks is given in brackets [ ] at the end of each question or part question.
The total of the marks for this paper is 50.

This document consists of **18** printed pages and **2** blank pages.

[Turn over

Section A

Answer **all** questions in this section.

1 Fig. 1 shows a door bolt made from steel for use in a bathroom. The bolt has a chrome finish.

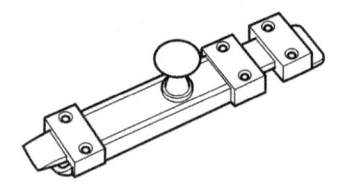

Fig. 1

Give **two** benefits of a chrome finish for the door bolt.

1 ....

2 .... [2]

2 Fig. 2 shows an incomplete leg fastening used to join a leg to the rails of a table.

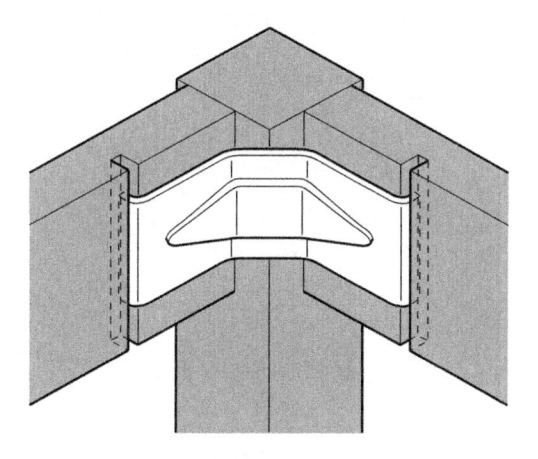

Fig. 2

Add to Fig. 2 to show how the leg fastening could be fixed to the leg and the rails. [3]

3 Complete the table below by adding the correct name from the list.

forstner   **countersink**   **flat**   **twist**   **centre**

Drill	Name
(arrow-shaped drill)	
(centre drill)	
(twist drill)	

[3]

4 Fig. 3 shows a skateboard. The deck is made by gluing thin layers of wood together.

Fig. 3

(a) Give the correct term for 'thin layers of wood'.

....[1]

(b) Complete the statement below by adding the correct term from the list.

casting   **machining**   **shaping**   **laminating**

Gluing thin layers of wood together is known as ....[1]

5   Fig. 4 shows a handle made from metal.

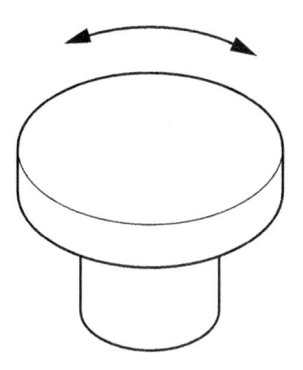

Fig. 4

Add sketches and notes to Fig. 4 to show a modification to the handle that would make it easier to grip and turn. [2]

6   Fig. 5 shows a canoe.

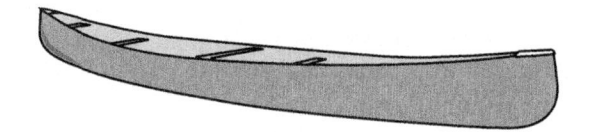

Fig. 5

Name **two** composite materials that could be used to make the canoe.

1 ....

2 ....[2]

7 Fig. 6 shows a piece of steel that has cracked due to work hardening during bending.

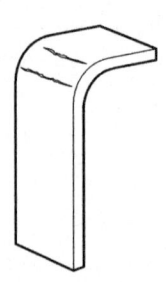

Fig. 6

Explain what is meant by the term 'work hardening'.

....

....

.... [2]

8 Fig. 7 shows views of a cabinet and a 6 mm thick sliding glass door to be fitted inside the cabinet. Add sketches and notes to Fig. 7 to show how **two** sliding glass doors could be fitted inside the cabinet.

glass door 6 thick

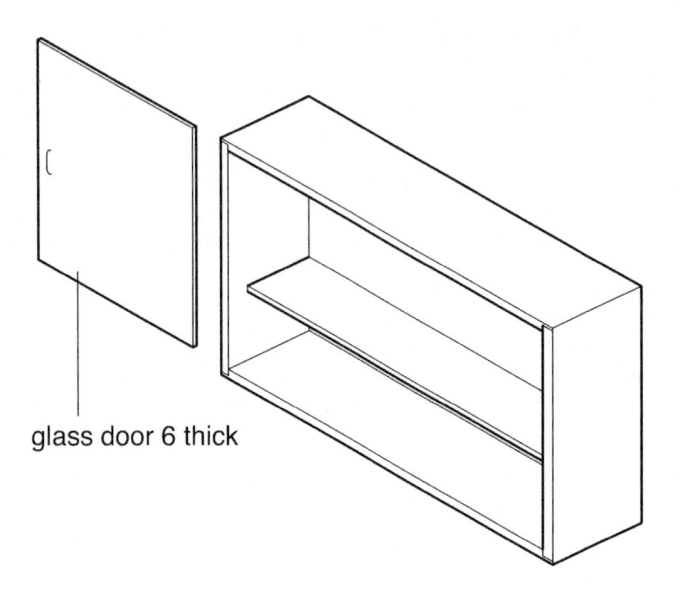

top of cabinet
15 thick

bottom of cabinet
15 thick

Fig. 7

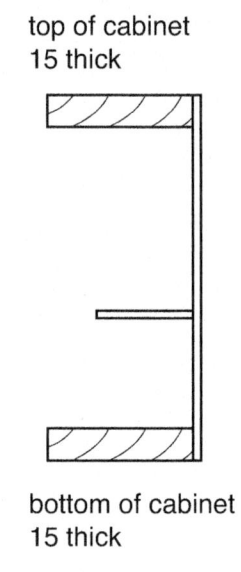

[3]

9 Complete the table by naming the correct plastic from the list below to match each description.

nylon   **melamine**   **PVC**   **polythene**   **polystyrene**

Material	Description of material
	hard, tough, weather resistant, used for pipes, guttering, window frames
	hard-wearing, strong, range of colours, used for decorative laminates
	lightweight plastic, absorbs shock, good heat and sound insulator

[3]

10 Fig. 8 shows a person sitting at a desk, using a computer. Three areas, where consideration of ergonomics is required, are labelled **A**, **B** and **C**.

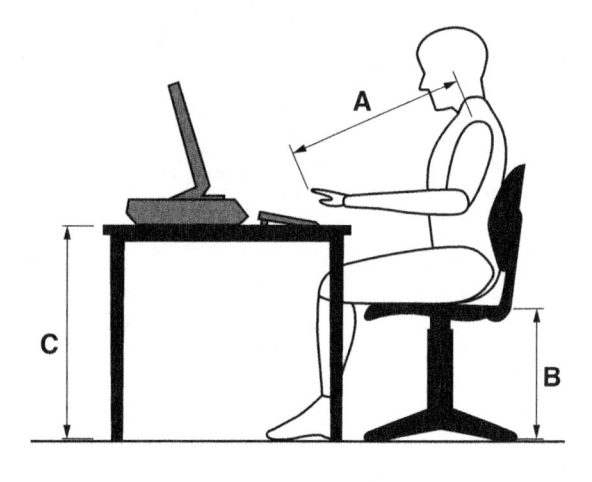

Fig. 8

Describe briefly the ergonomic consideration for **each** of the areas **A**, **B** and **C** shown.

A ....

B ....

C ....[3]

Section B

Answer **one** question from this section.

11 Fig. 9 shows a child's desk organiser made from 4mm thick acrylic. The desk organiser will store paints, brushes, marker pens, crayons and similar equipment.

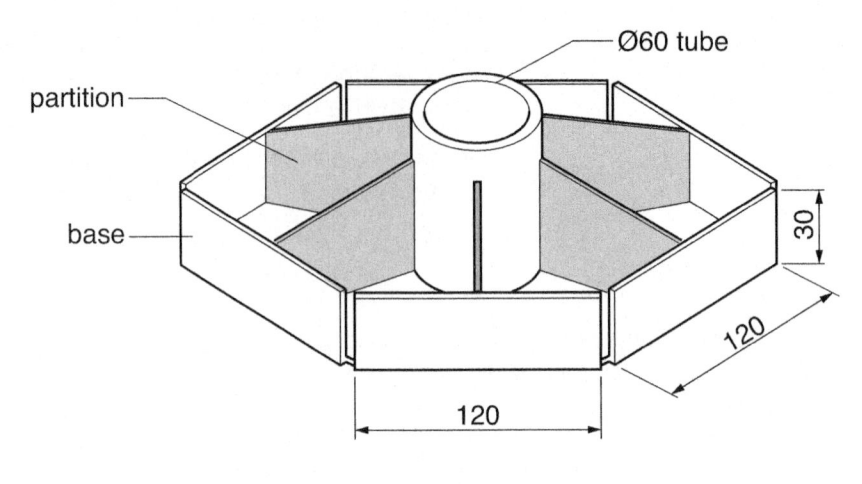

Fig. 9

(a) Fig. 10 shows the development (net) of the base of the desk organiser as a card template that will be glued to the acrylic.

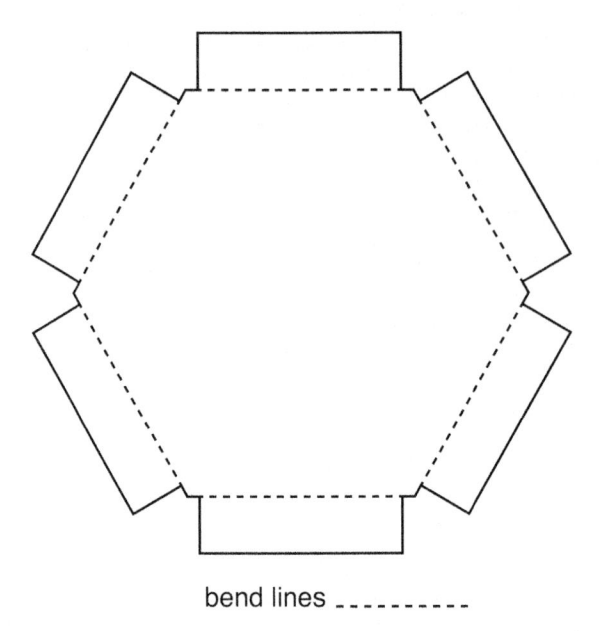

bend lines - - - - - - - - -

Fig. 10

(i) Give **one** advantage of using a template rather than marking the development (net) directly onto the acrylic.

....[1]

(ii) Use sketches and notes to show how the acrylic development (net) could be cut out by hand.
Include the following details:

- the method of holding the acrylic
- the name of a suitable saw
- **one** precaution that would be taken to prevent damage when sawing

[4]

(b) Fig. 11 shows a basic former around which the acrylic will be moulded to shape.

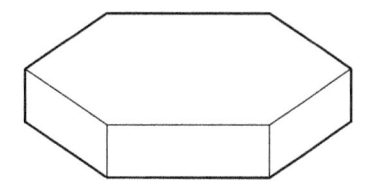

Fig. 11

Describe how the acrylic could be:
- made soft enough to be moulded to shape
- held securely while it cools

[4]

(c) The base of the desk organiser could also be produced by the vacuum forming process.

    (i) Name a suitable plastic, other than acrylic, that could be vacuum formed.

    ....[1]

    (ii) Describe **two** modifications that would need to be made to the former shown in Fig. 11 so that it could be used to vacuum form the base of the desk organiser.

    1 ....

    2 ....[2]

    (iii) Explain why vacuum forming would be a better method of producing the base of the desk organiser if it were to be batch produced.

    ....

    ....

    ....[2]

(d) The partitions will be joined permanently to the base and the Ø60 tube using acrylic cement. Describe **two** safety precautions that must be taken when using acrylic cement.

    1 ....

    2 ....[2]

(e) Many of the edges of the acrylic will need to be made smooth and highly polished.
List **three** tools or items of equipment that could be used to make the edges smooth and highly polished.

    1 ....

    2 ....

    3 ....[3]

[Turn over

(f) To make it easier for children to access the equipment in the desk organiser an additional base is required that will allow the desk organiser to rotate.
Children will then be able to turn the desk organiser to select the equipment they need.

Use sketches and notes to show how the desk organiser could be made to rotate freely on a base.
Include the following details:

- specific materials
- **two** important sizes

[6]

12 Fig. 12 shows a guitar stand made from hardwood. The stand can store up to four guitars.

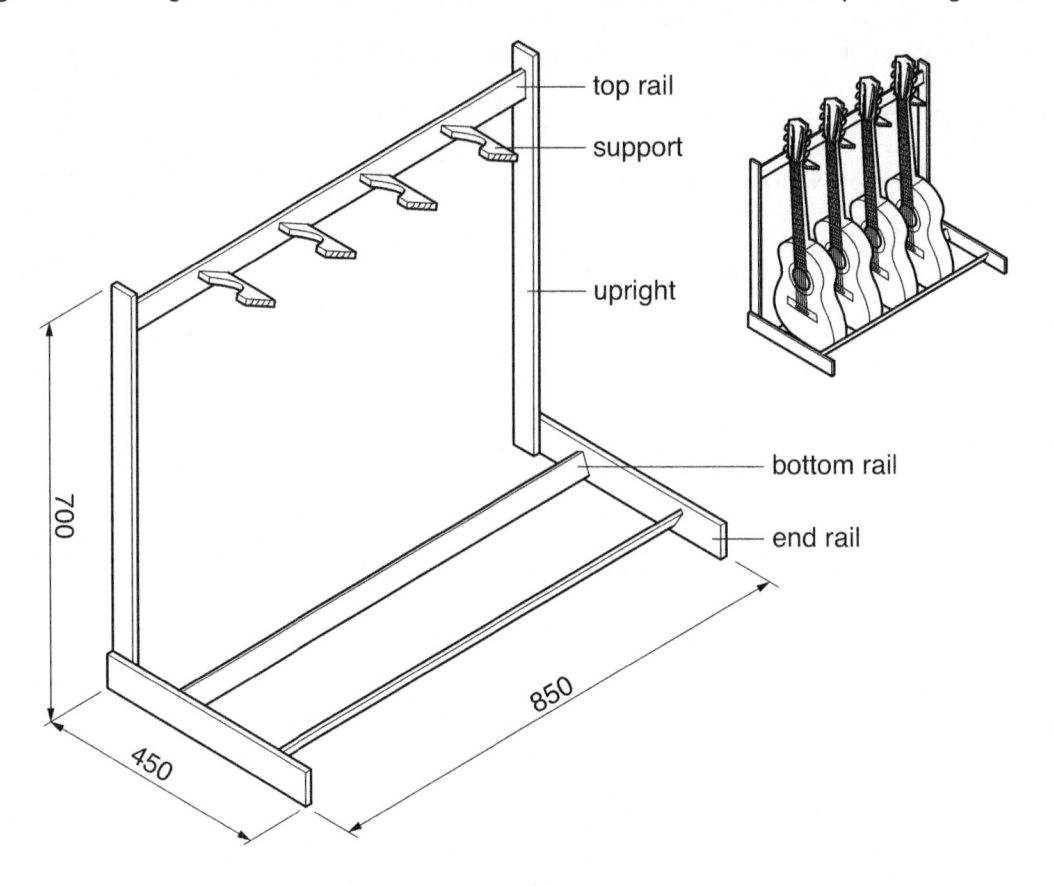

Fig. 12

(a) A parts list for the guitar stand is shown below.

Part	Number reqd.	Length × Width × Thickness	Hardwood
Upright	2	700 × 40 × 15	
Top rail	1	× 40 × 15	
Bottom rail	2	× 40 × 12	
End rail	2	450 × 60 × 15	
Support	4	120 × 50 × 12	

Complete the parts list by stating the **two** missing dimensions and naming **one** suitable hardwood for the guitar stand. [3]

(b) Give **three** items of research a designer would need to consider when designing the guitar stand.

1 ....

2 ....

3 ....[3]

(c) Fig. 13 shows one support marked out ready to be cut to shape.

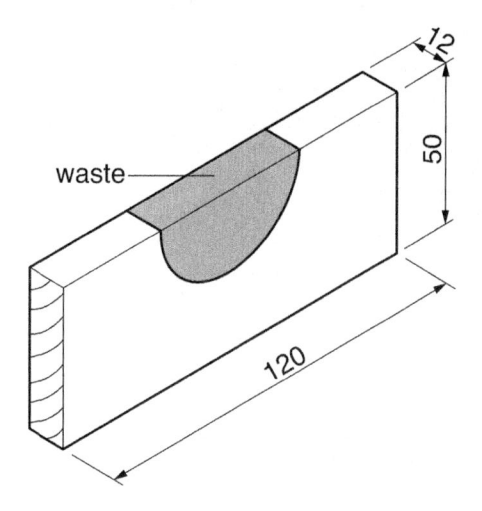

Fig. 13

Complete the table below by naming specific tools or items of equipment used to produce the final shape.

Stage	Process	Specific tool or item of equipment
1	Remove the waste	
2	Produce an accurately shaped curve	
3	Smooth the surfaces	

[3]

(d) Fig. 14 shows views of a bottom rail showing rounded edges.

marked out   after planing

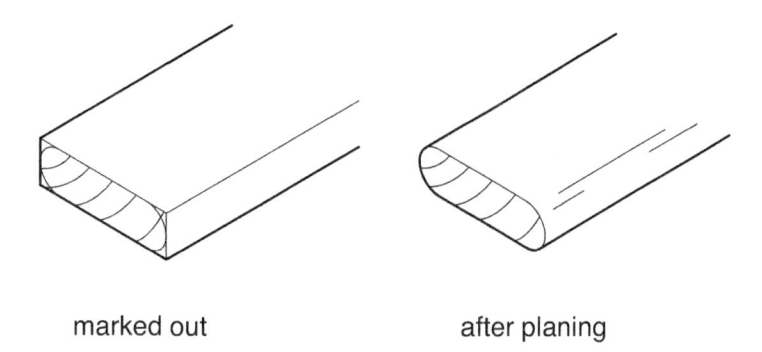

Fig. 14

(i) Name a suitable plane that could be used to produce the rounded edges.

....[1]

(ii) Give **one** reason why the bottom rails are covered with fabric.

....[1]

(e) The end rails will be joined to the uprights by means of 25 mm long screws. Complete the drawing of the screw shown below by:

- naming the type of head
- showing accurately the length of the screw
- naming a suitable material

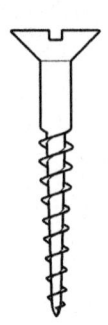

not to scale

[3]

(f) Fig. 15 shows one end of the top rail. The top rail is joined to the upright by means of dowels.

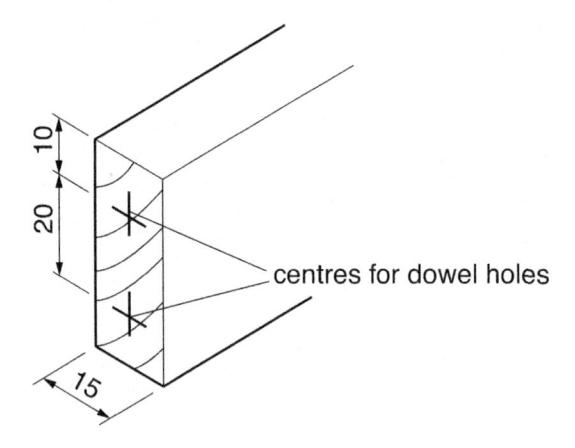

centres for dowel holes

Fig. 15

Use sketches and notes to show a design for a drilling jig that could be used to ensure that holes are drilled accurately in the ends of the top rails.
Name the material/s from which the drilling jig is made.

[5]

(g) Use sketches and notes to show how a set of 'feet' could be added to the guitar stand. Name the material used to make the 'feet'.

[3]

(h) A wax finish will be applied to the guitar stand.

  (i) Give **one** reason why two different grades of abrasive paper would be used to prepare the surfaces before the wax finish is applied.

  ....
  ....[1]

  (ii) Give **one** reason why the guitar stand would be waxed rather than painted.

  ....
  ....[1]

  (iii) Give **one** advantage of applying a wax finish rather than a polyurethane varnish finish to the guitar stand.

  ....
  ....[1]

13 Fig. 16 shows a card model for a safety glasses holder. The holder could be made from wood or metal. The safety glasses holder will be wall-mounted in a school workshop.

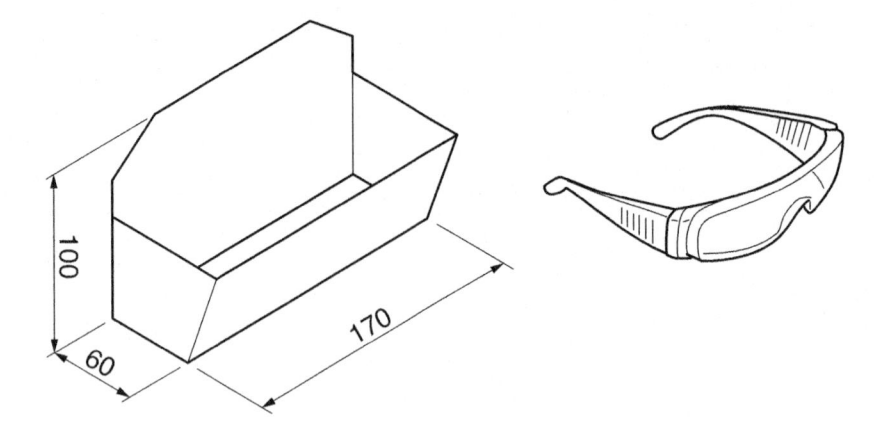

Fig. 16

(a) Give **two** benefits of making a card model of the holder before making it from wood or metal.

1 ....

2 ....[2]

(b) The development (net) of the safety glasses holder will be marked out on a sheet of metal.

  (i) Name a suitable ferrous metal for the holder.

  ....[1]

  (ii) Name a suitable non-ferrous metal for the holder.

  ....[1]

  (iii) The table below shows three marking out tools that could be used to mark out sheet metal.
  Complete the table by giving the specific name for each tool.

Tool	Name

[3]

(iv) Explain why tinsnips would be a more effective tool to cut out the shape of the holder rather than a hacksaw.

....

....

....[2]

(c) Fig. 17 shows a safety glasses holder made from plywood.

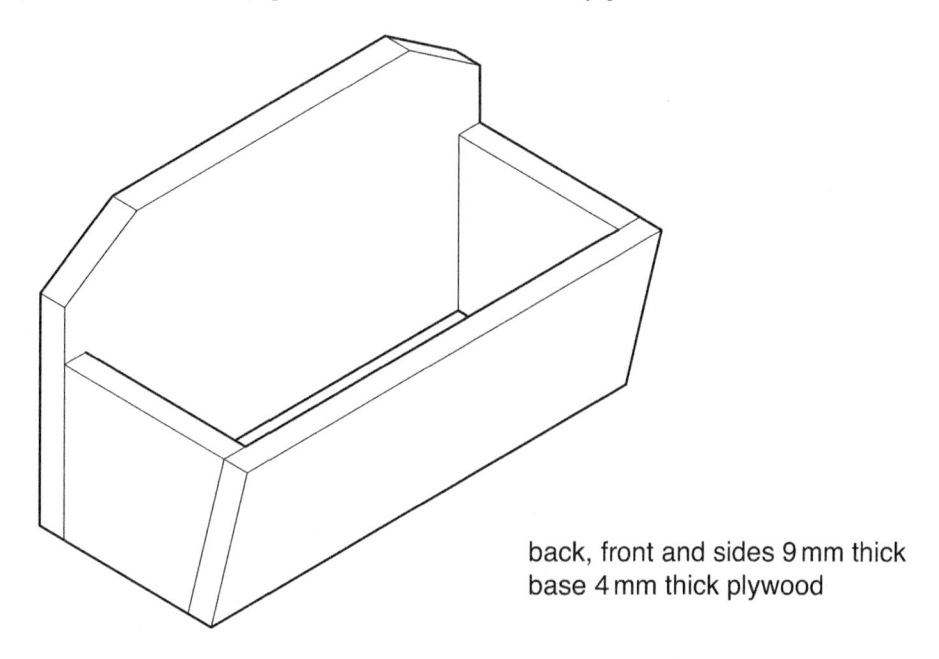

back, front and sides 9 mm thick
base 4 mm thick plywood

Fig. 17

(i) Plywood is a very stable manufactured board that is unlikely to twist or warp. Use sketches and notes to show the construction of plywood.

[3]

(ii) Name a different manufactured board that could be used to make the safety glasses holder.

....[1]

(iii) The parts of the safety glasses holder shown in Fig. 17 will be nailed and glued together. Name a specific type of nail that could be used to join the parts of the holder together.

....[1]

(iv) State a suitable length for the nail that could be used to join the front to the sides.

....[1]

(v) Name a suitable adhesive that could be used to glue the parts together.

....[1]

(vi) State approximately how long the adhesive named in part **(v)** would take to set.

....[1]

(d) Choose whether to make the safety glasses holder from metal or plywood.

(i) Use sketches and notes to show a modification to the safety glasses holder so that it could be fixed to a wall and easily removed for cleaning.

[3]

(ii) Use sketches and notes to show how a 'lid' could be fitted to the holder so that the safety glasses could be kept clean.
Include details of materials and constructions used.

[5]

Cambridge IGCSE

Cambridge International Examinations
Cambridge International General Certificate of Secondary Education

CANDIDATE NAME		
CENTRE NUMBER		CANDIDATE NUMBER

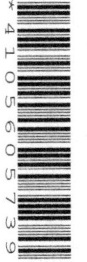

DESIGN AND TECHNOLOGY 0445/32

Paper 3 Resistant Materials   October/November 2018
1 hour

Candidates answer on the Question Paper.
No Additional Materials are required.

READ THESE INSTRUCTIONS FIRST

Write your Centre number, candidate number and name on all the work you hand in.
Write in blue or black pen.
You may use an HB pencil for any diagrams, graphs or rough working.
Do not use staples, paper clips, glue or correction fluid.
DO **NOT** WRITE IN ANY BARCODES.

Section A
Answer **all** questions in this section.

Section B
Answer **one** question in this section.

You may use a calculator.

At the end of the examination, fasten all your work securely together.
The number of marks is given in brackets [ ] at the end of each question or part question.
The total of the marks for this paper is 50.

This document consists of **19** printed pages and **1** blank page.

[Turn over

Section A

Answer **all** questions in this section.

1 Fig. 1 shows a length of wood marked to the required width.

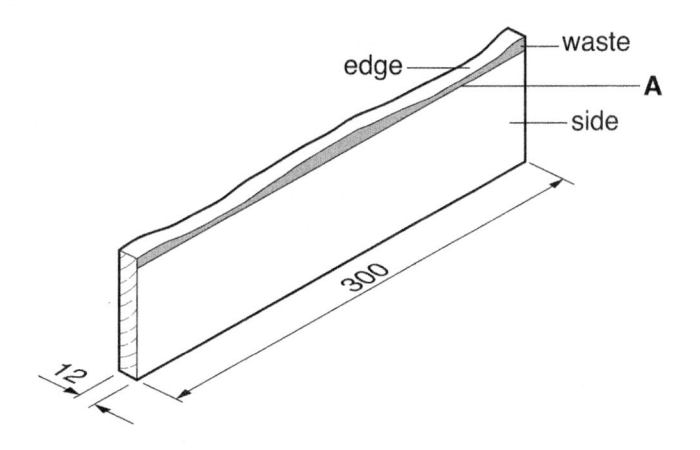

Fig. 1

(a) Name a tool, other than a pencil and steel rule, that could be used to mark the line **A**.

.... [1]

(b) Name a plane that could be used to remove the waste.

.... [1]

2 Fig. 2 shows a variety of different plastic tubes.

Fig. 2

Name the process used to make the plastic tubes.

.... [1]

3 Complete the table below by naming each tool and describing a specific use for each.

Tool	Name	Use
(pair of dividers)		
(centre punch)		

[4]

4 Fig. 3 shows two pieces of wood that will be joined together using a biscuit joint.

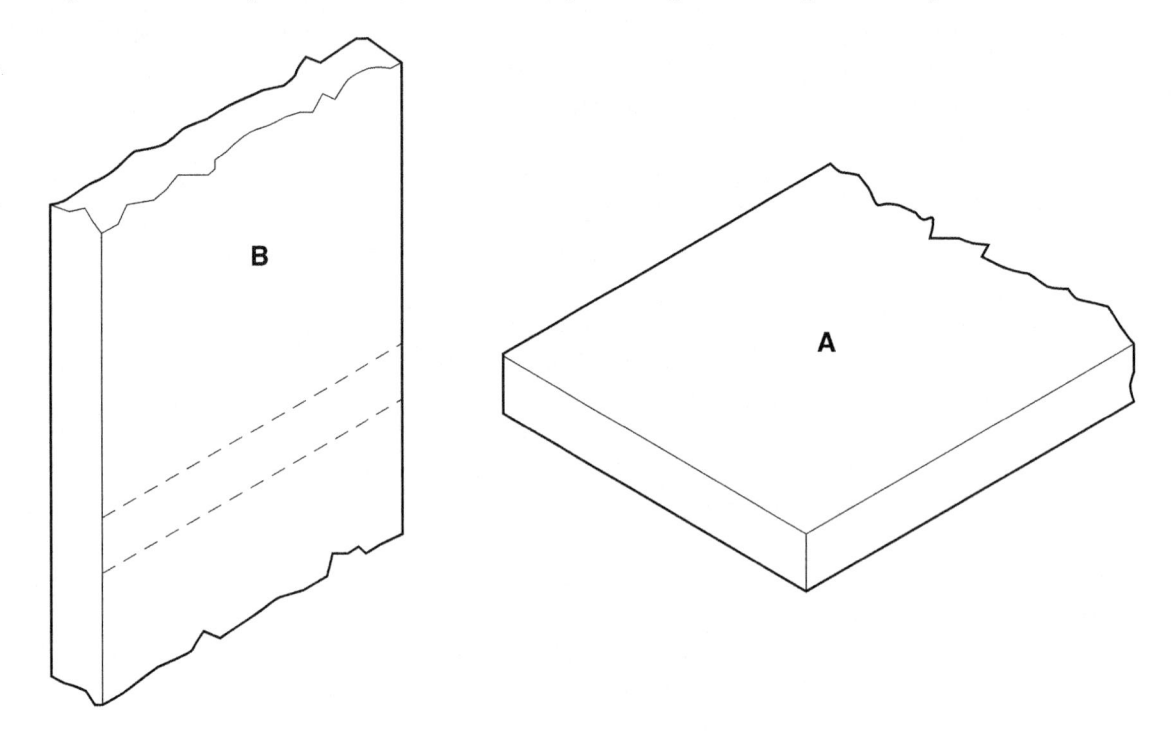

Fig. 3

Draw on Fig. 3 to show how **two** biscuits could be used to join **A** to **B**. [3]

5 Fig. 4 shows three products made from different thermosetting plastics.

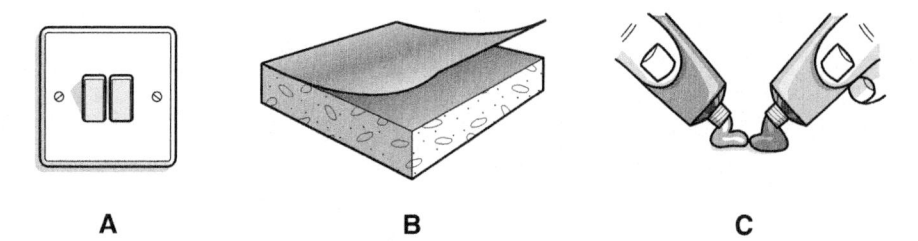

A   **B**   **C**

Fig. 4

Name a different thermosetting plastic that could be used to make **each** of the products.

A   Electrical fitting ....

B   Plastic laminate ....

C   Two-part adhesive .... [3]

6 Fig. 5 shows a three jaw and a four jaw chuck that are used with a centre lathe.

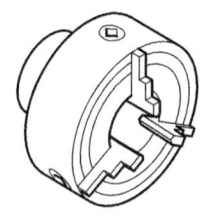

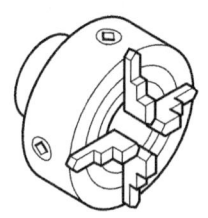

Fig. 5

(a) Describe a specific use for a three jaw chuck.

....

.... [1]

(b) Describe a specific use for a four jaw chuck.

....

.... [1]

7 Fig. 6 shows a pair of shin pads used by hockey players. The shin pads are made from a composite material.

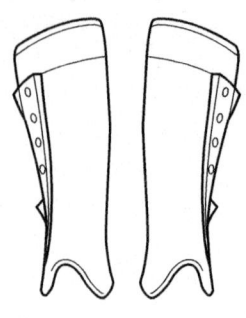

Fig. 6

(a) Name **one** composite material that could be used to make the shin pads.

.... [1]

(b) Describe **two** properties of a composite material that makes it suitable for the shin pads.

1..

2... [2]

8 Name the type of soldering that could be used when joining:

(a) electronic components to a circuit board;

.... [1]

(b) nickel silver jewellery.

.... [1]

9 Fig. 7 shows part of a leg and rail of a table and a knock-down (KD) fitting.

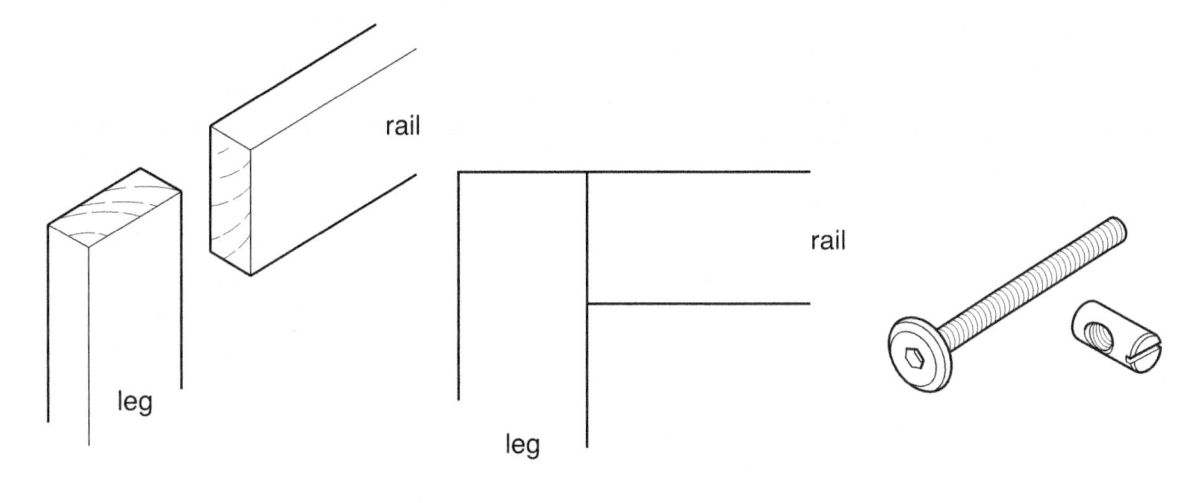

Fig. 7

Draw on Fig. 7 to show how the knock-down (KD) fitting could be fitted to the leg and rail to make a strong joint. [3]

10 Fig. 8 shows a process used to make a plastic bowl.

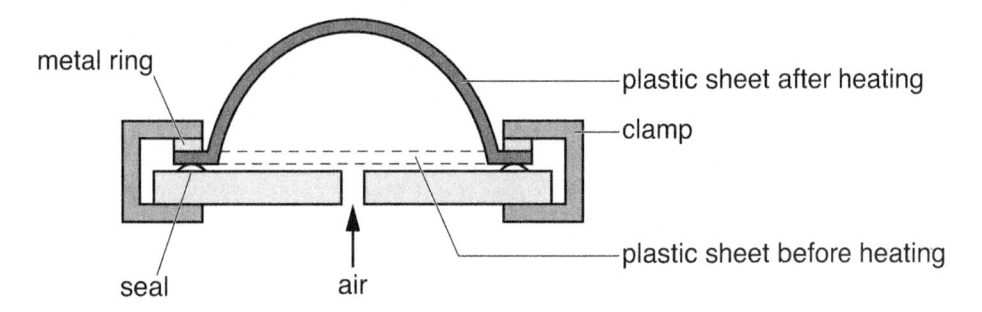

Fig. 8

(a) Name the process shown in Fig. 8.

.... [1]

(b) Add to Fig. 8 to show how the bowl could be produced with a flat bottom. [1]

Section B

Answer **one** question in this section.

11 Fig. 9 shows views of a toothbrush holder made from 4 mm thick acrylic.

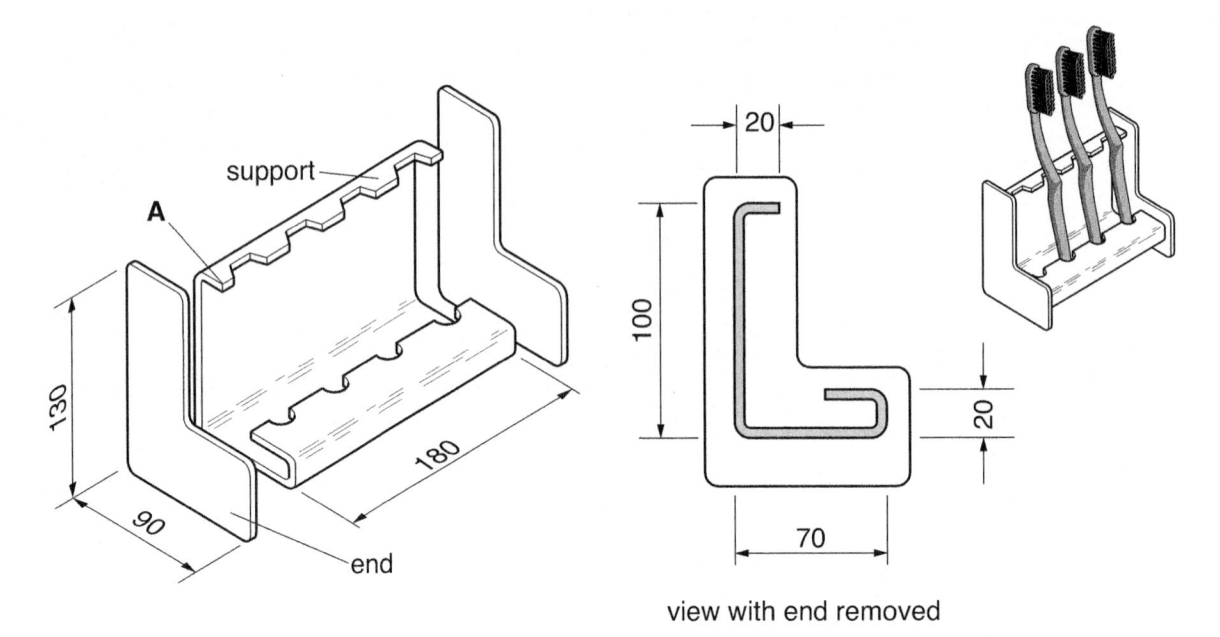

Fig. 9

(a) Fig. 10 shows a sheet of acrylic on which the development (net) of the support will be marked out. Corner **A** is shown in Figs. 9 and 10.

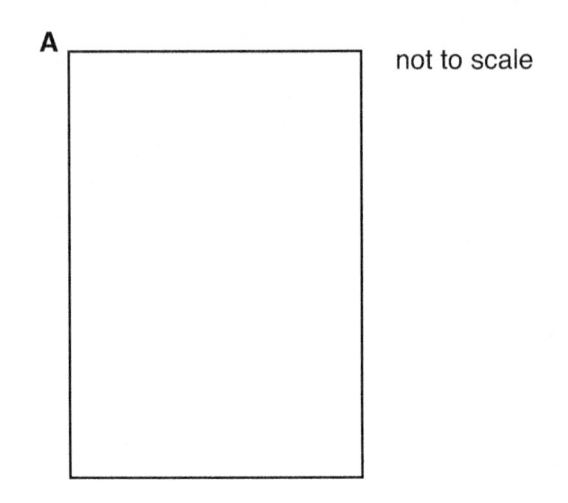

Fig. 10

(i) Draw on Fig. 10 to show **all** the bend lines. [4]

(ii) From the list below circle **one** item of equipment used to mark the bend lines on the surface of the acrylic.

lead pencil   biro   scriber   felt marker   marking knife [1]

(b) Use sketches and notes to show how the development (net) could be bent to shape. Include the following details:

- the method of softening the acrylic
- the method of producing an accurate shape

[5]

(c) Fig. 11 shows one end marked out, ready to be cut to shape.

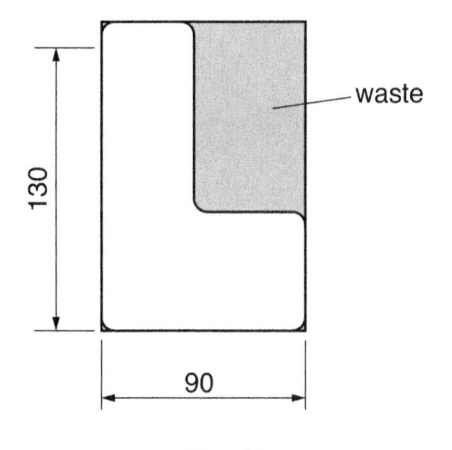

Fig. 11

Use sketches and notes to show how the waste could be removed and the rounded corners produced. Name **all** the tools and equipment used.

[4]

(d) The edges of the ends and support will be self-finished to a high quality before the parts are joined together.

   (i) Name the method of filing used to make the edges smooth.

   .... [1]

   (ii) Explain why two different grades of wet and dry (silicon carbide) paper would be used when self-finishing the edges.

   ....

   ....

   .... [2]

(e) The support will be joined to the ends by using acrylic cement.

   (i) Describe how the acrylic cement would be applied and how the parts would be held together while the acrylic cement sets.

   ....

   ....

   .... [2]

   (ii) State why it is important to work in a well-ventilated area when using acrylic cement.

   .... [1]

(f) Use sketches and notes to show how the toothbrush holder could be modified so that a tube of toothpaste could be stored.
Describe how the modification could be made in a school workshop.
Name all tools and equipment used.

[5]

12 Fig. 12 shows an incomplete design of a desk. The desk top is made from manufactured board and the legs and rails from hardwood.

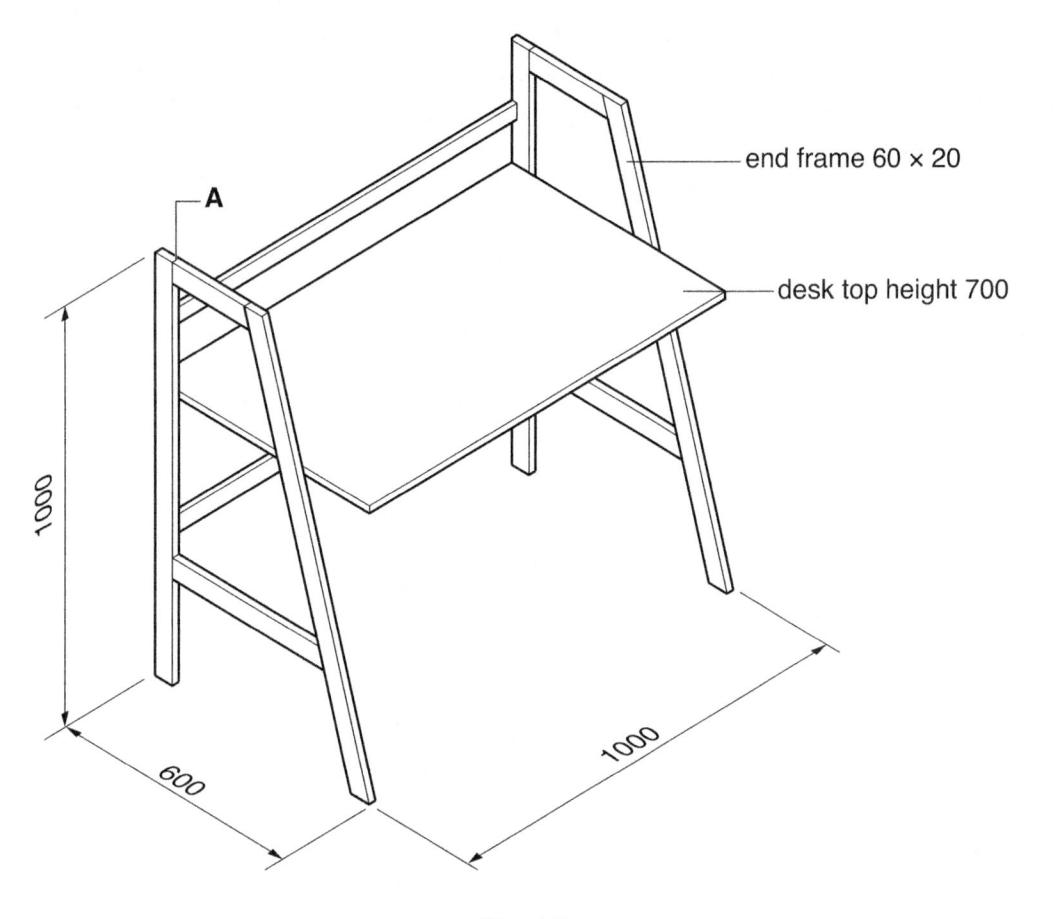

Fig. 12

(a) (i) Name a suitable manufactured board for the desk top.

.... [1]

(ii) Suggest an appropriate thickness of manufactured board for the desk top.

.... [1]

(iii) Name a suitable hardwood for the legs and rails.

.... [1]

(iv) Complete the statement below by adding the correct term from the list.

mechanisms   seasoning   anthropometrics   sustainability

The designer decided to make the desk 700 mm high after studying ....

.... [1]

(b) The corner bridle joint shown below could be used to join the leg and rail at corner **A** in Fig. 12.

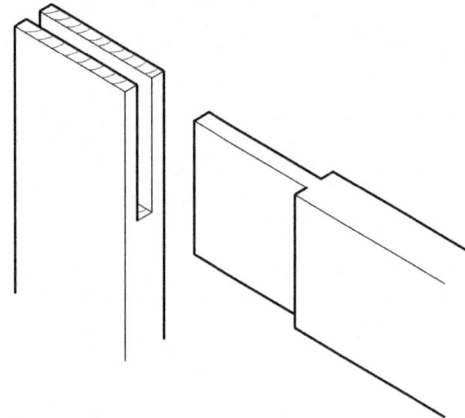

(i) Name **two** marking out tools, other than a pencil, that could be used to mark out the corner bridle joint.

1 ....

2 .... [2]

(ii) Name **two** tools that could be used to cut out the corner bridle joint.

1 ....

2 .... [2]

(c) Use sketches and notes to show how the desk top could be fixed to the end frames. Include details of constructions and fittings used.

[5]

(d) Fig. 13 shows the legs and rails of one frame ready to be glued and clamped.

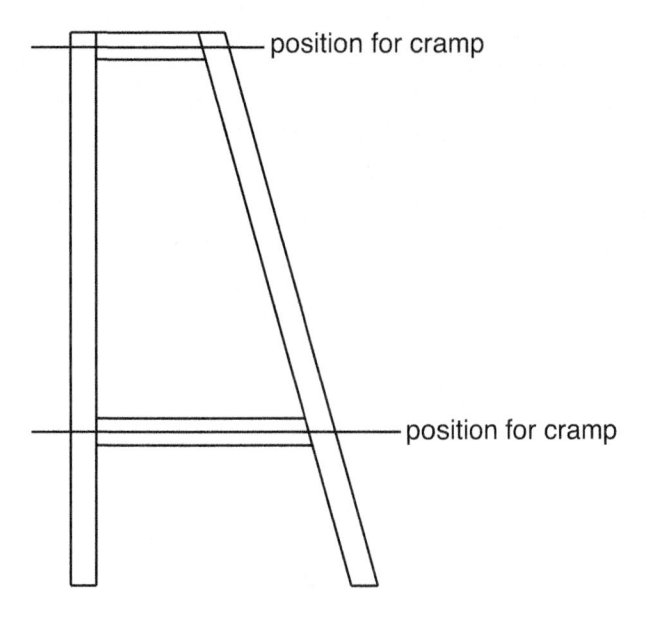

Fig. 13

(i) Name the cramps that would be used to secure the joints.

.... [1]

(ii) Name a suitable adhesive that could be used to glue the joint together.

.... [1]

(iii) Describe **two** checks that would need to be carried out when the legs and rails are glued and clamped together.

1 ....

2 .... [2]

(e) Fig. 14 shows the shape of one end frame marked out on a sheet of manufactured board. The end frame will be cut out of the sheet of manufactured board rather than using separate legs and rails.

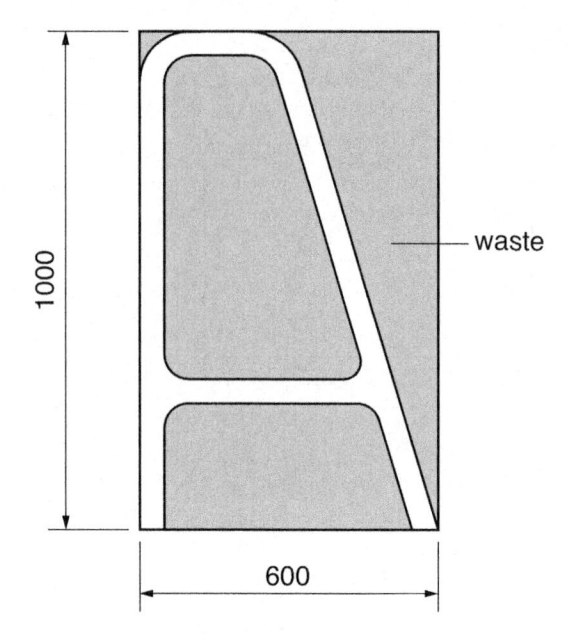

Fig. 14

(i) Give **one** advantage and **one** disadvantage of making the end frame from one piece of manufactured board rather than separate legs and rails.

Advantage ....

....

Disadvantage ....

.... [2]

(ii) Name a portable power tool that could be used to cut out the shape of the end frame.

.... [1]

(iii) Describe **two** safety precautions, other than personal protection equipment, that must be taken when using portable power tools.

1 ....

2 .... [2]

(f) Fig. 15 shows two desks. Desk **A** is a modern desk and desk **B** is a traditional design.

A

B

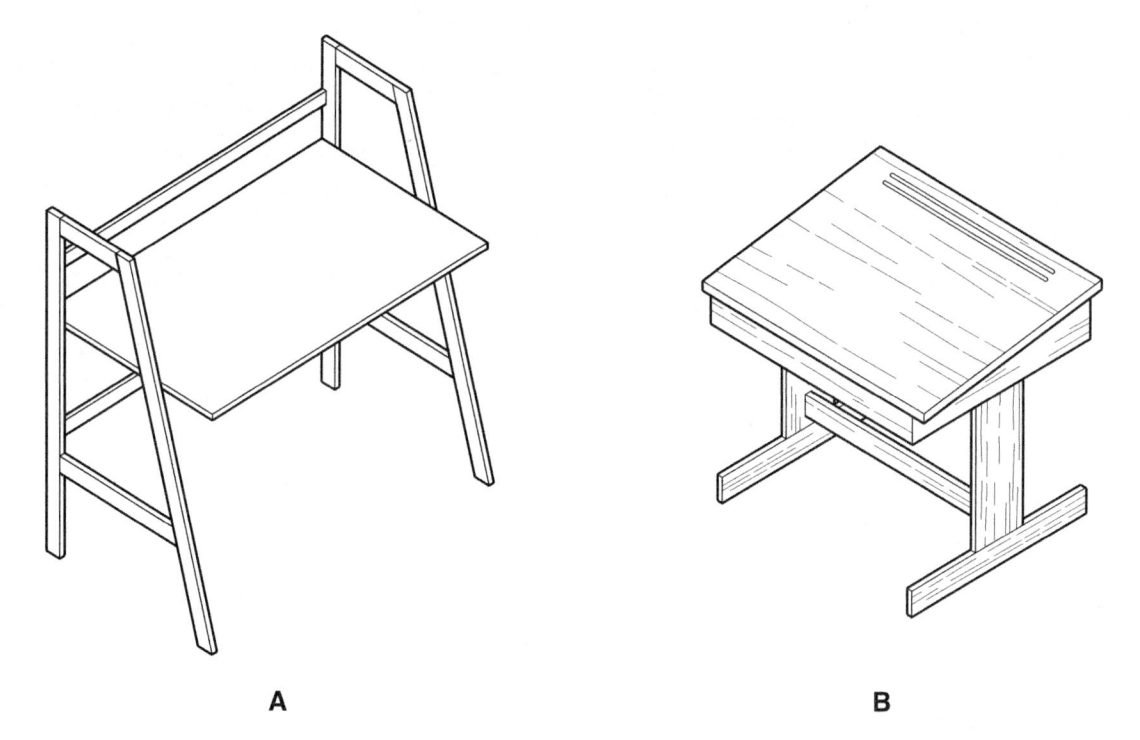

Fig. 15

Explain why the design of the desk has changed.

....

....

....

.... [3]

13 Fig. 16 shows a wall-mounted adjustable shelving system.

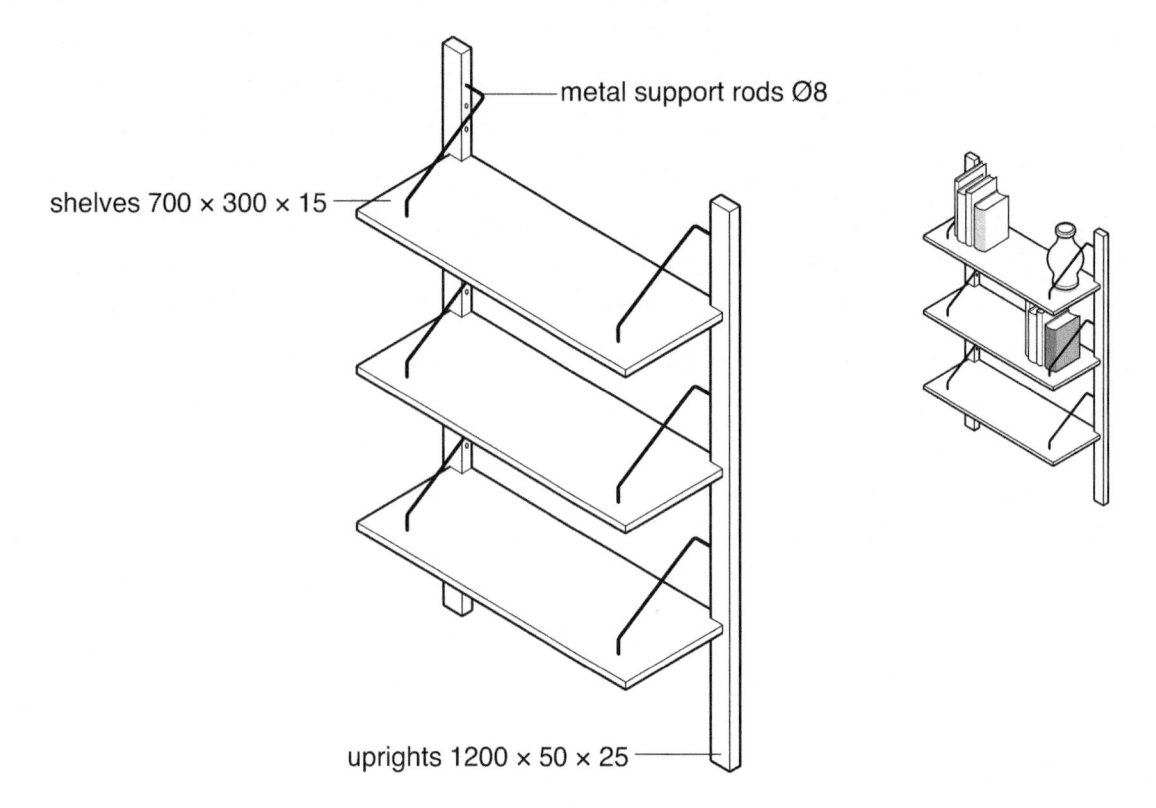

Fig. 16

(a) Name suitable specific materials for the parts of the shelving system:

- hardwood uprights ....

- metal support rods ....

- manufactured board shelves .... [3]

(b) The manufactured board used for the shelves is veneered.

(i) Give **one** benefit of covering the manufactured board with veneer.

.... [1]

(ii) Give **one** drawback of covering the manufactured board with veneer.

.... [1]

(c) Fig. 17 shows part of one upright with the centres for Ø8 holes marked out.

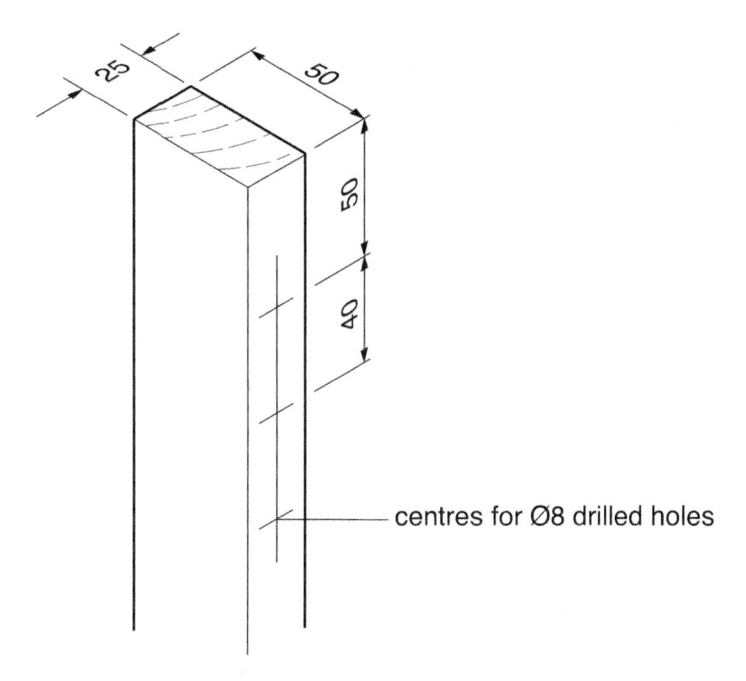

Fig. 17

centres for Ø8 drilled holes

Use sketches and notes to show a design for a jig to allow **three** holes to be drilled accurately. Include details of materials used.

[5]

(d) Fig. 18 shows details of one metal support rod.

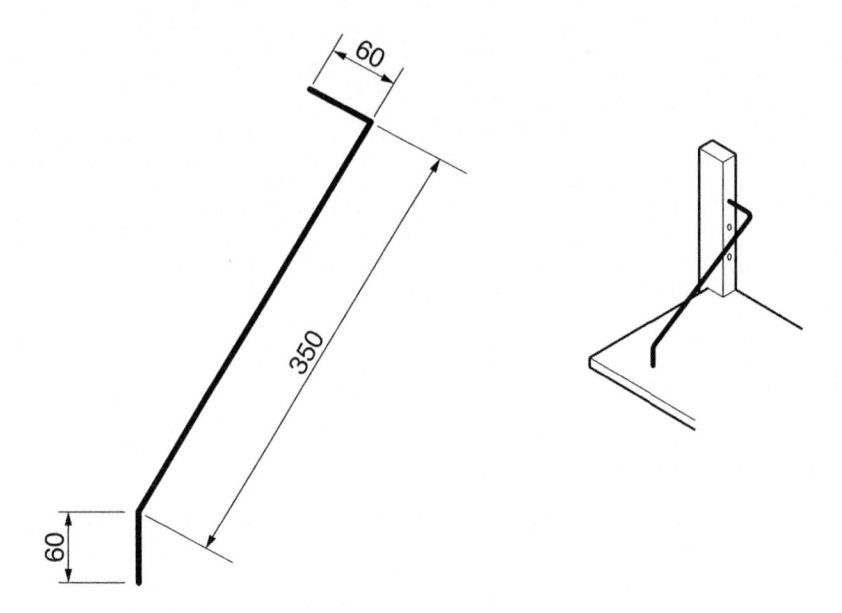

Fig. 18

Use sketches and notes to show how the **two** bends in the support could be produced.

[4]

(e) The metal support rods will have a clear lacquer finish.
Describe how the metal could be prepared **before** applying clear lacquer.

....

....

....

.... [3]

(f) Fig. 19 shows one corner of a shelf marked out ready to be cut out to take the upright.

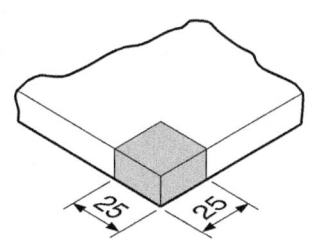

Fig. 19

(i) Name **one** marking out tool, other than a pencil and a steel rule, that could be used to mark out the shape.

.... [1]

(ii) Name a back saw that could be used to cut out the shape.

.... [1]

(g) Fig. 20 shows one metal support rod that fits into a Ø8 hole in a shelf.
Use sketches and notes to show how the metal support rod could be fixed to the shelf to support the weight when in use.

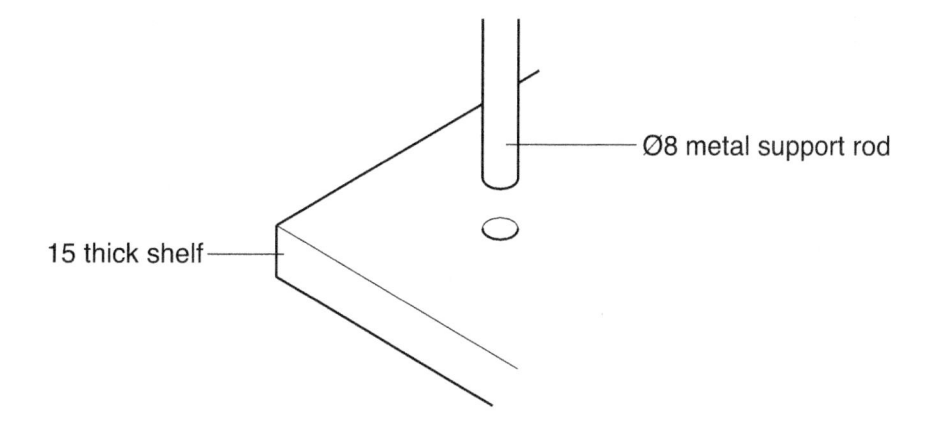

Fig. 20

[4]

(h) Describe **two** good design features of the shelving system.

1..

2... [2]

BLANK PAGE

Cambridge IGCSE

Cambridge Assessment International Education
Cambridge International General Certificate of Secondary Education

CANDIDATE NAME	

CENTRE NUMBER		CANDIDATE NUMBER	

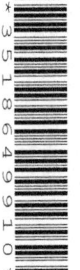

DESIGN AND TECHNOLOGY 0445/32

Paper 3 Resistant Materials May/June 2019

1 hour

Candidates answer on the Question Paper.
No Additional Materials are required.

READ THESE INSTRUCTIONS FIRST

Write your centre number, candidate number and name on all the work you hand in.
Write in dark blue or black pen.
You may use an HB pencil for any diagrams, graphs or rough working.
Do not use staples, paper clips, glue or correction fluid.
DO **NOT** WRITE IN ANY BARCODES.

Section A
Answer **all** questions in this section.

Section B
Answer **one** question in this section.

You may use a calculator.

At the end of the examination, fasten all your work securely together.
The number of marks is given in brackets [ ] at the end of each question or part question.
The total of the marks for this paper is 50.

This document consists of **18** printed pages and **2** blank pages.

DC (NH/SG) 168522/2
© UCLES 2019

Cambridge Assessment International Education

[Turn over

Section A

Answer **all** questions in this section.

1 Fig. 1 shows a kitchen pedal bin.

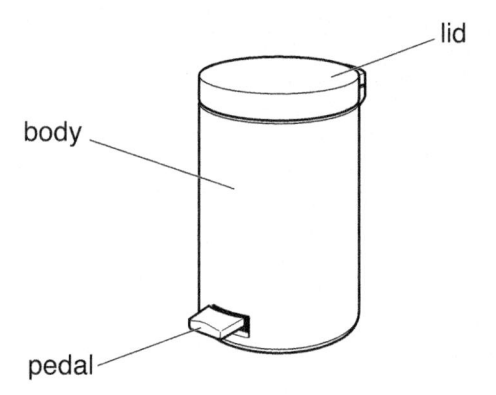

Fig. 1

Complete the list below by adding **two** specification points for the kitchen pedal bin.

1 The lid must open easily when the pedal is pressed.

2 ....

3 ....
[2]

2 Complete the table by stating the manufacturing process used to make each product.

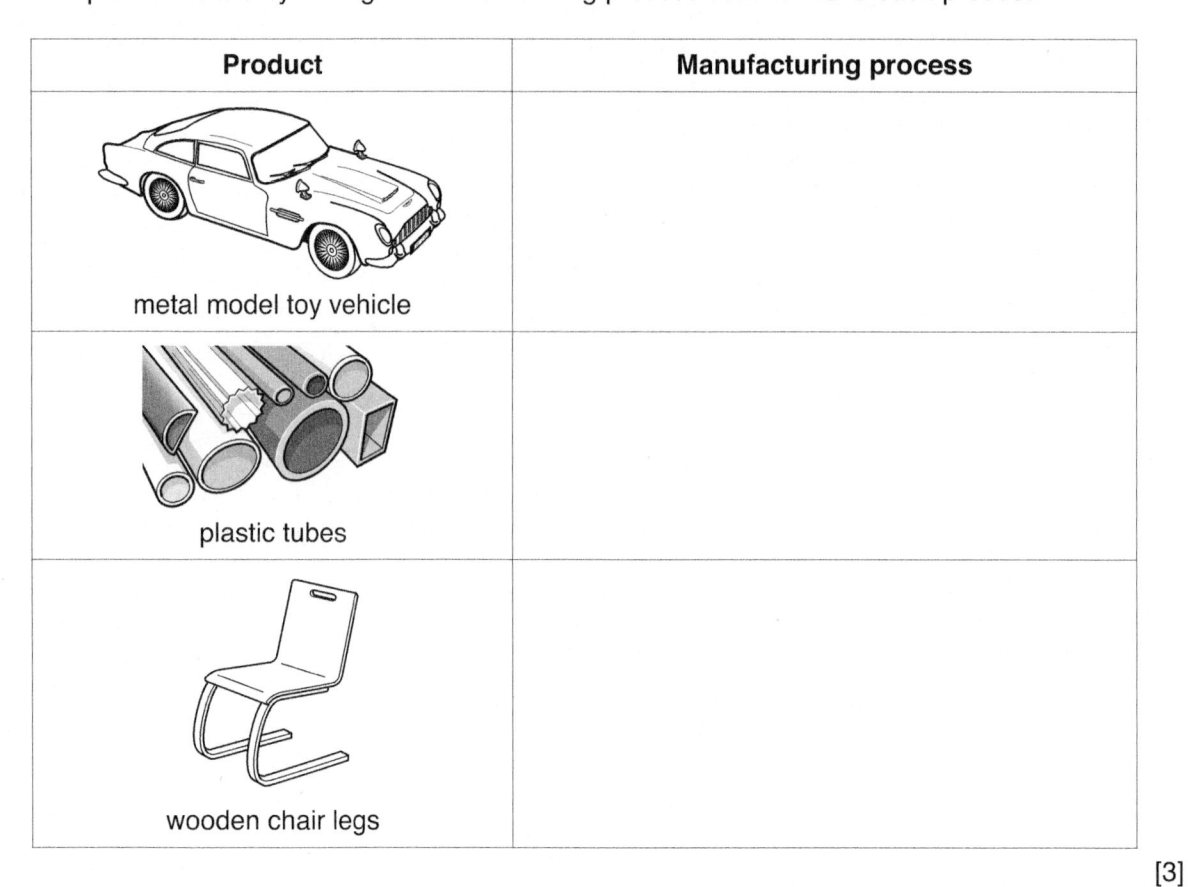

Product	Manufacturing process
metal model toy vehicle	
plastic tubes	
wooden chair legs	

[3]

3 Fig. 2 shows a length of veneered chipboard marked out, ready to be cut into four pieces.

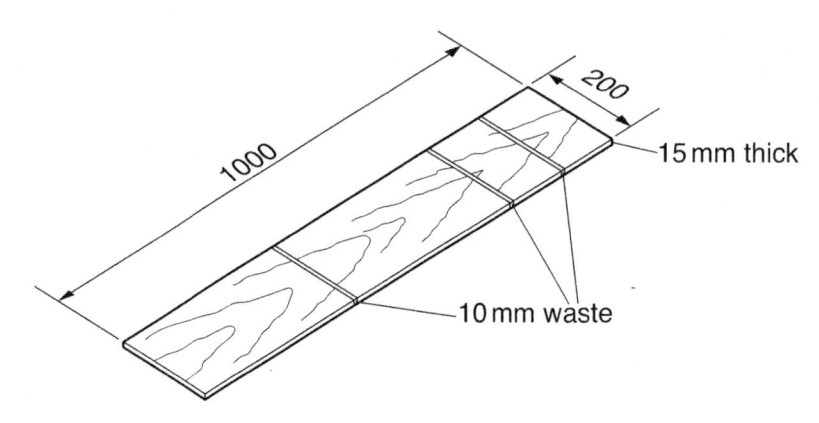

Fig. 2

(a) Give **one** reason why the lines would be marked out using a marking knife rather than a pencil.

.... [1]

(b) Give **one** reason why 10 mm waste has been allowed between the marked lengths.

.... [1]

4 Name the **three** standard metal sections shown below.

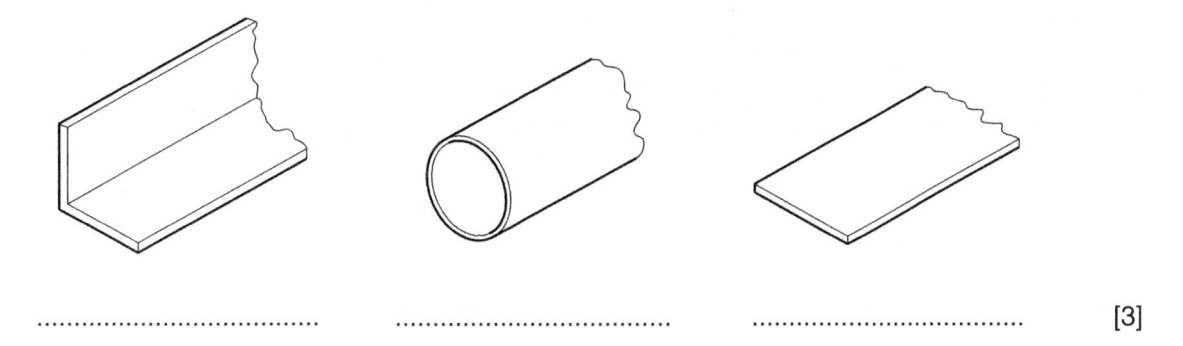

.... [3]

5 Complete the drawing below to show a finger (comb) joint.

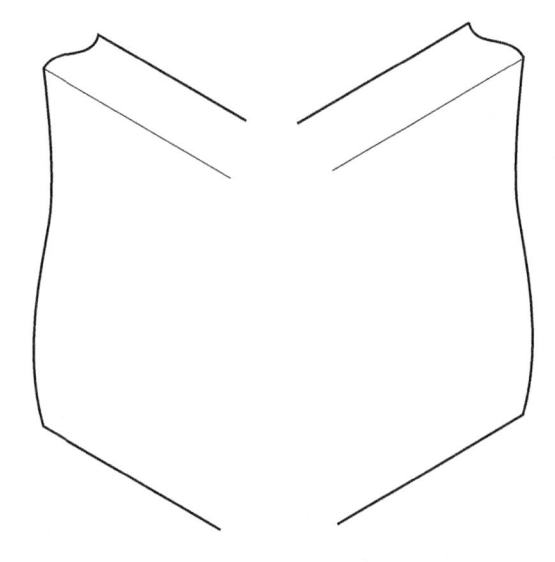

[3]

6 Composite materials are made by combining materials with different properties to make a material with more useful properties.
Name **two** composite materials.

1 ....

2 ....
[2]

7 The table shows two different centre lathe processes used when turning round metal bar. Complete the table by naming each process.

Process	Description of process	Name of process
	Cutting across the end of the round bar	
	Cutting off a length of round bar	

[2]

8 Fig. 3 shows hardwood strips being glued together to make a chopping board.

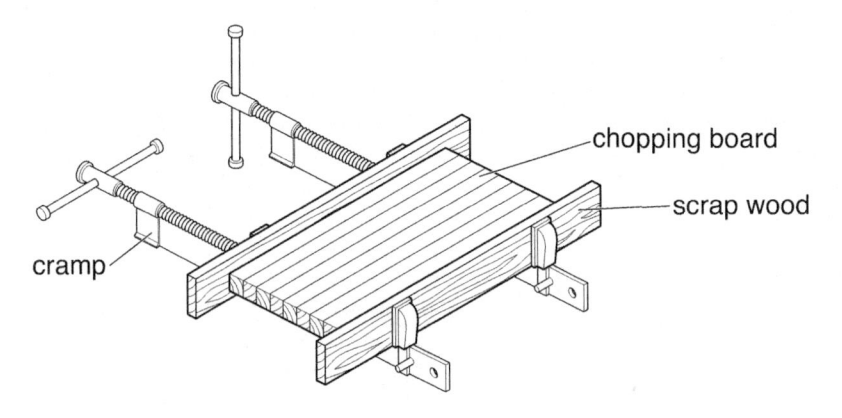

Fig. 3

(a) Name the type of cramps used.

.... [1]

(b) Give **two** reasons why scrap wood is used between the cramps and the chopping board.

1 ....

2 ....
[2]

9 Fig. 4 shows a toast rack made from stainless steel.

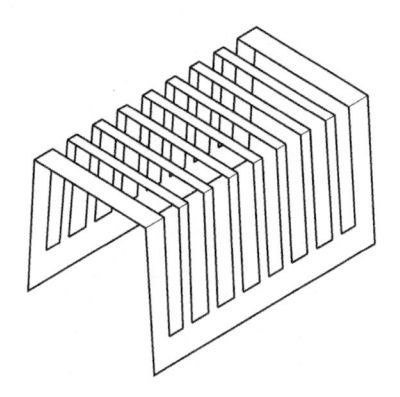

Fig. 4

Give **two** reasons why stainless steel is a suitable material for a toast rack.

1 ....

2 ....
[2]

10 Fig. 5 shows a wooden chair.

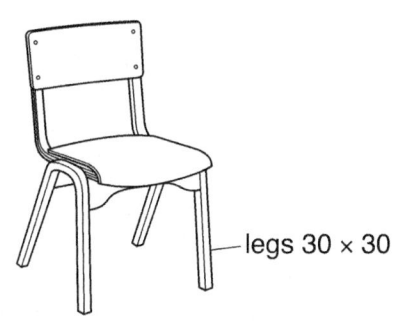

legs 30 × 30

Fig. 5

Use sketches and notes to show how the chair could be modified so that it can be linked, side by side, to an identical chair and could be easily separated for stacking.

[3]

Section B

Answer **one** question in this section.

11 Fig. 6 shows an incomplete design of a child's novelty clock.
The clock shape could be made from 5 mm thick manufactured board or 1.5 mm thick non-ferrous metal. The clock will be placed on a shelf.

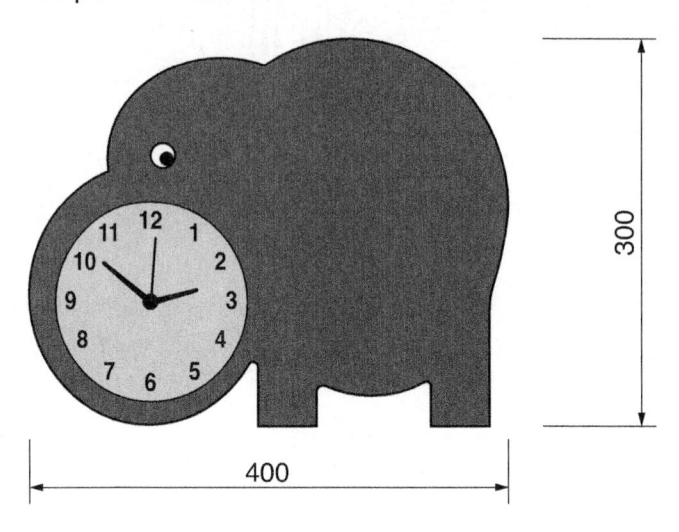

Fig. 6

(a) (i) Name a suitable manufactured board for the clock shape.

.... [1]

(ii) Name a suitable non-ferrous metal for the clock shape.

.... [1]

(b) Fig. 7 shows a template of the shape glued to a sheet of 5 mm thick manufactured board. The centre for a hole to be drilled for the clock mechanism is shown.

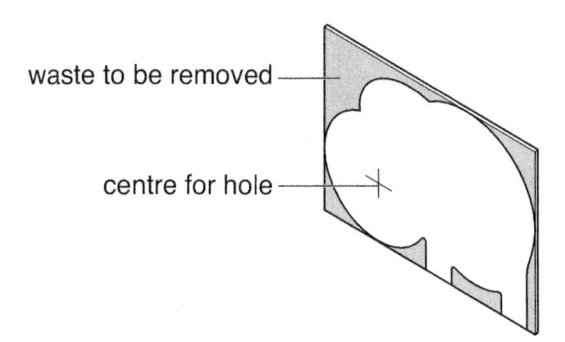

Fig. 7

(i) Give **two** reasons why the sheet of manufactured board must be clamped down securely when drilling the hole.

1 ....

2 ....
[2]

(ii) Use sketches and notes to show how the shape could be cut out by hand and the edges made smooth.

[3]

(c) Fig. 8 shows the clock shape made from manufactured board joined to a wooden base.

wooden base 400 × 40 × 10

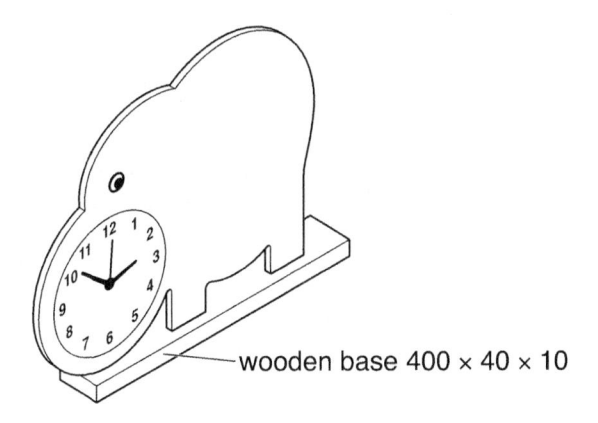

Fig. 8

Use sketches and notes to show how the clock shape could be joined to the base.

[3]

(d) The manufactured board clock shape will be finished with spray paint.
Give **two** advantages of spray paint rather than applying the paint with a brush.

1 ....

2 ....
[2]

(e) Fig. 9 shows the clock shape made from 1.5 mm thick non-ferrous metal.
Legs have been joined to the shape so that it could stand on a shelf.

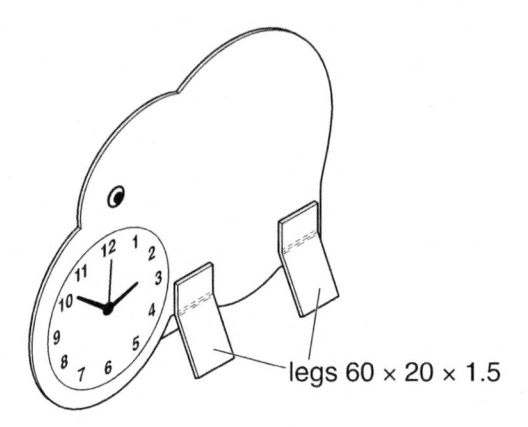

legs 60 × 20 × 1.5

Fig. 9

Use sketches and notes to show how the legs could be made from non-ferrous metal and joined permanently to the clock shape. Name **all** the tools and equipment used.

[5]

(f) When the clock shape is made from non-ferrous metal it could be self-finished.
Explain what is meant by the term 'self-finished'.

....

....

....
[2]

(g) Describe in detail how CAD/CAM could be used to produce the numbers 1 to 12 on the 5 mm thick manufactured board clock face.

....

....

....

....

....

.... [4]

(h) State **two** ways, other than shape and colour, by which designers make products used by young children appealing and exciting.

1 ....

2 ....
[2]

12 Fig. 10 shows views of a storage unit designed to hold a tablet, mobile phone and remote control.

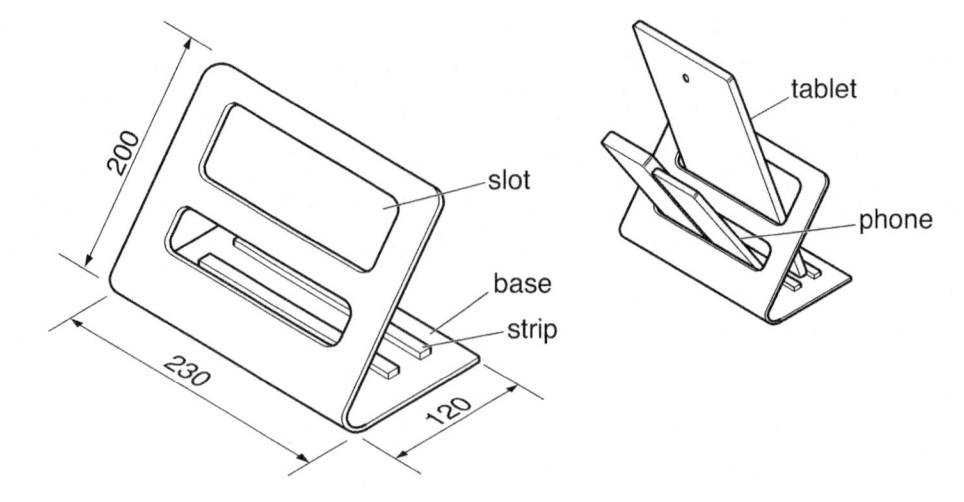

Fig. 10

(a) Give **two** reasons why acrylic would be a suitable material for the storage unit.

1 ....

2 ....
[2]

(b) Fig. 11 shows the development (net) of the storage unit made from 5 mm thick acrylic.

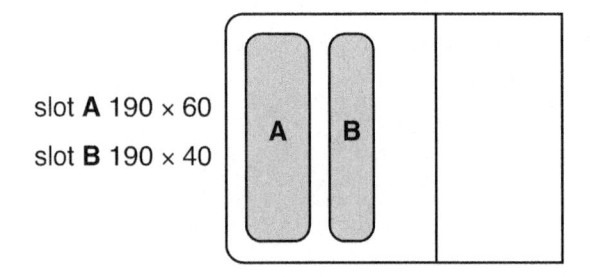

slot **A** 190 × 60
slot **B** 190 × 40

Fig. 11

Use sketches and notes to show how the slots could be cut out by hand and the edges made smooth.

[4]

(c) The development (net) and slots could be cut out using a CNC machine.
Describe the stages involved when using a CNC machine to cut out the development (net) and slots.

....

....

....

....

....

.... [4]

(d) Use sketches and notes to show how the acrylic development (net) could be bent to shape.

[3]

(e) Fig. 12 shows one of the strips that will be joined to the base of the storage unit using acrylic cement.

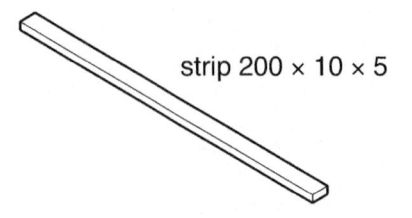

strip 200 × 10 × 5

Fig. 12

(i) Use sketches and notes to show how the strip could be held in place while the acrylic cement sets.

[2]

(ii) Give **one** reason why each of the following items would be worn when using acrylic cement:

disposable gloves

....

face mask.

....
[2]

(f) The storage unit could also be made by laminating five wood veneers, each 1 mm thick. Use sketches and notes to show how the laminate could be formed to the shape of the storage unit.

[4]

(g) Describe how you would evaluate the success of the final product.

....

....

....

.... [2]

(h) Explain why consumer demand for storage units of the type shown in Fig. 10 has increased in recent years.

....

....

....

.... [2]

13 Fig. 13 shows a child's ride-on toy made mainly from wood.

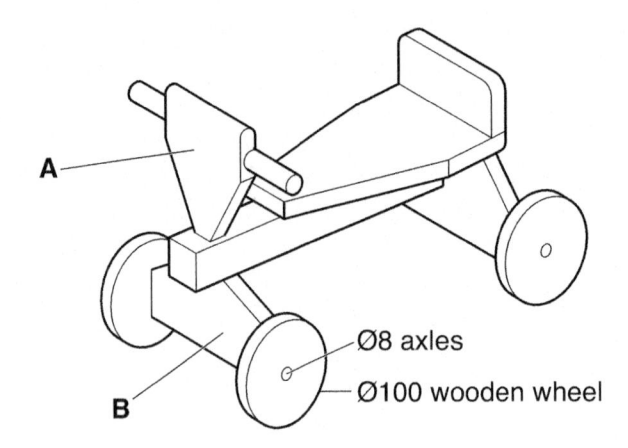

Fig. 13

(a) Fig. 14 shows details of part **A** and the hardwood from which it is made.

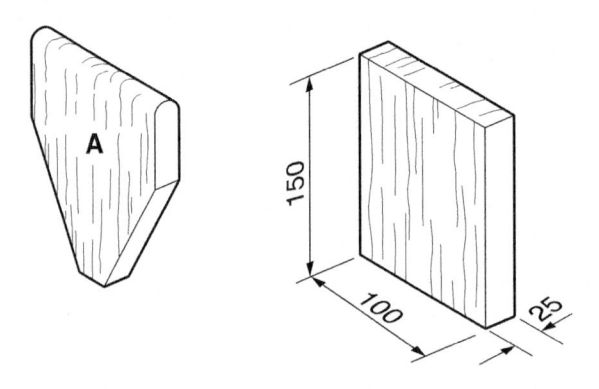

Fig. 14

Use sketches and notes to show how part **A** could be produced from the hardwood shown. Include details of marking out. Name all the tools and equipment used.

[5]

(b) Give **two** features of the ride-on toy that make it safe for children to use.

1 ....

2 ....
[2]

(c) Fig. 15 shows one wheel marked out ready to be shaped on a woodturning lathe.

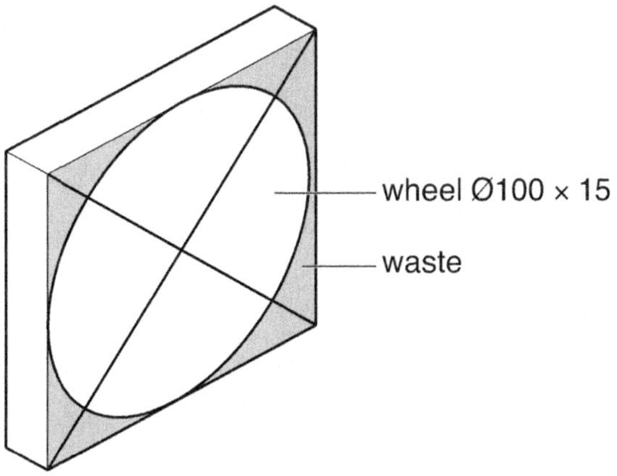

wheel Ø100 × 15

waste

Fig. 15

(i) Explain why the corners would be removed before the wood is set up on the woodturning lathe.

....

....

.... [2]

(ii) Name **two** tools or items of equipment that could be used when making the wheels on a woodturning lathe.

1 ....

2 ....
[2]

(iii) Give **two** advantages of making the wheels from plywood rather than hardwood.

1 ....

2 ....
[2]

(d) Fig. 16 shows details of part **B** of the ride-on toy. Holes will be drilled to take the axles.

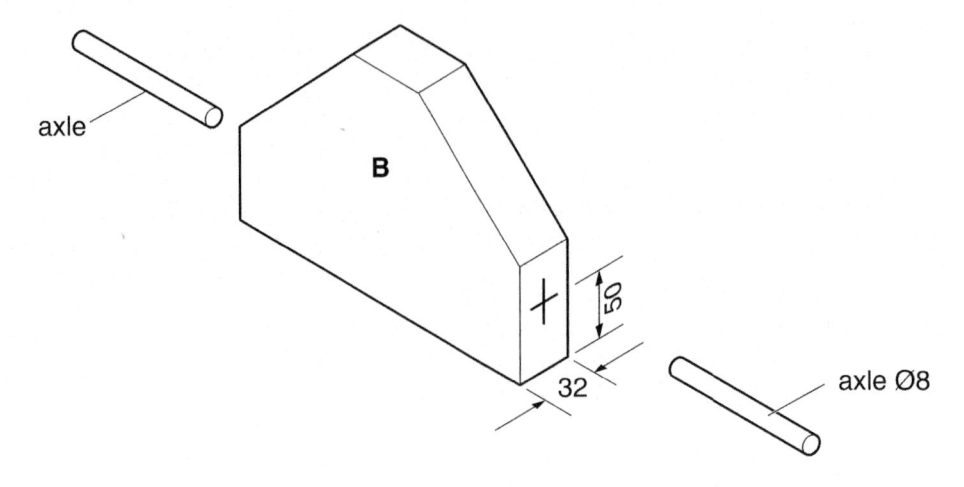

Fig. 16

(i) Use sketches and notes to show a design for a drilling jig to ensure the holes are drilled accurately. Name the material from which the jig is made.

[5]

(ii) The axles will be glued into part **B**.
Use sketches and notes to show how **one** wooden wheel, Ø100 × 15, could be fitted onto an axle and allowed to rotate freely.

[3]

(e) Fig. 17 shows a different design of a child's ride-on toy.

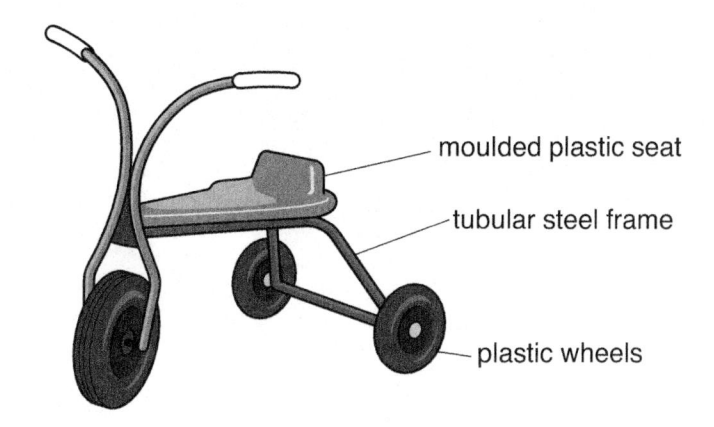

Fig. 17

(i) Name a process that could be used to produce the plastic wheels.

.... [1]

(ii) Give **one** method of joining lengths of steel tube permanently.

.... [1]

(iii) Name **two** types of finish that could be applied to the steel frame of the ride-on toy.

1 ....

2 ....
[2]

BLANK PAGE

	Cambridge Assessment International Education
Cambridge IGCSE	Cambridge International General Certificate of Secondary Education

CANDIDATE NAME

CENTRE NUMBER

CANDIDATE NUMBER

DESIGN AND TECHNOLOGY 0445/32

Paper 3 Resistant Materials October/November 2019

1 hour

Candidates answer on the Question Paper.
No Additional Materials are required.

READ THESE INSTRUCTIONS FIRST

Write your centre number, candidate number and name on all the work you hand in.
Write in blue or black pen.
You may use an HB pencil for any diagrams, graphs or rough working.
Do not use staples, paper clips, glue or correction fluid.
DO **NOT** WRITE IN ANY BARCODES.

Section A
Answer **all** questions in this section.

Section B
Answer **one** question in this section.

You may use a calculator.

At the end of the examination, fasten all your work securely together.
The number of marks is given in brackets [ ] at the end of each question or part question.
The total of the marks for this paper is 50.

This document consists of **18** printed pages and **2** blank pages.

Section A

Answer **all** questions in this section.

1 Complete the table by stating the manufacturing process used to make each plastic product.

Plastic product	Manufacturing process
electrical plug	
guttering	
sandwich container	

[3]

2 Fig. 1 shows a block of metal marked out ready to be drilled.

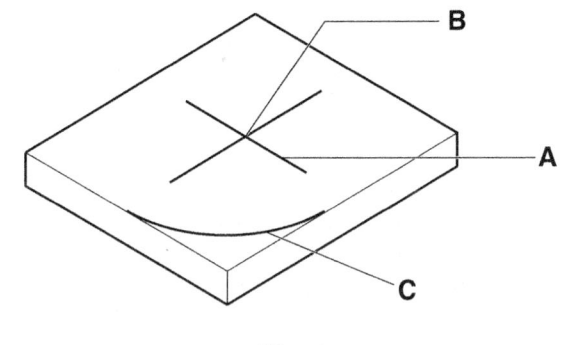

Fig. 1

Name the marking out tool used to mark line **A**.

....

Name the marking out tool used to mark centre **B**.

....

Name the marking out tool used to mark arc **C**.

....

[3]

3 Fig. 2 shows two basic designs for kitchen roll holders.

wall-mounted   freestanding

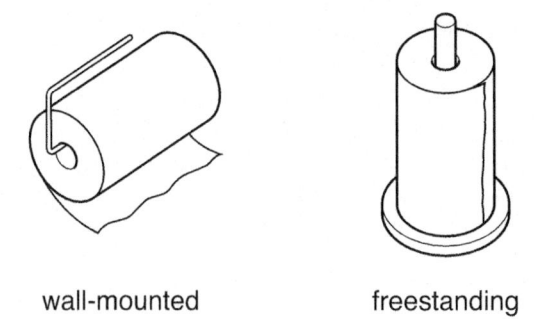

Fig. 2

Give **two** reasons why consumers may prefer to buy a wall-mounted kitchen roll holder rather than a freestanding kitchen roll holder.

1 ....

2 ....
[2]

4 Fig. 3 shows timber being seasoned in a kiln.

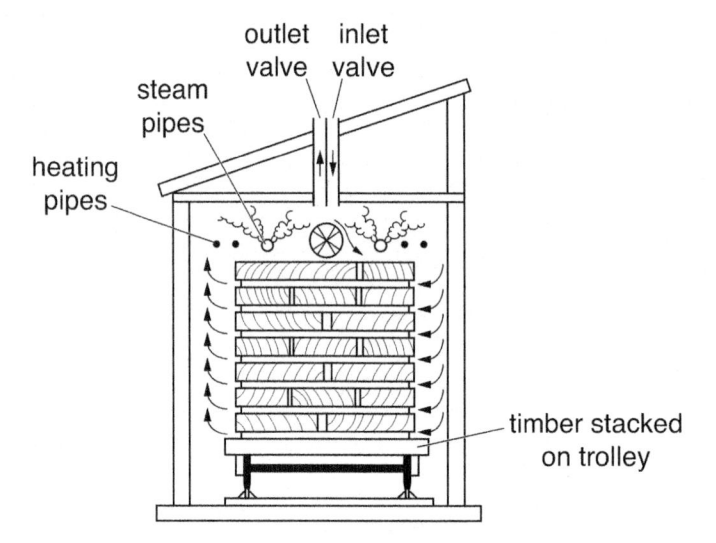

Fig. 3

(a) Explain why timber needs to be seasoned.

....

....

.... [2]

(b) Name a different method of seasoning timber.

.... [1]

5 A Ø10 hole will be drilled in a sheet of 4 mm thick acrylic.
Fig. 4 shows part of a drilling machine used to drill the hole.
Add to Fig. 4 to show how the acrylic sheet would be held when drilling the hole.

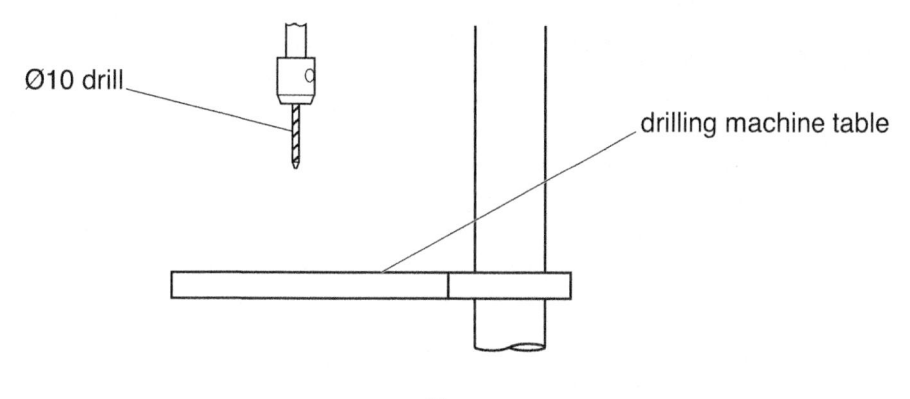

Fig. 4

[3]

6 Fig. 5 shows the end grain of a piece of hardwood being planed.
The wood is planed from each end to the centre, as shown by the arrows, to prevent it from splitting.

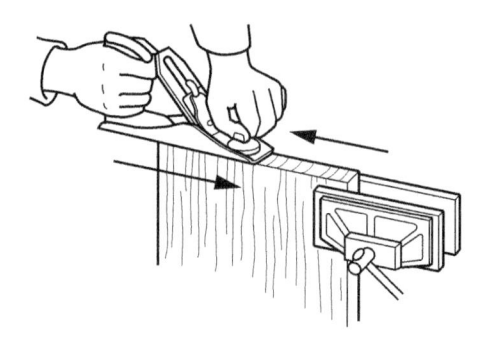

Fig. 5

Describe a different method of planing the end grain that will prevent the wood from splitting.

....

....

.... [2]

7 Circle from the lists below **one** material that is:

   (a) from a sustainable source

       acrylic   **stainless steel**   **oak**   **nylon**   [1]

   (b) biodegradeable.

       polystyrene   **cast iron**   **pine**   **copper**   [1]

8 Fig. 6 shows a computer desk.

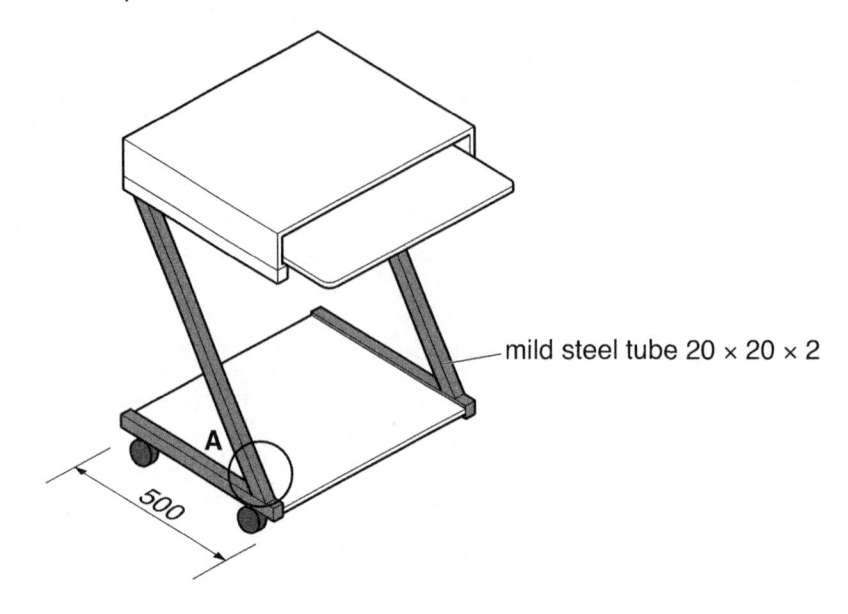

Fig. 6

Use sketches and notes to show how the corner joint at **A** could be strengthened.
State any constructions and fittings used.

[3]

9 (a) Name the centre lathe operation shown below.

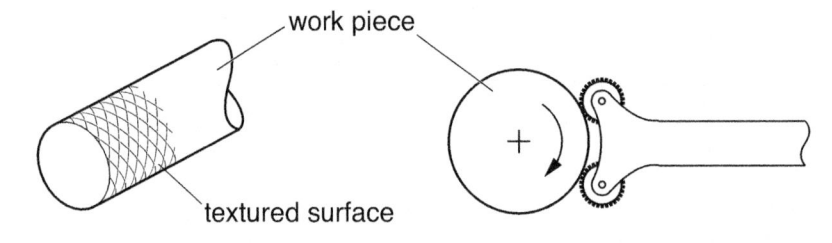

.... [1]

(b) State the purpose of the textured surface produced by the operation shown in part **(a)**.

.... [1]

10 Fig. 7 shows two small wooden tables. Both tables are the same overall size.
Table **A** is made by laminating. Table **B** is made by fabrication.

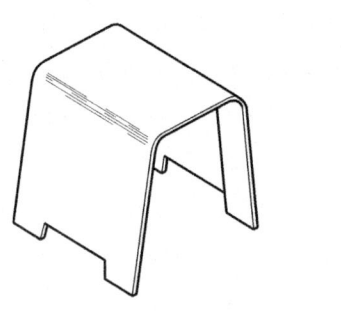

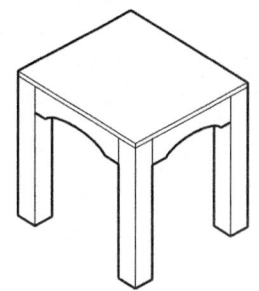

Table **A** laminated   Table **B** fabricated

Fig. 7

Compare the methods of manufacture and state which of the two tables would cost less to batch produce. Give **two** reasons for your decision.

Chosen table ....

Reason 1 ....

....

Reason 2 ....

....

[2]

Section B

Answer **one** question in this section.

11 Fig. 8 shows views of a planter box and stand.
The planter box is made from 12 mm thick marine plywood and the stand from Ø12 mild steel tube.

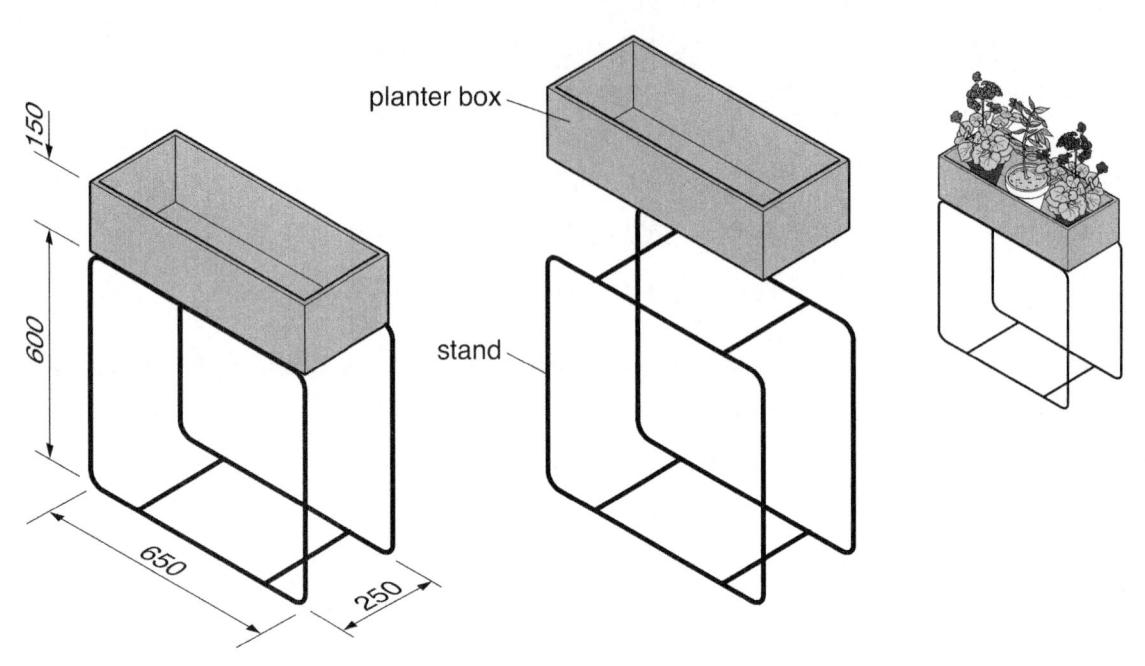

Fig. 8

(a) Give **two** benefits of using marine plywood for the planter box.

1 ....

2 ....
[2]

(b) The mild steel stand will have a dip-coated finish.
Give **two** benefits of a dip-coated finish for the mild steel stand.

1 ....

2 ....
[2]

(c) The planter box and stand is designed as flat-pack for self-assembly by the consumer. Fig. 9 shows the separate parts of the planter box.

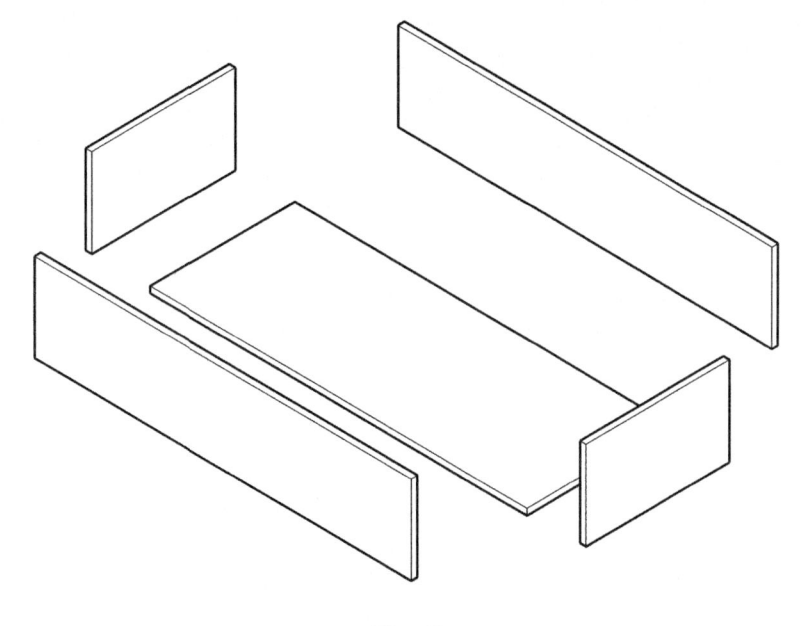

Fig. 9

Use sketches and notes to show how the parts could be joined together using basic tools.

[4]

(d) Details of the stand are shown in Fig. 10.
The stand is to be self-assembled from eight separate pieces of Ø12 mild steel tube.

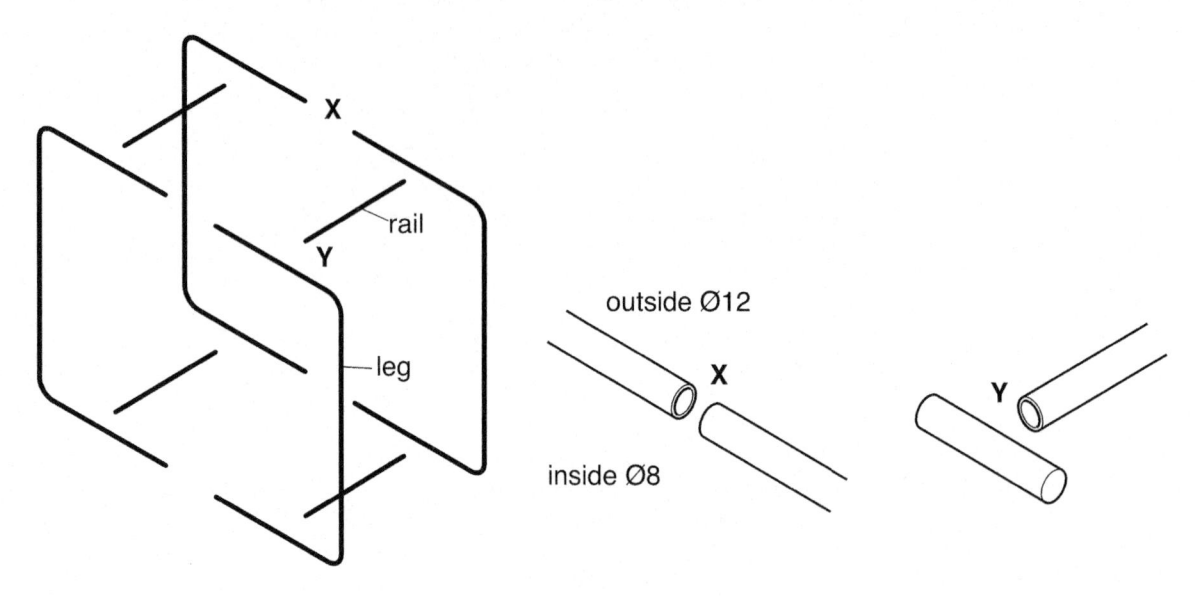

Fig. 10

Use sketches and notes to show details of connecting pieces that could be used to join:

(i) the legs together at **X**

[4]

(ii) a rail to a leg at **Y**.

[4]

(e) Use sketches and notes to show how the planter box could be fixed to the stand. The method of fixing must allow the planter box to be removed.

[4]

(f) Fig. 11 shows the basic shape of a box used to package all the parts of the planter box and stand for delivery to consumers.

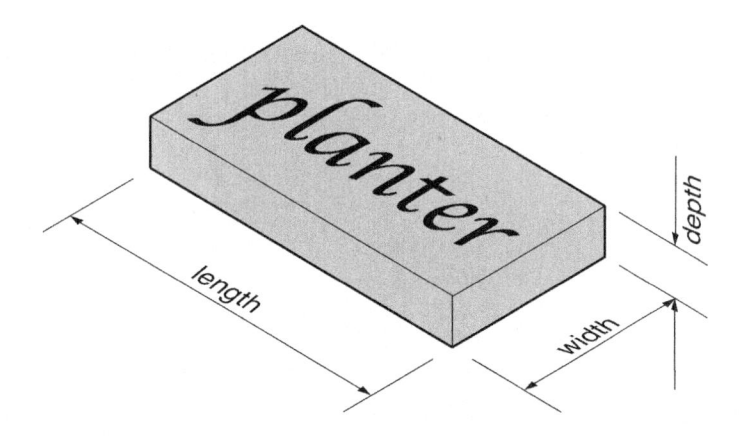

Fig. 11

Indicate on Fig. 11 a suitable length, width and depth for the box in which **all** the parts will fit.
[3]

(g) When designing and making products it is important to consider the choice of materials. Complete the following statement:

Using a manufactured board and a ferrous metal for the planter box and stand is not

harmful to the environment because ....

....

....

.... [2]

12 Fig. 12 shows views of an incomplete design for a toy helicopter made from 6 mm thick plywood.

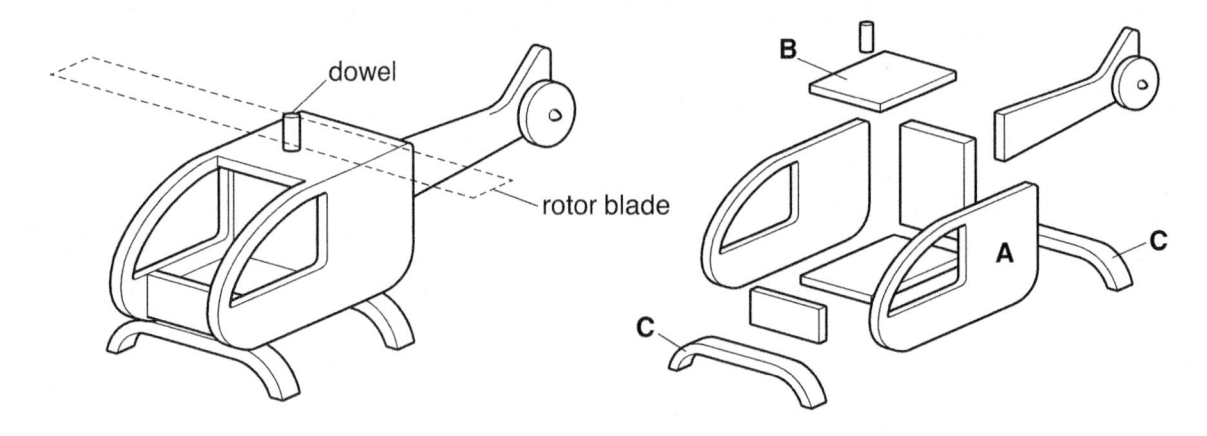

Fig. 12

(a) Give **two** reasons why 6 mm thick plywood is suitable for the toy helicopter.

1 ....

2 ....
[2]

(b) Fig. 13 shows side **A** marked out ready to be cut to shape.

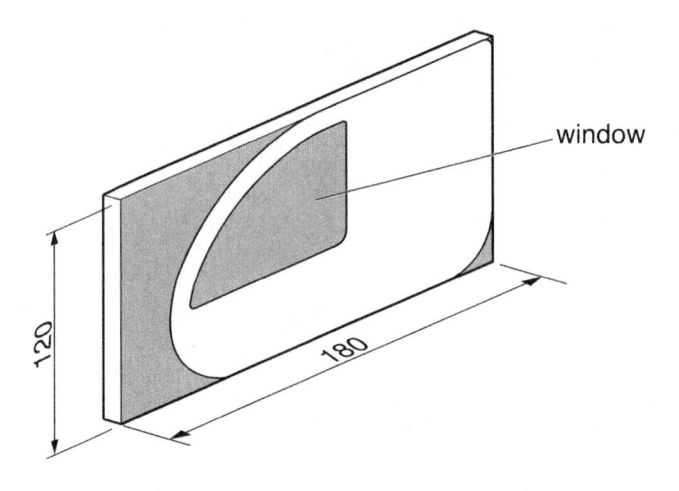

Fig. 13

Complete the table by naming the tools or items of equipment that could be used to make the side **A**.

Stage	Process	Tools / items of equipment
1	Mark out the shape	
2	Remove the window shape	
3	Smooth all cut edges	

[3]

[Turn over

(c) A contact adhesive will be used to join most of the parts of the toy helicopter.
Give **two** advantages of using a contact adhesive rather than PVA to join the parts.

1 ....

2 ....
[2]

(d) Fig. 14 shows the Ø6 dowel that will be glued into the roof, part **B**.

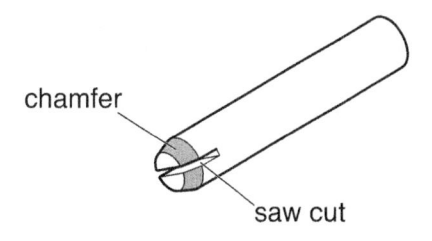

Fig. 14

Describe the purpose of the saw cut and the chamfer in the dowel.

Saw cut ....

Chamfer ....
[2]

(e) Fig. 15 shows one of the feet, part **C**, made from 5mm thick acrylic sheet.

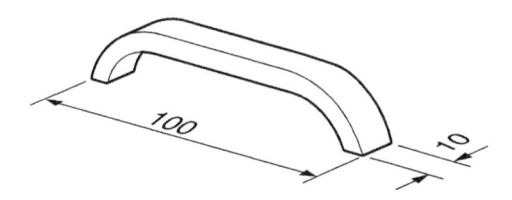

Fig. 15

Use sketches and notes to show how the foot could be made.
Include details of:
- marking out
- cutting out the shape
- producing the curved shape.

[5]

(f) The outline shape of a rotor blade that will be attached to the Ø6 dowel is shown in Fig. 12.

Choose a specific wood, metal **or** plastic for the rotor blade.
Use sketches and notes to show a design for a rotor blade that could be fitted to the Ø6 dowel.
The rotor blade must be able to turn freely.
Include all constructions, named materials and **two** important sizes.

[6]

(g) Identify **three** ways by which the designer has made the toy helicopter suitable for use by young children.

1 ....

2 ....

3 ....
[3]

(h) Plywood is a manufactured board. Explain why some manufactured boards can be considered environmentally friendly.

....

....

.... [2]

13 Fig. 16 shows a ladder plant stand.

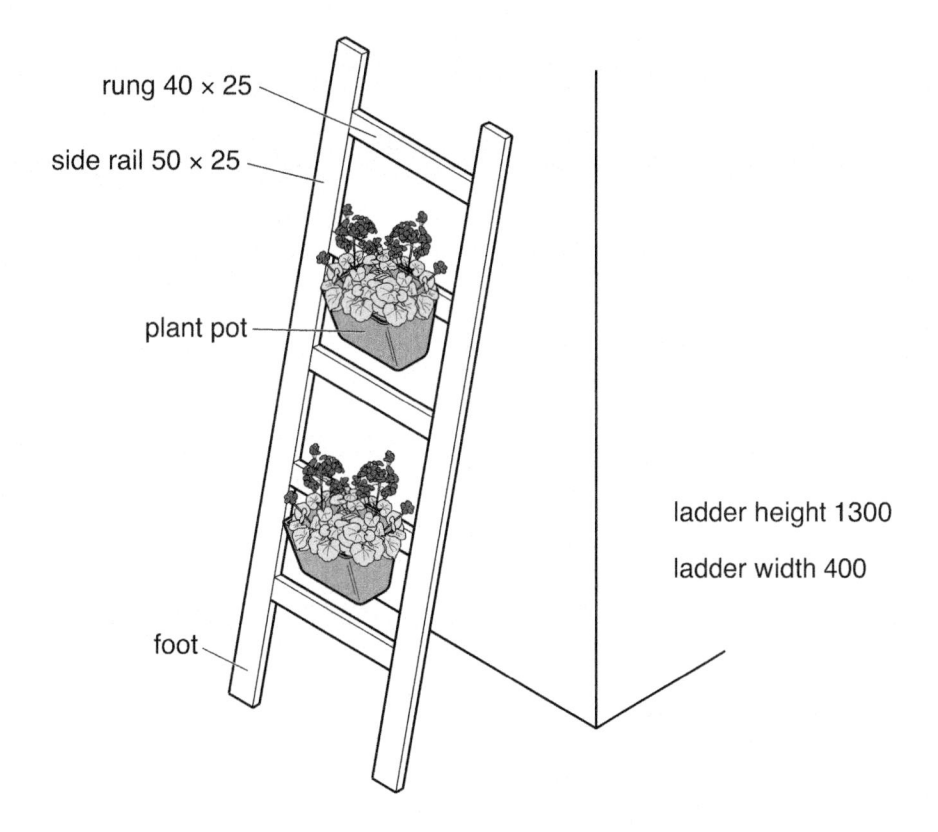

rung 40 × 25
side rail 50 × 25
plant pot
ladder height 1300
ladder width 400
foot

Fig. 16

(a) Name and sketch a permanent construction that could be used to join a rung to a side rail.

Name of construction ....

[4]

(b) Fig. 17 shows the side rails and rungs ready to be glued together.

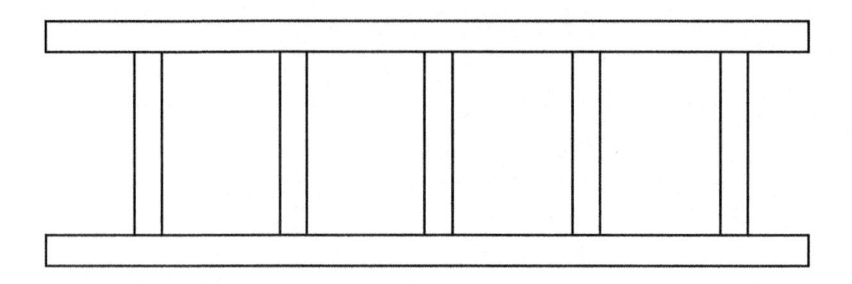

Fig. 17

(i) Add to Fig. 17 to show how cramps would be used to hold the side rails and rungs while the adhesive sets. [2]

(ii) Name the type of cramps used.

.... [1]

(iii) Name a suitable adhesive.

.... [1]

(iv) Describe **two** checks that would be made after the side rails and rungs have been glued and clamped.

1 ....

2 ....
[2]

(c) Fig. 18 shows views of one plant pot and a block of wood that will be made into the former used to vacuum form the plant pots.

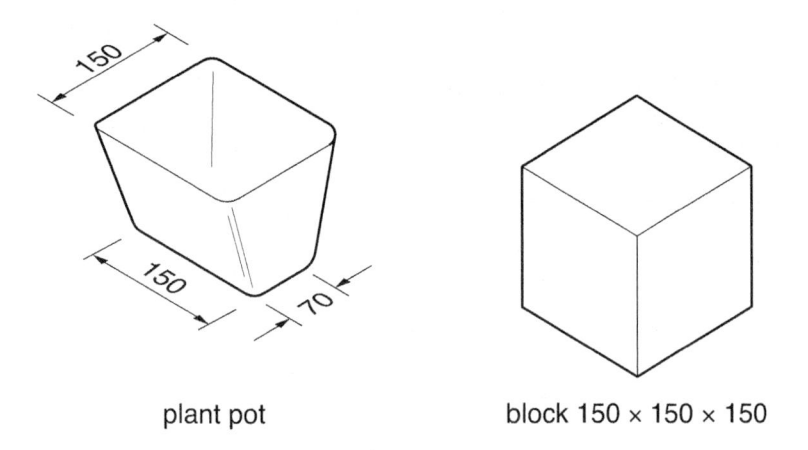

plant pot

block 150 × 150 × 150

Fig. 18

(i) Name a specific plastic that could be used to vacuum form the plant pots.

.... [1]

(ii) Draw on Fig. 18 to show the finished former ready to be used to make the plant pots. [2]

(iii) Use sketches and notes to show how the plant pots would be vacuum formed.

[6]

(d) The plant pots will be attached to the rungs securely but must allow for easy removal. Fig. 19 shows details of a plant pot and part of the ladder.

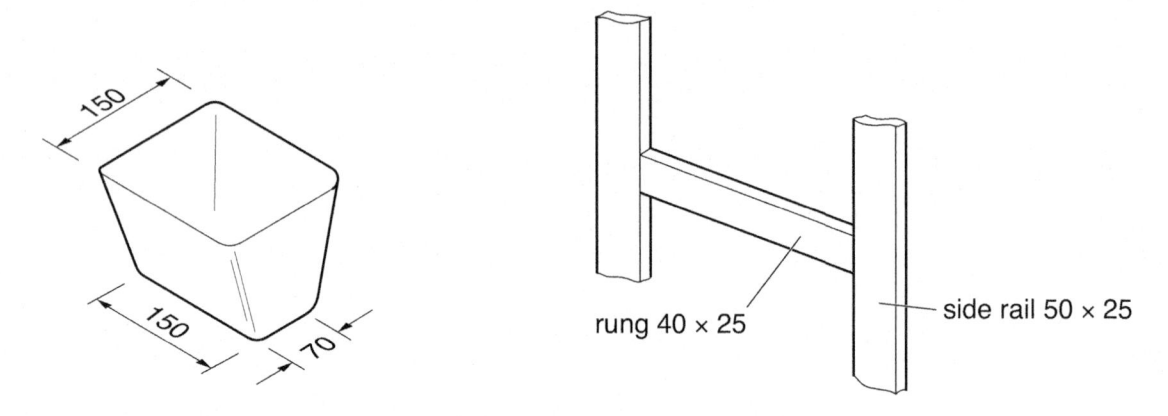

Fig. 19

Use sketches and notes to show how a plant pot could be attached to a rung while allowing for easy removal. Additional materials must be used.
Include details of materials used and any constructions.

[4]

Question 13 continues on page 18.

(e) Use sketches and notes to show a modification to the feet of the ladder that will prevent it from slipping away from a wall.

[2]

Cambridge IGCSE™

CANDIDATE NAME

CENTRE NUMBER

CANDIDATE NUMBER

DESIGN & TECHNOLOGY   0445/32

Paper 3 Resistant Materials   May/June 2020

                                                           1 hour

You must answer on the question paper.

No additional materials are needed.

INSTRUCTIONS
- Section A: answer **all** questions.
- Section B: answer **one** question.
- Use a black or dark blue pen. You may use an HB pencil for any diagrams or graphs.
- Write your name, centre number and candidate number in the boxes at the top of the page.
- Answer in the space provided.
- Do **not** use an erasable pen or correction fluid.
- Do **not** write on any bar codes.
- You may use a calculator.

INFORMATION
- The total mark for this paper is 50.
- The number of marks for each question or part question is shown in brackets [ ].
- All dimensions are in millimetres.

This document has **20** pages. Blank pages are indicated.

DC (ST/CB) 185041/3
© UCLES 2020   [Turn over

Section A

Answer **all** questions in this section.

1 Complete Table 1.1 by naming each of the tools that are used to mark out metal.

Table 1.1

Tool	Name of tool

[3]

2 Fig. 2.1 shows a drawer made from hardwood.
Sketch a suitable joint, other than a butt joint, that could be used at corner **A**.

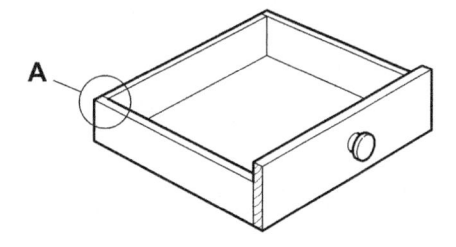

Fig. 2.1

[3]

3 Complete Table 3.1 by naming a suitable material for each product.

Table 3.1

Product	Suitable material
wooden building blocks	
metal toothbrush holder	
plastic cup and plate	

[3]

4 Fig. 4.1 shows details of a shelf bracket and a length of softwood from which the bracket is made.

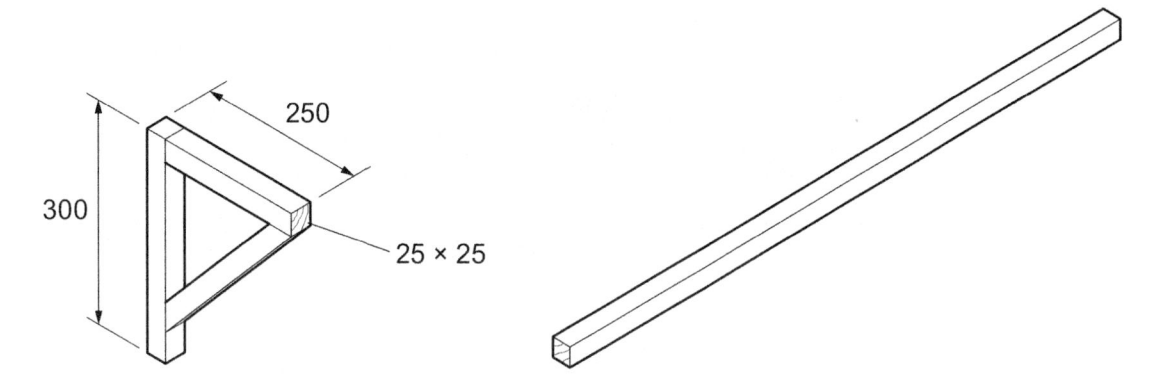

Fig. 4.1

State **three** processes that need to be carried out to produce the shelf bracket in Fig. 4.1.

1 ....
2 ....
3 ....
[3]

5 Fig. 5.1 shows a garden table made from plastic and the top of one of the removable table legs. The legs are fastened to the underside of the table top.

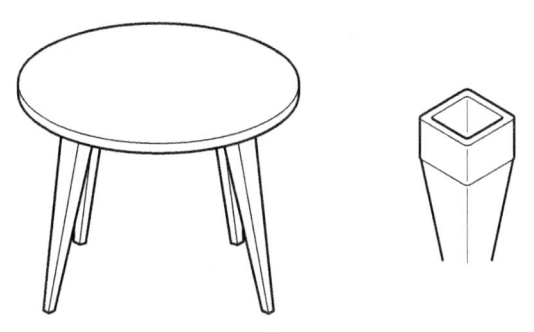

Fig. 5.1

Use sketches and notes to show how **one** leg could be fastened to the underside of the table top and be removable.

[2]

6 Fig. 6.1 shows a can opener in use.

Fig. 6.1

Give **three** specification points for the can opener.

1 ....
2 ....
3 ....
[3]

7 Fig. 7.1 shows views of a bracket made from 3 mm thick aluminium.

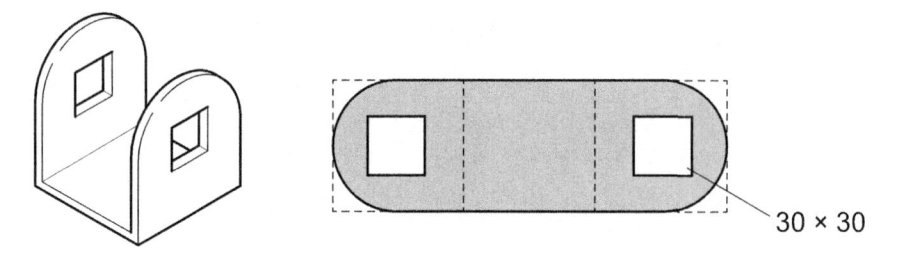

30 × 30

Fig. 7.1

Describe how the square holes 30 × 30 could be produced by hand.

....
....
.... [2]

8 Fig. 8.1 shows a draining rack used for drying crockery and cutlery.
The draining rack is made from steel and has a plastic coated finish.

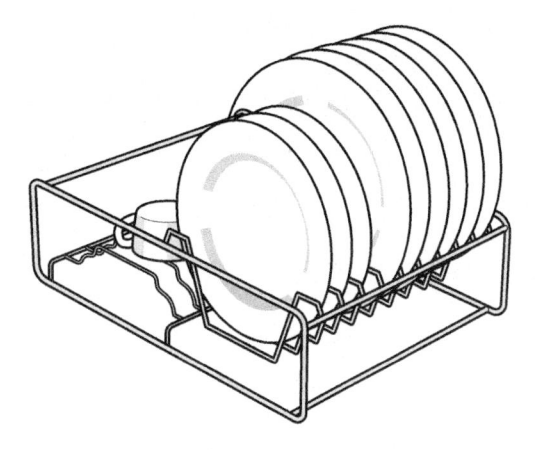

Fig. 8.1

(a) Give **one** benefit of a plastic coated finish on the draining rack.

.... [1]

(b) Give **one** drawback of a plastic coated finish on the draining rack.

.... [1]

9 Fig. 9.1 shows views of a coffee mug.
When hot liquid is added to the mug and the mug becomes warmer, a hidden image is revealed.

Fig. 9.1

Complete the statement:
The smart material that is added to the mug so that the image is revealed is known as

.... pigment. [1]

10 Fig. 10.1 shows views of a desk tidy made from 3 mm thick MDF.
The front, back and base fit into slots in the ends.

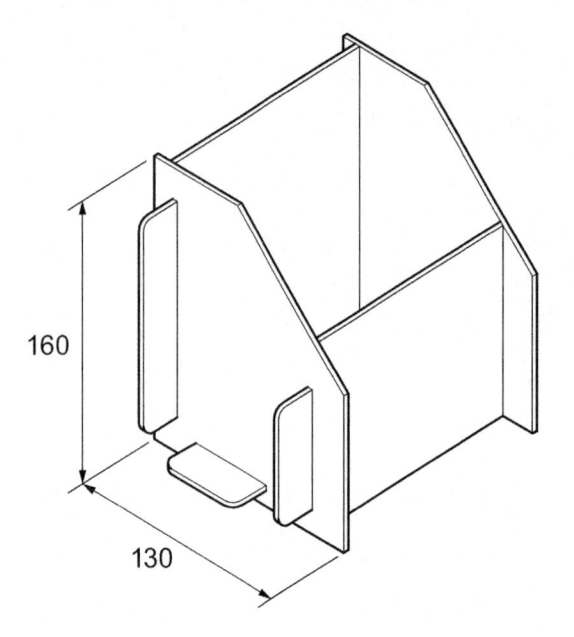

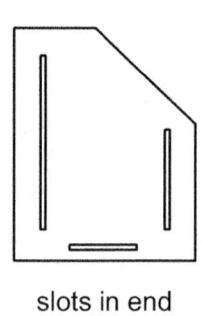

Fig. 10.1

slots in end

Use sketches and notes to show how the parts could be 'locked' in position without the use of an adhesive.

[3]

Section B

Answer **one** question in this section.

11 Fig. 11.1 shows views of an incomplete design for a key rack made from hardwood. The front of the key rack can swing open and closed as shown.

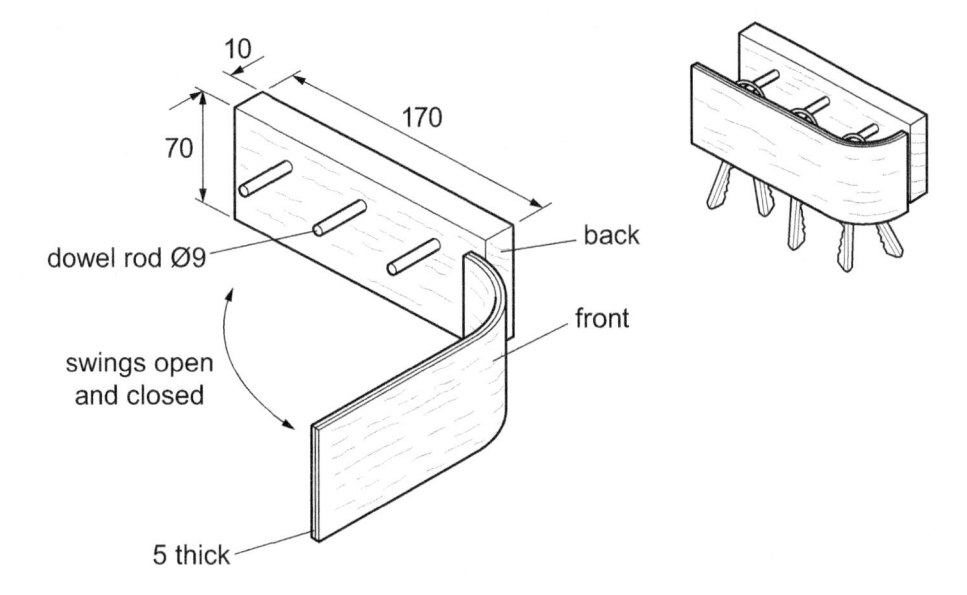

Fig. 11.1

(a) The front of the key rack is made by laminating wood veneers.
Use sketches and notes to show how the front could be produced.

[4]

(b) The keys will hang on Ø9 dowel pegs that are joined to the back of the key rack.
Use sketches and notes to show a modification to the dowel pegs so that the keys are prevented from sliding off.

[2]

(c) Use sketches and notes to show how the front could be joined to the back and allowed to open and close as shown in Fig. 11.1.
Include details of the materials and constructions used.

[4]

(d) (i) The front of the key rack will have a clear finish applied to it.
State **two** clear finishes, other than varnish, that would be suitable for the front of the key rack.

1 ....

2 ....
[2]

(ii) Give **two** stages of preparation that would need to be carried out before a clear finish could be applied to the front of the key rack.

1 ....

2 ....
[2]

(e) The key rack shown in Fig. 11.1 could be made completely from acrylic.

(i) Use sketches and notes to show how the front of the key rack could be formed when made from 5 mm thick acrylic sheet.

[3]

(ii) The dowel rods will be replaced with acrylic rod and the back replaced with acrylic sheet. Describe how the acrylic rod could be joined permanently to the back of the key rack.

....

....

.... [2]

(iii) The edges of the acrylic front and back will be self-finished to a high quality.
Complete Table 11.1 by describing **three** stages when self-finishing the edges of the acrylic.

Table 11.1

Stage	Process
1	Draw file edges using a hand file
2	
3	
4	

[3]

(f) When designing products, designers should select materials that are sustainable.
The key rack could be made from wood or plastic.
Explain why wood is considered to be more sustainable than plastic.

....

....

....

.... [3]

12 Fig. 12.1 shows an incomplete design for a rack to store items of equipment used for cycle maintenance. Three trays will be supported inside the rack.
The rack is made from 12 × 12 mild steel tube and the trays from high impact polystyrene (HIPS).

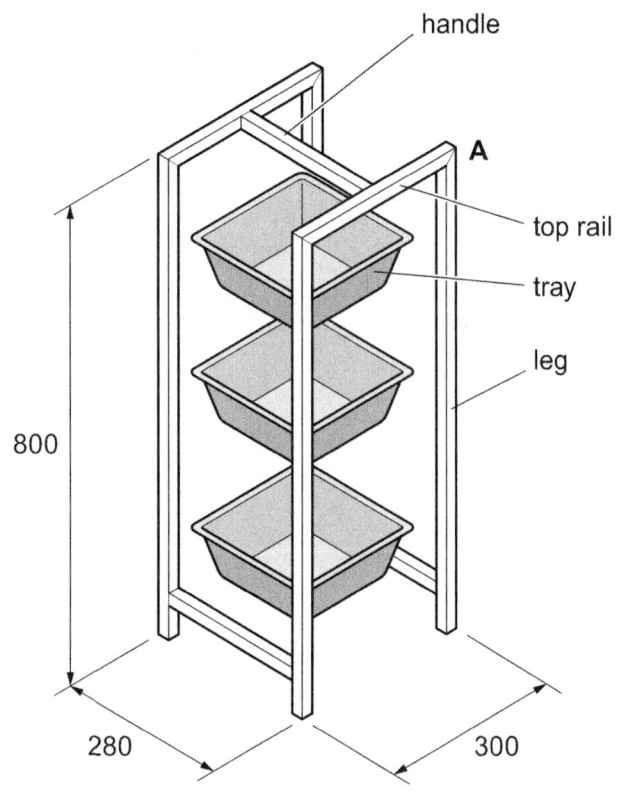

Fig. 12.1

(a) Fig. 12.2 shows parts of the top rail and leg of the rack marked out, ready to be cut, folded and brazed to form the corner at **A**.

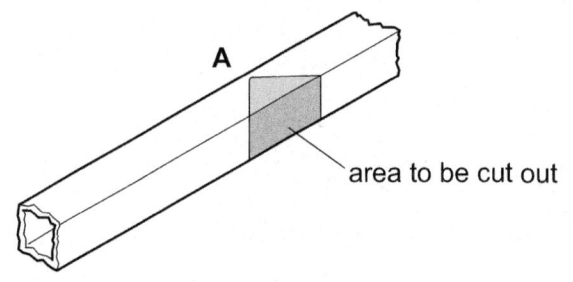

Fig. 12.2

Use sketches and notes to show how the joint could be cut out and the edges made flat using hand tools.

[4]

(b) The tubes will be joined together by brazing.
Complete Table 12.1 by stating the purpose of the items used when brazing the mild steel tube.

Table 12.1

Stage	Item of equipment	Purpose
1	emery cloth	
2	firebricks	
3	flux	
4	blow torch	
5	brazing rod	

[5]

(c) Fig. 12.3 shows part of the handle that will be joined to the top rail by means of an M8 screw.

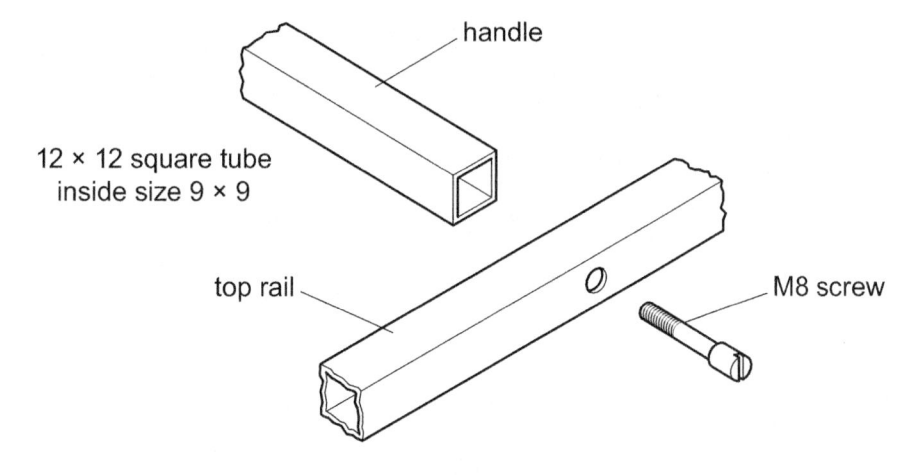

Fig. 12.3

Use sketches and notes to show a modification to the end of the handle so that the top rail and handle could be joined using the M8 screw.

[2]

(d) Use sketches and notes to show how the handle could be made more comfortable to hold when carrying the rack. Include details of materials used.

[2]

(e) Fig. 12.4 shows one of the trays and a block of wood that will be shaped into a former that will be used to vacuum form the trays.
Add sketches and notes to the block of wood to show the shape of a suitable former.

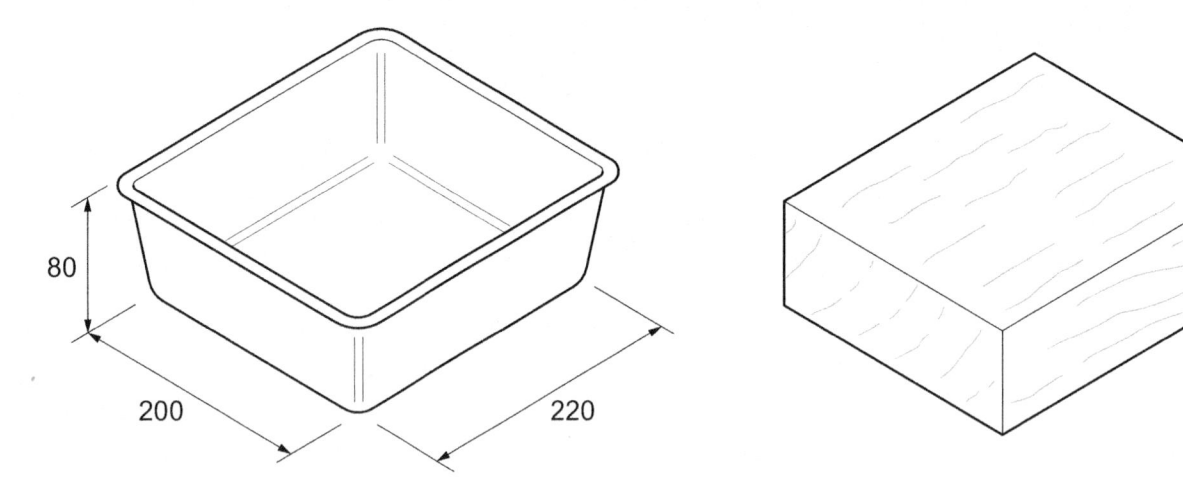

Fig. 12.4

[2]

(f) Give **two** benefits of the vacuum forming process when making a large quantity of products.

1 ....

2 ....

[2]

(g) Use sketches and notes to show modifications to the trays and/or the rack so that each of the three trays could be supported inside the rack and be able to be removed easily.
Include details of materials and constructions used.

[4]

(h) The rack is made from metal and the trays from plastic.
Explain the effects on the environment of using metal and plastic for the product.

....

....

....

....

.... [4]

13 Fig. 13.1 shows a small table to be made in a school workshop.

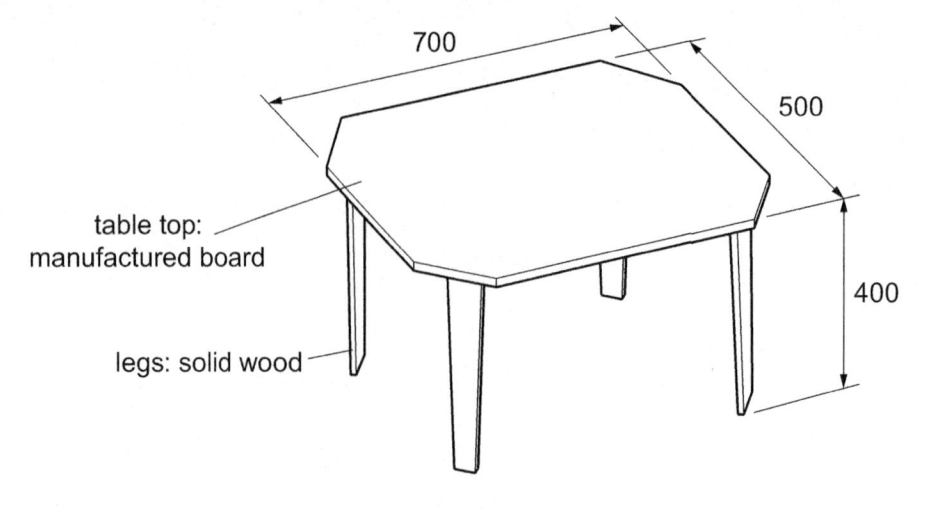

Fig. 13.1

(a) (i) Name a suitable manufactured board for the table top.

.... [1]

(ii) Give **two** reasons for your choice of manufactured board.

1 ....

2 ....
[2]

(b) Give **two** items of research that the designer would need to consider when deciding on the dimensions for the table.

1 ....

2 ....
[2]

(c) The legs are made from solid wood.
Fig. 13.2 shows one leg marked out ready to be shaped.

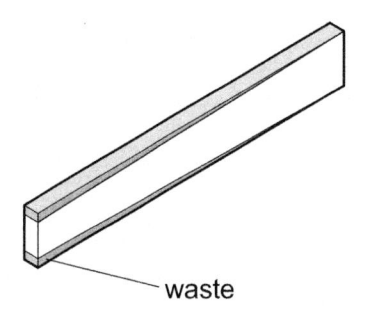

Fig. 13.2

(i) Name a suitable plane that could be used to remove the waste.

.... [1]

(ii) Show how the leg could be held securely while the waste wood is removed.

[2]

(d) Fig. 13.3 shows a palm sander.

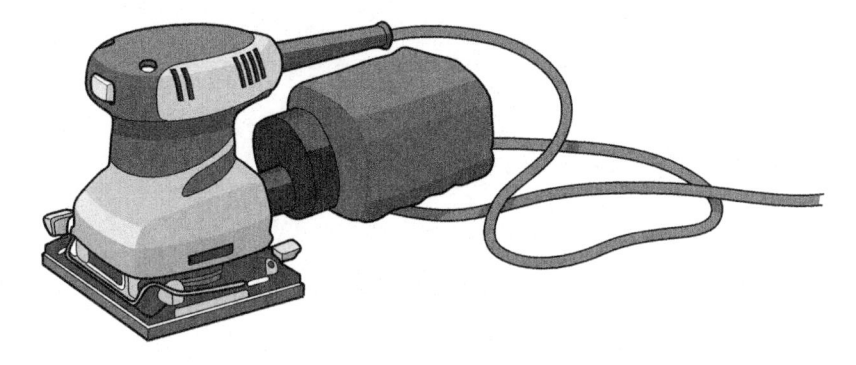

Fig. 13.3

(i) Give **two** benefits of using a palm sander to prepare the table top to take a finish.

1 ....

2 ....
[2]

(ii) Describe **two** safety precautions, other than items of personal protection equipment, that must be considered when using portable power tools.

1 ....

....

2 ....

....
[2]

(iii) The table top will be finished with clear lacquer.
Give **two** benefits of applying clear lacquer to the table top.

1 ....

2 ....
[2]

(e) Fig. 13.4 shows one leg in position to be hinged to the underside of the table top.

leg 60 wide × 20 thick

underside of table top

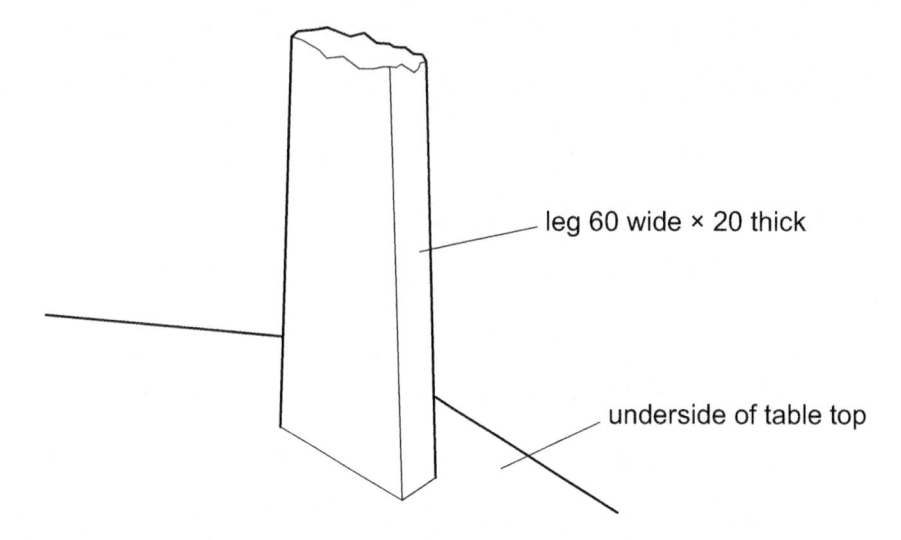

Fig. 13.4

(i) Add sketches and notes to Fig. 13.4 to show a suitable hinge that could be used to join the leg to the table top. [3]

(ii) Name the type of hinge used.

.... [1]

(iii) State the material from which the hinge is made.

.... [1]

(f) Use sketches and notes to show how the legs could be prevented from folding inwards when in use. Include details of materials and fittings used.

[6]

BLANK PAGE

MARKING KEYS

CAMBRIDGE INTERNATIONAL EXAMINATIONS

International General Certificate of Secondary Education

MARK SCHEME for the May/June 2014 series

0445 DESIGN AND TECHNOLOGY

0445/32　　Paper 3 (Resistant Materials), maximum raw mark 50

This mark scheme is published as an aid to teachers and candidates, to indicate the requirements of the examination. It shows the basis on which Examiners were instructed to award marks. It does not indicate the details of the discussions that took place at an Examiners' meeting before marking began, which would have considered the acceptability of alternative answers.

Mark schemes should be read in conjunction with the question paper and the Principal Examiner Report for Teachers.

Cambridge will not enter into discussions about these mark schemes.

Cambridge is publishing the mark schemes for the May/June 2014 series for most IGCSE, GCE Advanced Level and Advanced Subsidiary Level components and some Ordinary Level components.

Page 2	Mark Scheme	Syllabus	Paper
	IGCSE – May/June 2014	0445	32

Section A

1 **(a)** Aluminium [1]

   (b) Lightweight, light, corrosion resistant, good strength-weight ratio, low density [1]

2 Handle tight, pins in line, blade facing correct way, wood held securely, blade tight, blade is not damaged, blade is sharp   (2×1) [2]

3 **(a)** Accuracy of drawing: two parallel edges for 2 marks   (0–2) [2]

   (b) Safe edge correctly labelled [1]

4
Tool	Name	Specific use
	Guillotine, bench shears	Cutting thin metal/small section metal
	Jack plane	Preparation of material, quick removal of waste material

   (4×1) [4]

5 **(a)** Vacuum forming, injection moulding [1]

   (b) Release from mould [1]

   (c) To add strength, rigidity [1]

6 2 measurements indicated: floor to behind knee, behind knee to backside, backside to lumber area   (2×1) [2]

7 1 mm thick mild steel: scriber, odd legs, scribing gauge, scribing block

   3 mm thick acrylic: chinagraph pencil, marker pen, felt-tip, leave backing paper on or apply masking tape and use pen or pencil [2]

8 Sheet metal shown between folding bars (1)
   Folding bars shown in vice (1)
   Use of mallet or hammer and scrap wood (1) [3]

© Cambridge International Examinations 2014

Page 3	Mark Scheme	Syllabus	Paper
	IGCSE – May/June 2014	0445	32

9 (a) Soft solder [1]

(b) Tinplate work, plumbing [1]

10 Two advantages of moulded polypropylene include: weather resistance, durability, more easily moved around, comfortable armrests, will not rust, easier to clean, stronger must be qualified (2×1) [2]

Page 4	Mark Scheme	Syllabus	Paper
	IGCSE – May/June 2014	0445	32

Section B

11 (a) Suitable joints include: M&T, halving, bridle, dowel
Award 0–3 dependent upon accuracy of sketch (0–3)
Must be in correct orientation otherwise max. 2 marks
1 dowel only shown = 2 marks max.
Suitable joint named to match sketch (1) **[4]**
[Do not accept tenon or mortise on their own]

(b) (i) Variety of glues include: trade names such as Evo-Stik Resin W, Cascamite, or generic synthetic resin, PVA
[Do not accept epoxy resin]
Time to set to correspond with named glue: PVA 1–4 hours, synthetic resin 6–24 hours
[2]

   (ii) Sash cramps **[1]**

   (iii) 2 checks include: square, flat, joints pulled together, removal of excess glue, measure diagonals, use of scrap wood to spread pressure or prevent damage, clamped straight, clamps not over tightened, clamps tight/secure
(2×1) **[2]**

(c) Table of drilling machine shown (1)
Some form of 'wedge' to provide 20° angle or rotate table and lock (1)
Work piece secured/clamped (1) **[3]**

(d) Some form of base (1)
Male and female formers/rods (0–2)
Method of retention (1)

OR

Male and female formers (0–2)
Retention at start of bend (1)
Method of force (1) **[4]**

(e) Award up to 3 marks max. for practical method that is hidden behind frame (0–3)
Use of glued blocks/KD fittings/visible bracket/corner plates max. 2 marks
Award 0–1 for details of sizes and materials (0–1) **[4]**

(f) Frame:
Award 1 mark for recognition that frame needs to be in 4 separate parts (0–1)
Use of KD fittings/dowel/screws to connect separate pats (0–2)

Rods:
Award 1 mark for recognition that rods need to be in 3 separate parts (0–1)
Method of connecting 3 separate parts for each rod (0–1) **[5]**

© Cambridge International Examinations 2014

Page 5	Mark Scheme	Syllabus	Paper
	IGCSE – May/June 2014	0445	32

12 (a) 2 benefits include: check sizes, appearance, will it work, cheaper than making it from wood [Do not accept references to a template] (2×1) **[2]**

(b) Suitable method: dowel, M&T, added metal or wood support on surface of base
Award 0–3 dependent on technical accuracy (0–3)   (0–3)

Award up to max. 3 marks for support shown into mortise without shoulders
1 dowel only = max. 2 marks
Use of screws or nails from underneath = max. 2 marks
1 nail or screw = max. 1 mark
Name of method to correspond to sketch   (1) **[4]**

(c) (i) Quicker, more accurate, cuts fibres of wood, cannot be rubbed off (2×1) **[2]**

(ii) Acceptable methods:
Use of plane, hand-powered router, band saw table tilted at 45° angle (1)

Wood secured for plane and hand-powered router
Band saw requires fence/guide   (1)

Technical accuracy of named tools and equipment   (1) **[3]**

(d)

Process	Tools/equipment used
Mark out	Pencil, rule, sliding bevel, marking knife, mitre square
Saw off waste	Tenon saw, coping saw, various machine saws including Hegner, band saw, jig saw
Make sawn edges smooth	Sanding disc, file, chisel, plane, glasspaper/sandpaper

(3×1) **[3]**

(e) (i) Panel pins, oval wire, oval nail, round nail, round head, round wire, lost head **[1]**

(ii) PVA, synthetic resin, contact [impact], accept trade names such as Resin W. **[1]**
[Do not accept epoxy resin, animal or scotch glue]

(iii) Easier to clean, remove debris, allows water to escape **[1]**

(f) Problems involve weather/climate:
too hot or cold, too wet or dry, fungal/insect attack, windy conditions
woods can shrink or expand, rot
metals can rust, plastics can fade
award 1 mark for each sensible problem identified   (2×1)
award 1 mark for each method to overcome problem
e.g. painted to protect, choice of material for specific environment (2×1) **[4]**

© Cambridge International Examinations 2014

Page 6	Mark Scheme	Syllabus	Paper
	IGCSE – May/June 2014	0445	32

(g) End of **D** [or support] shaped to fit under roof (1)
Reinforced using block or strip of wood (1)
[Do not accept screwing of roof to shaped end of support]
Details of materials and constructions used (0–2) **[4]**

13

(a)

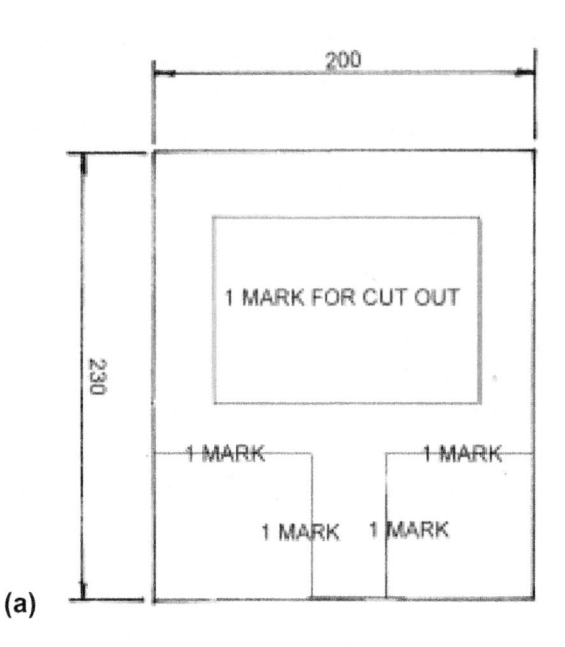

(i) Award 1 mark for each cut shown above (5×1) **[5]**
Incorrect orientation = 0 marks

(ii) Quicker, more accurate, repetitive accuracy
Template can be used as a 2D model (2×1) **[2]**

(b) (i) Sketch to show work low in the vice to prevent it cracking (0–2)
Added notes to describe how problem is overcome (0–1) **[3]**

(ii) Award work piece clamped in position/use of machine vice (1)
Award work piece supported underneath (1)
Award slow speed of drill/correct cutting angle/pilot drills (1) **[3]**

(c) Use of wet and dry paper, polishing wheel, mop and compound/polish
Award any 2 items of equipment described (2×1) **[2]**

(d) Heated over a line bender/strip heater/hot air gun to become soft (1)
Use of former or round bar (1)
Softened acrylic draped over former/round bar and held (1)
Technical accuracy (1) **[4]**

(e) Practical solution/ concept (0–3)
Details of sizes and constructions (0–3)
[Materials used must be appropriate for 4 mm thick acrylic otherwise 0 marks] **[6]**

© Cambridge International Examinations 2014

CAMBRIDGE INTERNATIONAL EXAMINATIONS

Cambridge International General Certificate of Secondary Education

MARK SCHEME for the October/November 2014 series

0445 DESIGN AND TECHNOLOGY

0445/32 Paper 3 (Resistant Materials), maximum raw mark 50

This mark scheme is published as an aid to teachers and candidates, to indicate the requirements of the examination. It shows the basis on which Examiners were instructed to award marks. It does not indicate the details of the discussions that took place at an Examiners' meeting before marking began, which would have considered the acceptability of alternative answers.

Mark schemes should be read in conjunction with the question paper and the Principal Examiner Report for Teachers.

Cambridge will not enter into discussions about these mark schemes.

Cambridge is publishing the mark schemes for the October/November 2014 series for most Cambridge IGCSE®, Cambridge International A and AS Level components and some Cambridge O Level components.

® IGCSE is the registered trademark of Cambridge International Examinations.

Page 2		Mark Scheme	Syllabus	Paper
		Cambridge IGCSE – October/November 2014	0445	32

Section A

| 1 | A | Mallet | 1 | |
| | B | Chisel | 1 | [2] |

2 (a) Dovetail [1]

(b) For added strength, more difficult to remove [1]

(c) Wide range available: PVA, accept trade names such as Resin W, Cascamite, animal glue [1]

3 (a) Press forming/moulding, plug & yoke, injection moulding, vacuum forming [1]

(b) acrylic, polystyrene, ABS [1]

| 4 | (a) | stainless steel | 1 | |
| | (b) | duralumin | 1 | [2] |

5	Plane to the centre and stop	1	
	Repeat from opposite end	1	
	OR		
	Use of scrapwood to support end grain	1	
	Plane straight across	1	[2]

6 Completed drawing of tee bridle.
Award 1 mark for top, 1 for lower part, 1 for overall accuracy [3]

7	Tenon saw	1	
	Used to cut small pieces of wood to length	1	
	Hacksaw	1	
	Used to cut small pieces of metal	1	[4]

8 (a) To prevent corrosion/rusting [1]

(b) Paint, galvanise [1]

© Cambridge International Examinations 2014

Page 3	Mark Scheme	Syllabus	Paper
	Cambridge IGCSE – October/November 2014	0445	32

9 (a) Completed drawing of back flap hinge. Award 0–2 dependent on technical accuracy. **[2]**

(b) Larger surface area, screw holes staggered for additional strength **[1]**

10 (a) Used for cut lines on joints, marked waste, across grain 1

(b) Marking, mortise and cutting gauges 1 **[2]**

Page 4	Mark Scheme	Syllabus	Paper
	Cambridge IGCSE – October/November 2014	0445	32

Section B

11 (a) (i) Dowel [1]

    (ii) Cascamite, [waterproof] PVA, synthetic resin [1]

(b) Two reasons: speed, repetitive accuracy   2 × 1   [2]

(c)

Stage	Process	Tool or item of equipment
1	Cut off the waste	Saw, chisel
2	Make the hole for the mast	Drill
3	Make edges smooth	File, glasspaper, disc sander

[3]

(d) Use of screw clearly shown   1
     Use of washers fitted appropriately   1   [2]

(e) Two properties: lightweight, water resistant, easily moulded   2 × 1   [2]

(f) Stages include:
set up mould/former on platen/in machine
lower into position
clamp plastic in position
heat plastic, check flexibility
raise platen/mould/former
turn on pump
wait to cool and release from mould/former

Award 0–5 for detailed stages   0–5
Award 0–3 for technically accurate sketches   0–3   [8]

(g) Deck must be clamped in position using G cramp
Award 0–2 dependent on technical accuracy.   [2]

(h) Two safety precautions:
gloves or barrier cream to protect skin, well ventilated space, face mask, goggles   2 × 1   [2]

Page 5	Mark Scheme	Syllabus	Paper
	Cambridge IGCSE – October/November 2014	0445	32

(i) Two ways of making toys appealing: shape, colour, movement, noise
Award 2 marks for one method well explained or 2 × 1 for two separate methods [2]

12 (a) (i) Suitable constructions: mortise and tenon, dowel
Award 0–3 dependent on technical accuracy   0–3   [3]

(ii) Sliding bevel can be adjusted and locked at a specific angle   1
Provides repetitive accuracy and speed   1   [2]

(b) (i) 25 mm, 32 mm   [1]

(ii) stages include:
preparation/cleaning of joint
apply flux
position on hearth/bricks
heat up metal
apply spelter
leave to cool

Award 0–4 for detailed stages   0–4
Award 0–2 for technically accurate sketches   0–2   [6]

(c) Some form of metal plate or block of wood attached to underside   0–2
Stand joined appropriately to plate or block   0–2
Accuracy of technical detail   0–2   [6]
Mortise and tenon directly into underside of tray = 0–2

(d) 2 methods:
1 mark out diagonals/circle   1
   cut off waste   1
   make round using sanding disc   1
   technical accuracy   1
   OR
2 faceplate turning: award 0–4 dependent on technical accuracy
   Stages include:
   prepare wood to 'octagonal' shape
   screw wood to faceplate
   set up on lathe
   set up tee rest
   turn to diameter   [4]

(e) (i) easily wiped clean, smooth surface, does not stain, heatproof, more durable   2 × 1   [2]

(ii) Impact/Contact adhesive. Accept trade names such as Thixofix.   [1]

© Cambridge International Examinations 2014

Page 6	Mark Scheme	Syllabus	Paper
	Cambridge IGCSE – October/November 2014	0445	32

13 (a) Smooth finish, consistent density, relatively easy to cut and shape, no splinters 2 × 1 [2]

(b) Location, items to be stored: how many, what sizes.
Accept any sensible research item carried out before designing. 2 × 1 [2]

(c) (i) Use of grove or rebate. Either cut out or applied beads.
Award 0–3 dependent on technical accuracy of drawing. 0–3 [3]
Award 0–2 for glued/screwed inside
Award 0 marks if base is visible

(ii) Partition could be pinned and glued, housing or dowelled
Award 0–3 dependent on technical accuracy of drawing. 0–3 [3]

(d) Method of location for stacking:
use of applied beads, metal pegs or wooden dowel 0–2

Constructional details and sizes 0–3 [5]

(e) (i) paint, stain [1]

(ii) use of glasspaper, different grades, wipe off dust 2 × 1 [2]

(f) Due to lack of thickness, traditional joints are not practical.
Methods should use applied strips and/or blocks to which the sides could be pinned or screwed and glued.
Butt + glue = 1 mark. Butt + pin + glue = 1 mark. Butt only = 0. Mitre = 1 mark.
Award 0–3 dependent on technical accuracy of drawing. 0–3 [3]

(g) Two functional improvements:
more partitions for increased storage, feet to lift off flat surface,
handholds to assist lifting.
Accept any sensible improvement showing understanding of the term 'functional'. 2 × 1 [2]

(h) Two advantages: ready coloured, easily moulded to shape, attractive colours available, durable material, requires no applied finish, easy to maintain/clean 2 × 1 [2]

© Cambridge International Examinations 2014

CAMBRIDGE INTERNATIONAL EXAMINATIONS

Cambridge International General Certificate of Secondary Education

MARK SCHEME for the May/June 2015 series

0445 DESIGN AND TECHNOLOGY

0445/32   Paper 3 (Resistant Materials), maximum raw mark 50

This mark scheme is published as an aid to teachers and candidates, to indicate the requirements of the examination. It shows the basis on which Examiners were instructed to award marks. It does not indicate the details of the discussions that took place at an Examiners' meeting before marking began, which would have considered the acceptability of alternative answers.

Mark schemes should be read in conjunction with the question paper and the Principal Examiner Report for Teachers.

Cambridge will not enter into discussions about these mark schemes.

Cambridge is publishing the mark schemes for the May/June 2015 series for most Cambridge IGCSE®, Cambridge International A and AS Level components and some Cambridge O Level components.

® IGCSE is the registered trademark of Cambridge International Examinations.

Page 2	Mark Scheme	Syllabus	Paper
	Cambridge IGCSE – May/June 2015	0445	32

Section A

1. Marking gauge (1)
    Micrometer (1)
    Odd legs/odd leg calipers/Jenny[s] calipers. (1) **[3]**

    Not calipers

2. Benefits: new blade is sharper, blades selected to cut different materials,
    new blade rather than replace whole tool, broken/blunt blades can be replaced,
    keeps blade sharp.
    Not different lengths. (2 × 1) **[2]**

3. Kevlar® (1)
    Glass reinforced plastic (1) **[2]**

4. (a) brazing, welding, epoxy resin, Araldite (1)

    (b) acrylic/plastic cement, Tensol [cement] (1) **[2]**
    Not epoxy resin, Araldite

5. (a) A dowel joint (1)
        B [corner] bridle joint, open mortise and tenon (1) **[2]**

    (b) greater surface area to be glued (1) **[1]**

6. (a) A [circular split] die (1)
        B tap, plug tap (1) **[2]**

    (b) cut screw thread on rod/bar, external [male] thread, (1) **[1]**

    (c) cut screw thread inside hole, internal [female] thread (1) **[1]**
        If 'cut a screw thread' is used for (b) and (c) award 1 mark only.

7. Award 0–3 dependent upon technical accuracy (0–3) **[3]**

Page 3	Mark Scheme	Syllabus	Paper
	Cambridge IGCSE – May/June 2015	0445	32

8   Hardwood not seasoned correctly, central heating,
    table top fixed to legs/rails without allowance for movement (2 × 1) **[2]**
    Award mark to answers relating to the wood drying out due to heat **not** excessive moisture.

9   Shape of sander fits into hand comfortably, quick replacement of abrasive paper,
    dust collection for health and safety, appropriate size to handle (2 × 1) **[2]**

10 (a) [High density] polyethelene/polythene. **[1]**

   (b) Can be recycled **[1]**
       Not 'it has been recycled'.

Page 4	Mark Scheme	Syllabus	Paper
	Cambridge IGCSE – May/June 2015	0445	32

Section B

11 (a) 4 stages: 4 × 1   Award any practical stage in process:
mark out length, mark out centres for holes, cut to length, square cut end,
drill holes (4)
Do **not** reward references to glasspaper/cork block

Award 0–1 for technical accuracy (1)
Award 1 mark for Technical Accuracy **only** if minimum 3 stages are given
If no sketches are provided maximum mark 3 dependent on overall
quality of answer. **[5]**

(b) Jig with minimum of 3 holes correctly spaced (0–2)
Award 1 mark for 1 or 2 holes shown only.
Award 1 mark only if not correctly spaced.

Jig fits over width of strip **and** block or fits into base board (0–2)
Award 1 mark only if not positively located.

'Stopped' at one end (0–2)
Named materials (0–1) **[7]**

(c) (i) Advantage: preserve, protect, enhance appearance, create interest,
more durable/hardwearing (1)

(ii) Disadvantage: paint or varnish can chip and look unattractive,
children may put in their mouth (1) **[2]**
Not 'increased cost' or 'takes longer'.

(d) Specific materials used (0–1)
Appropriate processes (0–3)
2 relevant/appropriate sizes: e.g. minimum Ø50 of wheel (0–2)
Technical accuracy (0–2) **[8]**

If CAM/CNC machining is given answers must include details of process;
e.g. designed by CAD and downloaded to machine, machine parameters set,
material positioned in machine.

(e) Round section wood: dowel **[1]**

(f) Advantages: inherent colour, self-finished, moulded/intricate shapes possible,
hygienic, lightweight, no splinters, durable/hardwearing,
better resistance to weathering/external use. (2 × 1) **[2]**

Not cheaper, more attractive, easy to mass produce.

© Cambridge International Examinations 2015

Page 5	Mark Scheme	Syllabus	Paper
	Cambridge IGCSE – May/June 2015	0445	32

12 (a) 4 bend lines (4 × 1) **[4]**
Award 4 marks for correctly **stated** sizes even if drawing is not accurately proportioned.

(b) 3 stages, **in correct sequence** include:
use of scraper,
wet and dry [silicon carbide] abrasive paper [medium grit],
wet and dry abrasive paper [silicon carbide] [fine grit],
polishing mop and compound
Brasso, acrylic polish. (3 × 1) **[3]**

Do not award marks for any filing process.
Do not award marks for emery cloth.
Award **2 stages** with different grades of wet and dry paper only.
Do accept 'wet and dry sand paper'.

(c) (i) **Do not** award marks for marking out.
drill hole in acrylic (1)
insert blade of coping saw, Hegner saw, abra file and cut out waste (1)
file edges smooth **or** use of wet and dry paper (1) **[3]**

If chain drilling is described, award 2 marks for chain drilling and 1 mark for filing.

If CAM/CNC machining is given answers must include details of process;
e.g. designed by CAD and downloaded to machine, machine parameters set, material positioned in machine.

(ii) 2 precautions: appropriate drill speed, clamp acrylic securely,
slow feed for drill, support under acrylic, use of masking tape, drill pilot hole,
use gradually increasing diameters of drill, little pressure (2 × 1) **[2]**

(d) Method of softening acrylic: strip heater or line bender (1)
Do not accept oven or hot air gun to heat acrylic.

Appropriate shaped former (1)
Clamp acrylic to retain shape (1)
Technical accuracy (1) **[4]**

Award 1 mark for Technical Accuracy only if minimum 2 stages are provided.

(e) Practical idea: some form of 'shelf' or extended base. (0–2)

Appropriate materials and constructions (0–2) **[4]**
Allow use of Araldite/epoxy resin **only** to join acrylic to wood or acrylic to metal.

Page 6	Mark Scheme	Syllabus	Paper
	Cambridge IGCSE – May/June 2015	0445	32

(f) **Do not** award marks for marking out.
Accept any 3 stages: (3 × 1)

Use of a wooden former/folding bars/jig
Aluminium sheet secured while bent to shape [vice or cramps]
Method of force: mallet or hammer **and** scrap wood.

Do not award marks for hammer **without** scrap wood. **[3]**
Accept bending machine: for maximum marks details must be provided. (0–3)

(g) Self-finished: no applied finish (1)
material is cleaned and prepared with appropriate abrasives (1) **[2]**

13 (a) Smooth finish, consistent density, relatively easy to cut and shape, no splinters, takes paint well, easier to work with, better finish, finer grain, no need to glasspaper,
(2 × 1) **[2]**
Not 'cheaper'.

(b) Rounded corners, appropriate size, interesting puzzle shapes, different colours, lightweight, simple puzzle, tray to keep pieces, pieces too small to swallow (3 × 1) **[3]**

(c) (i) Construction shown clearly (0–2)
Notes to explain alternating grain producing stability/strength (0–1) **[3]**

1 mark   2 marks   1 mark for drawing &
                       2 marks explanation

(ii) **Do not** award marks for marking out **or** use of a hole saw to remove shape.

Accept **any 3 stages** from the following:
Drill hole inside circular shape
Insert blade of appropriate saw and cut out shape or use of Surform tool or rasp to remove most of waste
Use of file to make smooth [**not** rasp]
Use of abrasive paper to make smooth (3 × 1)

Technical accuracy:
appropriately named saw and file and wood held securely (0–2) **[5]**
e.g. coping, Hegner, scroll, fret, pad
e.g. half-round, round or rat tail file

Page 7	Mark Scheme	Syllabus	Paper
	Cambridge IGCSE – May/June 2015	0445	32

    (iii) Top and bottom pieces of plywood shown clamped together   (0–2)
        At least 2 cramps shown **or** statement refers to use of cramps plural.
        Suitable glue: PVA, Cascamite, synthetic resin, Gorilla glue.   (1)

        Do not award marks for Araldite/epoxy resin.

        Suitable cramps: G cramps, F cramps.   (1)   **[4]**

    (iv) Two advantages: speed of production, lighter weight, colours available, comfortable moulded shape, coloured without painting, easier to clean, consistent quality when batch produced.   (2 × 1)   **[2]**
        Do not award marks for 'easier to make', 'cheaper'.

(d) Computer Aided **Design/Drafting**   (1)

    Computer Aided **Manufacture/Machining**   (1)   **[2]**

(e) Two quality control checks applied to the puzzle and/or the tray: checks for dimensional accuracy/sizes/tolerances, overall finish, surface finish, consistency of materials used.   (2 × 1)   **[2]**

(f) Manufactured boards can be made from recycled materials, therefore reducing the impact on the number of trees grown. Use of manufactured boards can reduce need for oil based products, plastics do not decompose, some manufactured boards use waste materials.   (2 × 1)   **[2]**

CAMBRIDGE INTERNATIONAL EXAMINATIONS
Cambridge International General Certificate of Secondary Education

MARK SCHEME for the October/November 2015 series

0445 DESIGN AND TECHNOLOGY

0445/32 Paper 3 (Resistant Materials), maximum raw mark 50

This mark scheme is published as an aid to teachers and candidates, to indicate the requirements of the examination. It shows the basis on which Examiners were instructed to award marks. It does not indicate the details of the discussions that took place at an Examiners' meeting before marking began, which would have considered the acceptability of alternative answers.

Mark schemes should be read in conjunction with the question paper and the Principal Examiner Report for Teachers.

Cambridge will not enter into discussions about these mark schemes.

Cambridge is publishing the mark schemes for the October/November 2015 series for most Cambridge IGCSE®, Cambridge International A and AS Level components and some Cambridge O Level components.

® IGCSE is the registered trademark of Cambridge International Examinations.

Page 2	Mark Scheme	Syllabus	Paper
	Cambridge IGCSE – October/November 2015	0445	32

Section A

1 Three pieces of information: length, thread diameter, type of head, quantity, material

(3 × 1) [3]

2 Completed drawing of coping saw
Award (0–2) dependent on technical accuracy [2]

3 (a) Sash cramp/F cramp (1)

(b) To protect, apply even pressure (1) [2]

4 Polymorph, nitinol (2 × 1) [2]

5

Tool	Specific name	Specific use
	Outside calipers	Measuring outside diameters
	Brace	Drilling/boring holes

[4]

6 (a) Allows cheaper manufactured boards to appear as solid wood (1)

(b) Less durable, can be damaged easily (1) [2]

7 Corner strengthened: triangular plates, corrugated fastener, dowel, metal pins, feather, wooden block, modesty block
Use of nails: award 1 mark only if 2 nails are shown
Do not accept use of screws or bolts through end
Award (0–2) dependent on technical accuracy [2]

8 (a) [sand] Casting, die-casting (1)

(b) Self-finished, anodised, spray paint, dip coat, lacquer (1) [2]

© Cambridge International Examinations 2015

Page 3	Mark Scheme	Syllabus	Paper
	Cambridge IGCSE – October/November 2015	0445	32

9 Accept any 3 from: drill hole, insert blade of coping or scroll saw and cut out waste, file flat, chisel, glasspaper (3 × 1) **[3]**

10 (a) Lamination, steam bending (1)

   (b) Mortise and tenon, dowel (1)

   (c) Less constructions to produce, stronger overall form, inherent flexibility in chair, more stable, more comfortable (1) **[3]**

Section B

11 (a) (i) Lower costs than ready assembled furniture, ready collected, satisfaction of assembling at home (2 × 1) **[2]**

       (ii) Less storage space required, fewer manufacturing processes means quicker production, competitive costs (2 × 1) **[2]**

   (b) Recognised KD fitting: corner/modesty block (0–2)
       Added notes (0–2)
       Use of dowel or screws award 1 mark max. **[4]**

   (c) Accurate sketch of pre-manufactured component runner or use of grooves [cut or applied]
       Award (0–2) dependent on technical accuracy (0–2)
       Additional notes (0–2) **[4]**

   (d) (i) Two advantages: even application possible, no brush strokes, faster, smoother (2 × 1) **[2]**
       (ii) Well ventilated room, face mask, safety glasses (2 × 1) **[2]**

   (e) Accept any sensible positive or negative evaluative comments about computer desks generic

       (i) Safety: corners are rounded, the desk is stable in use **[2]**

       (ii) Good space for keyboard monitor etc. attractive painted finish, clean simple form **[2]**

       (iii) Use of manufactured board is economical, minimal constructions/self-assembly reduces cost of product **[2]**

Page 4	Mark Scheme	Syllabus	Paper
	Cambridge IGCSE – October/November 2015	0445	32

(f) Limited lifetime issues include:

- materials such as manufactured board may not be as long lasting as solid wood

- constructions such as KD fittings dependent on strength of screw thread may not be considered long lasting; over time, in use, KD fittings may become worn

- fashion can dictate the change for furniture of this type

- technological developments means that tables to accommodate computers etc. may become obsolete

Award (0–3) dependent on quality of explanation [3]

12 (a) Durable metal, relatively cheap, easily worked/shaped, resist high temperatures
(2 × 1) [2]

(b) Steel will rust if not protected, improved appearance [1]

(c) Cutting: mild steel sheet cut using bench shears or tinsnips (0–2)
partial success using hacksaw or cold chisel (1 maximum)
Award 1 mark for sketch of correct tool
Award 1 mark for correctly named tool
Holding: mild steel sheet held by hand or clamped to a bench (0–2) [4]

(d) Mild steel sheet held in vice (1)
Use of former/block of wood (1)
Method of force: hammer and scrapwood or mallet (1) [3]

(e) Sketch showing use of: riveting, weld, braze (0–2) [2]

(f) Practical idea for support (0–2)

Named materials (0–2)

Two important sizes [500 mm height given] (0–2)

Method of joining temporarily (0–2) [8]

(g) Practical idea: three tools safely held allowing for ease of access (0–3)
Details of materials and constructions (0–2) [5]
Use of wood joined to barbecue body inappropriate

© Cambridge International Examinations 2015

Page 5	Mark Scheme	Syllabus	Paper
	Cambridge IGCSE – October/November 2015	0445	32

13 (a) (i) Polystyrene, acrylic, polypropylene, ABS, HIPS [1]

    (ii) No grain marks, stable, will not warp, smooth surface, easy to shape, no splinters   (2 × 1) [2]

    (iii) Draft angle, rounded corners, no undercuts, smooth finish, air vents   (2 × 1) [2]

(b) Award 0–5 for specific stages: (0–5)
Place mould in machine [on platen]
Clamp plastic in place
Bring heater across to soften plastic
Check flexibility of plastic
Bring up mould into soft plastic
Turn pump on to remove air
Remove from moulded plastic
Lower mould [on platen] and leave to cool

Award (0–3) for technical quality of sketches (0–3) [8]

(c) (i) Injection moulding [1]

    (ii) Manufactured board top needs to be clamped down on drilling machine table or to a workbench (1)
Use of scrap wood under work piece (1)
Method of clamping (1) [3]

    (iii) Appropriate method:
pin or screw (1)
glue top to sides (1)
Added details   (0–2) [3]

(d) Practical idea showing 3 paintbrushes safely stored with ease of access (0–3)
Details of materials, constructions, sizes (0–2) [5]

© Cambridge International Examinations 2015

… Cambridge International Examinations
Cambridge International General Certificate of Secondary Education

DESIGN AND TECHNOLOGY 0445/32
Paper 3 Resistant Materials May/June 2016
MARK SCHEME
Maximum Mark: 50

Published

This mark scheme is published as an aid to teachers and candidates, to indicate the requirements of the examination. It shows the basis on which Examiners were instructed to award marks. It does not indicate the details of the discussions that took place at an Examiners' meeting before marking began, which would have considered the acceptability of alternative answers.

Mark schemes should be read in conjunction with the question paper and the Principal Examiner Report for Teachers.

Cambridge will not enter into discussions about these mark schemes.

Cambridge is publishing the mark schemes for the May/June 2016 series for most Cambridge IGCSE®, Cambridge International A and AS Level components and some Cambridge O Level components.

® IGCSE is the registered trademark of Cambridge International Examinations.

This document consists of 6 printed pages.

Page 2	Mark Scheme	Syllabus	Paper
	Cambridge IGCSE – May/June 2016	0445	32

Section A

1. **A** Screwdriver [not posidrive or Phillips]   1
    B Spanner, socket, wrench, torque wrench   1
    C Allen key, hexagon key   1   [3]

2. Award 0–2 dependent upon accuracy of sketch   0–2   [2]

3. **(a)** **A** finger or comb joint   1
          B dovetail joit   1   [2]

    (b) Reason: finger joint can be pulled apart in two directions and the dovetail joint can only be pulled apart in one direction   [1]

4. Round tube   1
    Angle, angle iron   1   [2]

5. **(a)** Knurled   [1]

    (b) To provide grip   [1]

    (c) Centre lathe, lathe, CNC lathe, metal lathe   [1]

6. **A** Cutting gauge   1
    B Marking gauge [not mortise gauge]   1   [2]

7. 2 advantages: lighter weight means greater fuel economy, speed, environmentally more friendly, does not corrode, more suitable for small production runs, less dense, higher strength-weight ratio.

    Not: more impact resistant, easier to mould/shape, stronger   2 × 1   [2]

8. 3 ways suitable for children: colourful parts, appropriate height/reach, hardwearing materials, sound construction, rounded edges, non-toxic paint.
    Accept individual anthropometric features.
    Not: lightweight, aesthetically pleasing, simple to use [must be justified with specific feature]
    no small pieces that could be swallowed   3 × 1   [3]

9. High voltage, electric shock hazard, danger electricity. Not: electric current.   [1]
    Flammable, fire hazard   [1]

© Cambridge International Examinations 2016

Page 3	Mark Scheme	Syllabus	Paper
	Cambridge IGCSE – May/June 2016	0445	32

10 Malleable: aluminium, copper, brass, gilding metal, lead, low carbon steel, wrought iron, mild steel, precious metals. Not: iron, tin.

Corrosion resistant: aluminium, copper, brass, gilding metal, lead, zinc, stainless steel. Precious metals, titanium.

Electrical conductivity: aluminium, copper, brass, silver, steel, gold. Not: iron   [3]

Section B

11 (a) 2 advantages: lighter weight appearance, lightweight, less weight, less expensive than solid piece, fewer problems of warping/shrinkage, less waste

Not: easy to make, stronger   2 × 1   [2]

(b) Only acceptable:
mortise and tenon, dowel, biscuit, butt [nailed or screwed and glued]   1

Award 0–3 dependent upon accuracy of sketch   0–3   [4]
Award max 2 marks for butt joint nailed or screwed and glued
Award 0 marks if butt has no nails or screws and glue
Award max 3 for 2 dowels shown in proportion with correct orientation
Award max 1 mark if 1 dowel only is shown

(c) (i) Name of cramps: sash, F cramp   1
2 or 3 cramps shown spaces appropriately across frame   1
Use of scrap wood   1   [3]

(ii) Frame held in vice   1
Use of smoothing, jack or bench plane   1
Use of glasspaper to make smooth   1
Correctly named tools and equipment   1   [4]

(d) Use of screws, dowels and adhesive.
Award 0–2 dependent upon accuracy of sketch   [2]
Do not reward modified stand

(e) Practical idea: [do not reward increased height of ledge]
Must be separate, additional components   0–2
Details of materials and fittings used, including sizes   0–2   [4]

(f) Practical idea: some form of stand or support   0–2
Adjusts to 3 positions and held securely   0–2
Materials, constructions and fittings   0–2   [6]

© Cambridge International Examinations 2016

Page 4	Mark Scheme	Syllabus	Paper
	Cambridge IGCSE – May/June 2016	0445	32

12 (a) 2 reasons: hardwearing, close-grained, will not chip/splinter easily, takes a good finish, hardwood.   2 × 1   [2]
Tough, durable and strong acceptable **only** if justified: e.g. Strong enough to withstand knocks.
Not: easy to work with, lightweight, non-toxic, aesthetically pleasing.

(b) (i) Chinagraph pencil, marker pen, felt-tip pen, marking pen, permanent marker   [1]

(ii) Reward 4 separate stages 4 × 1 **OR** 3 stages 3 × 1 + good technical accuracy + 1
Drill hole   1
Insert blade from appropriate saw and cut out shape   1
Use of files/scraper/wet and dry to make smooth   1
Technical accuracy   1
If laser cutter is used for maximum 4 marks full details **must** be provided.
If no sketches are provided award maximum 2 marks.   [4]

(iii) Process: drilling   1
Solution: clamp securely, support with scrapwood, drill speed   1

Process: sawing **or** filing   1
Solution: clamp securely, low in the vice   1

Process: bending   1
Solution: heat to the correct temperature before bending   1   [4]

(c) Practical acceptable method named: 1
Acceptable methods: plough plane, power router, CNC router, circular saw [bench or portable], chisel and mallet, drilled holes, tenon saw.

Award 0–2 dependent upon technical accuracy of sketches   0–2   [3]
Do not reward marking out or cleaning up with glasspaper

(d) Acceptable methods:
band saw [tilted table/jig for correct angle]
tenon saw [from both ends]
handsaw [vertical]
use of smoothing, jack and bench plane
linisher, belt sander

Look for 3 stages: secure work piece, remove waste, clean up to final shape   3 × 1
Accuracy of named tools and equipment   0–1   [4]

(e) Preparation:
mark diagonals on end
centre drill, centre punch, bradawl
draw circle on end
make saw cut along one diagonal
plane off corners to 45°   3 × 1   [3]

© Cambridge International Examinations 2016

Page 5	Mark Scheme	Syllabus	Paper
	Cambridge IGCSE – May/June 2016	0445	32

(f) (i) 3 advantages: ready coloured, wide range of colours available, hygienic/easily cleaner, smooth surface finish, no danger of splinters, no finish required, water proof/resistant, will not warp or shrink, less waste material
Not: lighter than beech, faster to make 3 × 1 **[3]**

(ii) Process: extrusion, injection moulding **[1]**

13 (a) (i) A scriber/odd leg calipers/odd legs 1
   B centre/dot punch 1
   C dividers 1 **[3]**

(ii) marking/engineers blue, spirit marker **[1]**

(b) Drill hole/s in sheet 1
Insert blade of abra file saw, piercing saw, Hegner saw and cut out. 1
Not: hacksaw, jig saw
File to shape 1
Use of abrasive paper 1 **[4]**

(c) (i) Self-finishing: use of emery cloth and/or wet and dry paper, polishing mop/compound. Not: filing
Award 0–3 for specific stages and/or specific information relating to the grade of paper used. **[3]**

(ii) Reason for anodising: to protect, enhance appearance, prevent tarnishing, change colour. **[1]**

(d) (i) 2 tools/equipment: chisel, mallet, router, mortise machine, mortise drill, drilling machine and saw tooth/forstner bit, drill.
Accept 2 different types of router.
Accept any appropriate tool or item of equipment. 2 × 1 **[2]**

(ii) Suitable adhesive: epoxy resin, Araldite, impact adhesive 0–1
Not: superglue
Clamp in position or use of weights 0–1
Use of scrap wood to protect surface and distribute pressure 0–1 **[3]**

(e) 2 benefits: great accuracy, more accurate, each keyhole will be identical, quicker than traditional methods 2 × 1 **[2]**

(f) Practical ideal
Method includes use of brackets attached to back of keyrack and to wall or use of keyhole slot in plate recessed into back. 0–2
Holes drilled in wall and use of dowel, screws or pins = 1 mark max.
Accept screw holes visible in brackets or support strips used.

Materials, constructions and fittings 0–2 **[4]**

© Cambridge International Examinations 2016

Page 6	Mark Scheme	Syllabus	Paper
	Cambridge IGCSE – May/June 2016	0445	32

(g) Environmental impact of aluminium in products:
aluminium is plentiful in terms of the ore bauxite.
greenhouse gases are produced during extraction and processing.
aluminium can be recycled.

Description 0–1
Expanded/explained 0–1 **[2]**

![Cambridge IGCSE logo]

Cambridge International Examinations
Cambridge International General Certificate of Secondary Education

DESIGN AND TECHNOLOGY 0445/32

Paper 3 Resistant Materials October/November 2016

MARK SCHEME

Maximum Mark: 50

Published

This mark scheme is published as an aid to teachers and candidates, to indicate the requirements of the examination. It shows the basis on which Examiners were instructed to award marks. It does not indicate the details of the discussions that took place at an Examiners' meeting before marking began, which would have considered the acceptability of alternative answers.

Mark schemes should be read in conjunction with the question paper and the Principal Examiner Report for Teachers.

Cambridge will not enter into discussions about these mark schemes.

Cambridge is publishing the mark schemes for the October/November 2016 series for most Cambridge IGCSE®, Cambridge International A and AS Level components and some Cambridge O Level components.

® IGCSE is the registered trademark of Cambridge International Examinations.

This document consists of **5** printed pages.

© UCLES 2016 [Turn over

Page 2	Mark Scheme	Syllabus	Paper
	Cambridge IGCSE – October/November 2016	0445	32

Section A

1. **A** rip saw, cross cut saw, panel saw (1)
   B tenon saw, dovetail saw [not backsaw] (1)
   C coping saw (1) [3]

2. Metal spoon: stainless steel (1)
   Metal wire: copper, aluminium (1)
   Plastic bowl: polypropylene, PP, HDPE (1) [3]

3. Award 0–2 dependent upon accuracy of sketch   0–2 [2]

4. Marking gauge (1)
   Scriber (1)
   Odd legs, odd leg calipers [not calipers] (1) [3]

5. (a) Lines to be sawn down use a marking knife. Wood fibres are cut [1]

   (b) Sliding bevel, mitre square, combination square [1]

6. Channel: extrusion (1)
   Container: blow moulding (1) [2]

7. (a) Sketch shows tenon (1)
   Sketch shows haunch (1)
   Must be shown in correct orientation [2]

   (b) To lock the tenon to prevent it from moving/twisting
   stability/ more gluing area/increased strength [1]

8. **A** Countersink drill (1)
   B Flat bit (1) [2]

9. [Cold] chisel (1)
   Guillotine (1)
   Tinsnips (1) [3]

10. (a) Pine: wide range of adhesives. Accept generic and trade names such as PVA and Evo Stik Resin W, Cascamite, synthetic resin, Gorilla glue, contact/impact adhesive (1)

    (b) Epoxy resin, Araldite (1) [2]

Page 3	Mark Scheme	Syllabus	Paper
	Cambridge IGCSE – October/November 2016	0445	32

Section B

11 (a) 2 specification points: must be large enough to be seen at distance, must have clear and easy to read numbers, must be able to move hands freely, must be freestanding/wall-mounted
Accept any sensible spec. points 2×1 **[2]**

(b) (i) 2 safety precautions include: wear safety glasses, mask, secure work, no trailing leads, tie hair/clothing out of the way, no obstructions below work piece
2×1 **[2]**

(ii) Award 0–2 on quality of description: for example, use of sanding disc fully described with plywood rotated against the disc to ensure smooth finish.
Accept use of files. **[2]**

(c) Use of:
coping saw, Hegner saw or equivalent, junior hacksaw saw to cut out waste (1)
files to achieve shape (1)
wet and dry paper to achieve smooth surface (1)
polishing mop/compound to produce high quality finish (1) **[4]**

(d) Benefit: range of colours, inherent colours/self-finished, attractive **[1]**

(e) Some form of screw, bolt, pin or dowel (1)
Hands retained at back and front (1)
Spacers/washers to allow for movement (1) **[3]**

(f) CAD to design numbers: easy to change design, wide variety of fonts to try out. **[1]**
CAM to make numbers: extremely accurate, more professional appearance and quicker to produce than alternative methods, identical quality. **[1]**
Not faster/quicker without qualification.

(g) Some form of practical stand or support 0–3
For maximum marks the stand/support must be clearly drawn showing how it functions
Materials, fittings and constructions 0–2 **[5]**

(h) Some form of practical bracket attached to the back of the clock with provision for fixing to wall. Alternative method: plate with keyhole slot.
Award 0–2 dependent upon accuracy of drawing. 0–2
Materials, fittings and constructions 0–2 **[4]**

Page 4	Mark Scheme	Syllabus	Paper
	Cambridge IGCSE – October/November 2016	0445	32

12 (a) 2 advantages: cheaper, does not warp/shrink, more readily available.
                                                                                                                                              2×1 [2]

    (b) (i) Use of blocks and pegs to position the mild steel rod against former   0–2
              Retention of end of rod (1)   [3]

       (ii) Work hardened: metal is shaped by hammering (1)
            as a result metal becomes harder (1)   [2]

    (c) Preparation of ends before brazing: degreasing, filing, emery cloth
                                                                                                                                0–2

        Accept 4 stages in brazing process:
        Clamp ends together
        Set up on hearth
        Apply flux
        Apply heat
        Apply brazing rod/spelter
        Allow to cool   4×1
        Award 0–2 for technical accuracy of sketches   0–2 [8]

    (d) Method of fixing allows for use of brackets, modifications to length and/or width
        of shelves. Practical idea   0–2
        Fix to shelf   0–1
        Fix to end frame   0–1
        Details of materials, fittings and fixings   0–2 [6]

    (e) 2 reasons about aesthetics: for example, different appearance is more interesting, prefers
        combination of materials, lighter appearance   2×1 [2]

    (f) Environmentally friendly materials:
        mild steel can be melted down and recycled   [1]
        veneered chipboard uses waste materials not requiring trees to be chopped down   [1]

Page 5	Mark Scheme	Syllabus	Paper
	Cambridge IGCSE – October/November 2016	0445	32

13 (a) 2 properties: very hardwearing, tough, water resistant, attractive, gives a good finish
                                                                                                    2×1 **[2]**

(b) Method of support: vice or bench stop shown (1)
Use of saw (1)
Use of plane to remove waste (1)
Use of glasspaper to make smooth (1)
Technical accuracy: for example, named plane, saw, different grades of glasspaper
                                                                                                     0–1 **[5]**

(c) Some sort of bracket to which the rails can be attached   0–2
Use of pin, rod or dowel through rails to allow them to rotate   0–2
Method to keep rails apart: some form of spacer   0–2
Details of materials and fittings used   0–2 **[8]**

(d) Practical idea. For maximum marks the method must be clear   0–2
Holder must not rotate   0–1
Some form of bracket attached to the back of the towel holder
with provision for fixing to wall.
Alternative method: plate with keyhole slot.
Materials, fittings and constructions   0–2 **[5]**

(e) (i) 2 reasons: hardwearing, attractive, allows natural colour/grain of wood to be seen, waterproof, protects wood   2×1 **[2]**

    (ii) 3 stages include:
use of glasspaper [medium grade]
wipe down surface/ remove dust
use of glasspaper [fine grade]
use of cork rubber/block stated   3×1 **[3]**

© UCLES 2016

Cambridge International Examinations
Cambridge International General Certificate of Secondary Education

DESIGN AND TECHNOLOGY 0445/32

Paper 3 Resistant Materials May/June 2017

MARK SCHEME

Maximum Mark: 50

Published

This mark scheme is published as an aid to teachers and candidates, to indicate the requirements of the examination. It shows the basis on which Examiners were instructed to award marks. It does not indicate the details of the discussions that took place at an Examiners' meeting before marking began, which would have considered the acceptability of alternative answers.

Mark schemes should be read in conjunction with the question paper and the Principal Examiner Report for Teachers.

Cambridge will not enter into discussions about these mark schemes.

Cambridge is publishing the mark schemes for the May/June 2017 series for most Cambridge IGCSE®, Cambridge International A and AS Level and Cambridge Pre-U components, and some Cambridge O Level components.

® IGCSE is a registered trademark.

This document consists of **6** printed pages.

Question	Answer	Marks
1	PVA	1

Question	Answer	Marks
2	Point = 1 mark 'Step' = 1 mark	2

Question	Answer	Marks
3	Smart	1

Question	Answer	Marks
4	Award 1 mark for each correctly drawn groove and rebate	2

Question	Answer	Marks
5	A nut and bolt B [pop] rivet C screw D nail Accept incorrectly named screw or nail. **Not** cut tack.	4

Question	Answer	Marks
6	Completed drawing showing grain at 90° to previous layers	1

Question	Answer	Marks
7	Electric plug body Urea/phenol formaldehyde 1 Plastic blister packaging Polythene, PVC, PET 1 Knife handle Phenol formaldehyde, ABS 1	3

Question	Answer	Marks
8(a)	Chipboard	1
8(b)	Very small particles of scrap/wood chips 1 With an adhesive 1 **Not** sawdust. Ignore references to recycled wood	2
8(c)	Cost	1

Question	Answer	Marks
9(a)	1.5–3 mm. Do **not** accept ranges of thicknesses.	1
9(b)	Two methods of permanent joining: brazing [soldering], welding, riveting **Not** pop rivets, epoxy resin	2

Question	Answer	Marks
10(a)(i)	Stainless steel, mild steel	1
10(a)(ii)	Aluminium, brass, copper	1
10(b)	Base fitted: to collect crumbs, add rigidity to rack, stability Prevent scratches to surfaces, pick up more easily **Not** wider surface area.	2

Section B

Question	Answer	Marks
11(a)	Two good design features include: angled for comfort [ergonomics], storage unit useful, ledge prevents pens/pencils/paper sliding off, rounded corners for safety	2
11(b)	Board — plywood, **faced** chipboard only, MDF, Blockboard, Laminboard, **not** chipboard — 1 Storage unit — PVC, ABS, HIPS, acrylic polystyrene — 1 Ledge — accept any suitable named hardwood — 1 Support — mild steel, stainless steel, aluminium, **not** steel — 1	4
11(c)(i)	Power saw: jig saw, circular saw	1
11(c)(ii)	No trailing leads, no loose clothing, long hair tied back, work secured, face mask, safety of hands, ear defenders **Not** goggles, gloves	1
11(d)(i)	Two features of mould design: draft angle, rounded edges/corners, no undercuts **Not** vent holes	2
11(d)(ii)	If the plastic is overheated = 1 it will melt = 1 If the plastic is not hot enough = 1 it will not form to the mould = 1 Plastic can be moulded to the shape of the former = 1 Plastic is made soft = 1	2
11(e)(i)	The drawing board is only 15mm thick and the metal rod would not be secure or the holes would wear and the support work loose. Additional blocks provide a thicker material to provide deeper holes Makes more stable/stronger Hole will be visible	2
11(e)(ii)	Metal rod bent: Held in vice or clamped to a bench — 1 Vice, former or anvil around which the rod can be bent — 1 Method of force hammer **and** scrap wood or mallet — 1 **Not** hammer on its own	3
11(f)	Practical method: Angled — 1 Stable and secure — 0–2 Named materials — 1 Constructions — 0–2 Total redesign of board = max 3	6
11(g)	Portable sander benefits: faster than by hand, more even pressure exerted. Produces a smooth surface, removes marks and scratches.	2

Question	Answer	Marks
12(a)	Two reasons include: easily formed, self-coloured, durable outdoors, waterproof, easily cleaned, corrosion resistant, windproof **Not** self-finishing.	2
12(b)	Hole saw	1
12(c)(i)	Hegner saw or equivalent, scroll saw, band saw, jig saw	1
12(c)(ii)	Half-round file, round [rat tail] file, spokeshave, scraper, bobbin sander	1
12(c)(iii)	Safety glasses, goggles, eye protection, no loose clothing, long hair tied back, finger safety	1
12(d)	Sketch showing: butt joint glued and pinned/screwed, dowel, half-lap, dovetail, finger, biscuit Award use of adhesive 1 Technical accuracy of joint 0–2 **Not** mitre joint, hot glue gun	3
12(e)(i)	Two items of equipment: chinagraph pencil, marker pen, wax pencil, crayon, pencil on protective paper, felt-tip pen. **Not** scriber	2
12(e)(ii)	lower acrylic in vice, support behind acrylic while sawing, fine tooth blade, speed of sawing, clamping/securing acrylic. Award 1 mark for 1 point and 1 mark for additional description **OR** Award 2 marks for 2 separate points.	2
12(f)	Method of shaping roof: 3 stages: 3 Heat plastic in oven, hot air 'gun' use of former over which to shape acrylic Method of retention Technical accuracy of stages/equipment used 0–1	4
12(g)(i)	Two features of mould include draft angle, smooth surfaces, radiused edges/corners, no undercuts	2
12(g)(ii)	Vacuum forming process involves numerous stages: Position mould on platen, clamp plastic to machine, heat plastic, test for flexibility, lift platen into plastic, turn on blower to suck out air, lower platen, leave to cool, trim edges of plastic, finish edges appropriately Award 1 mark for 6 specific stages	6

Question	Answer	Marks
13(a)	MDF, plywood, chipboard, blockboard, laminboard	1
13(a)(ii)	Reason for choice: durable, hardwearing, stable, references to recycled materials, cheaper than...[qualified], MDF [**only**] low risk of splinters **Not** cheap.	1
13(b)(i)	Suitable joint: mortise and tenon, dowel, bridle named 1 Technical accuracy of joining method 0–3 **Not** butt joint, screwed joint, mitre joint Must be in correct orientation/proportion for maximum marks	4
13(b)(ii)	Support joined using screws/KD fitting/nuts and bolts, brackets 1 technical accuracy of details provided 0–2	3
13(c)(i)	Medium grade glasspaper: used to clean hardwood and remove small scratches and marks 1 Fine grade glasspaper: used **after** medium grade to produce an even smoother finish 1 **Progression** through 2 grades of glasspaper Damp cloth: used to remove dust following glasspapering 1 Cork block: used to wrap glasspaper around to provide more even pressure 1	4
13(c)(ii)	Polyurethane varnish is hardwearing, tough, easily cleaned, stain resistant, durable, gives protection, attractive/aesthetic, waterproof/resistant.	2
13(d)(i)	Length of computer desk top dependent on items to be positioned on the top, anthropometric measurements	1
13(d)(ii)	Height of desk dependent on seat height of user	1
13(e)	Drawer supported under desk top and made to slide in and out Use of runners, rebates or grooves for drawer to run on and be supported 0–2 Award 0–2 for practical idea Joined to supports = 1 mark Two important sizes 0–2 Details of materials and constructions used 0–2	6
13(f)	Two drawbacks: some methods of construction may not be as durable, parts sometimes missing, limited consumer skill, difficult instructions, tools not available. References to strength of materials and/or constructions must be qualified otherwise 0 marks.	2

Cambridge IGCSE

Cambridge Assessment International Education
Cambridge International General Certificate of Secondary Education

DESIGN AND TECHNOLOGY 0445/32

Paper 3 Resistant Materials October/November 2017

MARK SCHEME

Maximum Mark: 50

Published

This mark scheme is published as an aid to teachers and candidates, to indicate the requirements of the examination. It shows the basis on which Examiners were instructed to award marks. It does not indicate the details of the discussions that took place at an Examiners' meeting before marking began, which would have considered the acceptability of alternative answers.

Mark schemes should be read in conjunction with the question paper and the Principal Examiner Report for Teachers.

Cambridge International will not enter into discussions about these mark schemes.

Cambridge International is publishing the mark schemes for the October/November 2017 series for most Cambridge IGCSE®, Cambridge International A and AS Level components and some Cambridge O Level components.

® IGCSE is a registered trademark.

This document consists of **6** printed pages.

[Turn over

0445/32   Cambridge IGCSE – Mark Scheme   October/November
PUBLISHED   2017

Section A

Question	Answer	Marks
1	Award 0–2 dependent on technical accuracy Top and bottom plies =1 Strips shown correctly =1 Blocks drawn on 2 edges =0	2

Question	Answer	Marks
2(a)	cast iron.	1
2(b)	hard, hardwood, hardwearing. **Not** durable	1

Question	Answer	Marks
3	temperature	1

Question	Answer	Marks
4(a)	injection moulding, blow moulding	1
4(b)	mild steel will rust when in contact with water 1 galvanising mild steel prevents rusting 1	2
4(c)(i)	A	1
4(c)(ii)	injection moulding is a quick process, fewer processes, mould can be reused, whereas **B** would require fabrication of parts taking longer to make and involve more material	1

Question	Answer	Marks
5	Award 0–2 dependent on technical accuracy. 2 curved legs = 2 with points = 1 only	2

Question	Answer	Marks
6	**Joining acrylic** Danger – flammable, toxic fumes, irritant to skin 1 Prevention – ventilation, wear gloves, barrier cream, mask [any form accepted] 1 **Pouring molten aluminium** Danger – 'spitting' of hot metal, spillages 1 Prevention – wear visor, gauntlets, leather apron, overshoes 1 Must be **specific** equipment	4

Question	Answer		Marks
7	**A** diameter/gauge of thread **B** length/height of screw **C** type of head/countersink head. **Not** type of screw	1 1 1	3

Question	Answer	Marks
8	Award 0–2 dependent on technical accuracy Tongue = 1 Groove = 1 Award 1 mark for separate tongue	2

Question	Answer	Marks
9(a)	to dry out wood, remove moisture, to minimise shrinkage/warping/rotting Minimise attack from woodboring insects	1
9(b)	kiln, artificial	1

Question	Answer		Marks
10	phenol formaldehyde nylon	1 1	2

Section B

Question	Answer	Marks
11(a)	The types of [suitable] outdoor materials and finishes,, constructions, appropriate dimensions to consider, the sizes of car 'boots', space saving devices to make the table compact 3 × 1	3
11(b)(i)	mild steel, aluminium	1
11(b)(ii)	two heat processes: soldering **or** brazing, welding Aluminium: award 1 mark only for welding. Award 2 marks for 2 different types of welding. 2 × 1	2
11(c)	Plastic laminate: heatproof, stainproof, waterproof, attractive, easier to clean. 2 × 1	2
11(d)(i)	**Some form of hinge or pivot method** 0–2 Use of hinge or similar method shown without description 1 Clear sketch [and name if appropriate] 2 **Details of materials, fittings and constructions** 0–2 Named material/s 1 Fittings/constructions: e.g. award 1 mark for stating screws, named, braze 1	4
11(d)(ii)	**Some form of 'catch'/bracket to support end frames** 0–2 Accurate sketch showing method clearly 2 **Materials** named 1 **Fittings and constructions** named 1	4
11(e)	**Method to remain level** 0–3 some form of adjustment to legs/'telescopic' principle 1 method of locking/securing 1 details of rods, pins, screws, nuts and bolts 1 **Details of materials, fittings and constructions** 0–2 e.g. length of rod/pin, types of head of screw, named materials	5

Question	Answer	Marks
12(a)(i)	Sliding bevel evident in sketch 0–1 Correct position of sliding bevel 0–1	2
12(a)(ii)	Wide variety of saws: tenon, coping, jig, band, Hegner or equivalent	1
12(a)(iii)	Jack, smoothing plane, block	1
12(b)(i)	Nail: round wire, round, oval, panel pin	1
12(b)(ii)	Outdoor adhesive: PVA, Cascamite. Accept any appropriate trade names 1 **Not** superglue or Araldite [epoxy resin] Time to set must correspond with named adhesive 1	2

Question	Answer	Marks
12(c)	Suitable hinge: butt or piano Award 0–3 dependent on technical accuracy of sketch of hinge 0–3 Correctly named 1	4
12(d)(i)	acrylic held securely in vice or clamped to bench 1 use of coping saw, Hegner saw or equivalent, band saw 1 use of files to make flat and smooth 1	3
12(d)(ii)	acrylic window fitted by means of grooves or applied beads Award 0–2 dependent on technical accuracy 0–2 Constructional details: tools used, sizes, processes involved 0–2	4
12(e)	Method of attachment: some form of screw thread and nut to fasten parts together Award 0–3 dependent on technical accuracy Award max. 0–2 for simple bend dependent on added notes Award 1 mark for simple 'stop' Award 1 mark for details of 'stop': e.g. method of fixing to rod Award 1 mark for details of materials	3
12(f)	Problems include: climate [heat, cold, wet, wind], theft, vandalism Solutions include: weather resistant materials, protective finishes, secure mounting of products and 'vandal proof'/tough/durable materials Award 1 mark for any sensible problem identified and award 1 mark for any practical solution. 4 × 1	4

Question	Answer	Marks
13(a)	MDF is more stable, cheaper, readily available, larger sheets, easier to cut/work **Not** lighter in weight 2 × 1	2
13(b)(i)	Quicker, easier, accurate, repetitive accuracy	1
13(b)(ii)	Coping, band, jig, Hegner or equivalent	1
13(b)(iii)	Half-round file, round/rat tail file. **Must** be specific name	1
13(c)(i)	positions drawn along centre of thickness 1 accept holes drawn in appropriate position positions for centres 20–50 mm **in** from each edge 1 dimensions noted on drawing 1	3
13(c)(ii)	Ø6 or Ø9 dowel	1
13(c)(iii)	chamfer: to help guide the dowel into the hole 1 Grooves: to provide space for the glue 1	2

Question	Answer		Marks
13(c)(iv)	template + 2 inaccurately drawn holes shown template + 2 accurate holes shown template + 2 accurate holes shown with location in **one** direction template + 2 accurate holes shown with location in **two** directions	1 2 3 4	4
13(c)(v)	Quality of explanation of use	0–2	2
13(d)	Use of drill to drill out one or more holes Use of piercing saw or Hegner [with metal cutting blade] to cut out Use of files to achieve shape Correctly named tools	1 1 1 1	4
13(e)	MDF is unattractive without some form of opaque 'covering'. Paint used can be colourful and vibrant Clear varnish would not hide the unattractive surface	1 1	2
13(f)	Self-assembly products popular: Can be collected and transported immediately, self-satisfaction of assembling correctly, wide range of purpose built products, good value for money/generally cheaper than some ready-assembled products	2 × 1	2

Cambridge Assessment International Education
Cambridge International General Certificate of Secondary Education

DESIGN AND TECHNOLOGY 0445/32

Paper 3 Resistant Materials May/June 2018

MARK SCHEME

Maximum Mark: 50

Published

This mark scheme is published as an aid to teachers and candidates, to indicate the requirements of the examination. It shows the basis on which Examiners were instructed to award marks. It does not indicate the details of the discussions that took place at an Examiners' meeting before marking began, which would have considered the acceptability of alternative answers.

Mark schemes should be read in conjunction with the question paper and the Principal Examiner Report for Teachers.

Cambridge International will not enter into discussions about these mark schemes.

Cambridge International is publishing the mark schemes for the May/June 2018 series for most Cambridge IGCSE™, Cambridge International A and AS Level and Cambridge Pre-U components, and some Cambridge O Level components.

IGCSE™ is a registered trademark.

This document consists of **9** printed pages.

© UCLES 2018 [Turn over

0445/32 Cambridge IGCSE – Mark Scheme
PUBLISHED
Generic Marking Principles

These general marking principles must be applied by all examiners when marking candidate answers. They should be ap specific content of the mark scheme or generic level descriptors for a question. Each question paper and mark scheme w marking principles.

GENERIC MARKING PRINCIPLE 1:

Marks must be awarded in line with:

- the specific content of the mark scheme or the generic level descriptors for the question
- the specific skills defined in the mark scheme or in the generic level descriptors for the question
- the standard of response required by a candidate as exemplified by the standardisation scripts.

GENERIC MARKING PRINCIPLE 2:

Marks awarded are always **whole marks** (not half marks, or other fractions).

GENERIC MARKING PRINCIPLE 3:

Marks must be awarded **positively**:

- marks are awarded for correct/valid answers, as defined in the mark scheme. However, credit is given for valid answ scope of the syllabus and mark scheme, referring to your Team Leader as appropriate
- marks are awarded when candidates clearly demonstrate what they know and can do
- marks are not deducted for errors
- marks are not deducted for omissions
- answers should only be judged on the quality of spelling, punctuation and grammar when these features are specific question as indicated by the mark scheme. The meaning, however, should be unambiguous.

GENERIC MARKING PRINCIPLE 4:

Rules must be applied consistently e.g. in situations where candidates have not followed instructions or in the application descriptors.

0445/32   Cambridge IGCSE – Mark Scheme
                                                    PUBLISHED

GENERIC MARKING PRINCIPLE 5:

Marks should be awarded using the full range of marks defined in the mark scheme for the question (however; the
be limited according to the quality of the candidate responses seen).

GENERIC MARKING PRINCIPLE 6:

Marks awarded are based solely on the requirements as defined in the mark scheme. Marks should not be award
grade descriptors in mind.

0445/32 Cambridge IGCSE – Mark Scheme
PUBLISHED

Question	Answer
1	Attractive finish, protects against corrosion, matches existing fittings 2 × 1

Question	Answer
2	Screws in left, right and centre = 3. 2 screws in left and 2 screws in right = 3. 1 screw in left and 1 screw in right = 2. 1 screw in centre = 3. 1 screw/bolt in centre with wing nut = 2.

Question	Answer
3	From the top to bottom: countersunk, centre, twist 3 × 1

Question	Answer
4(a)	Veneers
4(b)	laminating

Question	Answer
5	Examples of modifications include: knurling to edge, insertion of shaped piece into top surface of handle, sa provide space for screwdriver blade. Award 1 mark for practical idea. Award 1 mark for notes that expand upon drawing*

0445/32   Cambridge IGCSE – Mark Scheme
PUBLISHED

Question	Answer
6	GRP, CFRP 2 × 1

Question	Answer
7	As work is done to the metal it becomes hard and brittle = 1 Hammer/hammering stated = 1

Question	Answer
8	Grooves or applied beads in top = 1 Grooves or applied beads in bottom = 1 Depth of grooves/beads in top twice as deep = 1

Question	Answer
9	From the top to bottom: PVC melamine polystyrene 3 × 1

Question	Answer
10	**A** reach from head to fingers for comfortable access to keyboard/desk = 1 **B** seat height set at comfortable height appropriate for the individual = 1 **C** desk height appropriate for individual seated at the computer with space for legs = 1

0445/32   Cambridge IGCSE – Mark Scheme
PUBLISHED

Question	Answer
11(a)(i)	Quicker than having to draw, more accurate, repeated accuracy, no risk of damaging acrylic
11(a)(ii)	Holding acrylic: vice, clamped down = 1 Named saw; coping, hacksaw, Hegner [or equivalent], band = 1 One precaution: low in vice, well supported, use of scrap wood to protect sides = 1 Technical accuracy: terms used, accuracy of sketches = 1
11(b)	Acrylic shown above strip heater/line bender, oven 0–2 Method of holding: use of strips/blocks and some form of clamping 0–2
11(c)(i)	HIPS, polystyrene, ABS
11(c)(ii)	Draft angle on sides, rounded edges/corners 2 × 1
11(c)(iii)	Quicker process because the mould can be reused and provides repetitive accuracy, less waste
11(d)	Well-ventilated area, no naked flames, wearing of PPE [e.g. nose and mouth masks, gloves, goggles], use cream 2 × 1
11(e)	File, scraper, various grades of wet and dry [silicon carbide] paper, polishing mop, buffing wheel, polishing compound 3 × 1
11(f)	Recognised base 1 Constructional details: e.g. how the rod is inserted, grooves routed, some form of rod or ball bearings/marb in a groove 0–2 Named materials appropriate 1 2 important sizes 2 × 1

0445/32 Cambridge IGCSE – Mark Scheme
PUBLISHED

Question	Answer
12(a)	Top rail = 790–820 Bottom rail =820–850 2 × 1 Hardwood: accept **any** named hardwood 1
12(b)	Important areas of the guitar to measure to determine sizes, number of guitars to be stored, types of of the guitar are suitable for holding/supporting, environment in which the stand is located 3 × 1
12(c)	Stage 1: coping, Hegner or equivalent, band, Scroll, jig saws = 1 Stage 2: half-round, round [rat-tail] files, spokeshave, Surform tools, bobbin sander = 1 Stage 3: glasspaper, sandpaper, bobbin sander = 1
12(d)(i)	Jack, smoothing, block, moulding
12(d)(ii)	To protect the guitar from scratches
12(e)	Head: countersink = 1 length = 1 Material: steel, brass, copper, stainless steel = 1
12(f)	2 holes drilled in 'plate' = 1 location on 1 side = 1, location on 2 sides = 2, location on 3 sides = 3. Named material = 1
12(g)	Practical idea: some form of 'foot' accurately drawn 1 Method of attaching 'foot' 1 Appropriate material 1
12(h)(i)	2 different grades means one grade will be finer to remove scratches of previous grade
12(h)(ii)	Hardwood is used to show off its colour, grain, figure that would be covered by paint, paint could ch mark guitar
12(h)(iii)	Wax finish is quicker to apply, more even finish, easy to maintain, easier to apply, does not chip/fla

0445/32   Cambridge IGCSE – Mark Scheme
PUBLISHED

Question	Answer
13(a)	Saves material if errors are made, allows faults to be seen and rectified, gives visual impression of final des used as a template
13(b)(i)	Mild steel, stainless steel
13(b)(ii)	Aluminium, brass, copper, duralumin
13(b)(iii)	From the top to bottom: try square, engineers square, odd-legs[calipers], Jenny callipers, scriber 3×1
13(b)(iv)	Hacksaw limited to the depth of the frame, thin sheet can bend = 1 Tinsnips provide more control = 1
13(c)(i)	2 layers shown with same grain = 1 3 layers shown with same grain = 2 2 layers shown with alter. grain = 2 3 layers shown with alter. grain = 3
13(c)(ii)	MDF, chipboard
13(c)(iii)	Panel pin, round wire, oval nail/brad
13(c)(iv)	Accept a single number between 15–25 mm
13(c)(v)	PVA, Cascamite, Synthetic resin, Gorilla glue
13(c)(vi)	Time must correspond to named adhesive: e.g. PVA 1–4 hours, Gorilla glue 1 hour
13(d)(i)	1 hook/bracket/screw = 1 2 screw holes only [no screws shown] = 1 2 screws + 2 holes in back of holder = 2 2 screws and 2 keyholes in back of holder = 3 Added hooks/brackets and screws = 3 Additional notes to expand on drawings = 1

0445/32

Question	Answer
13(d)(ii)	Lid can be hinged or 'lift-off' design. Practical design: 0–2 Constructional details: 0–2 Named materials: 0–1

Cambridge IGCSE

Cambridge Assessment International Education
Cambridge International General Certificate of Secondary Education

DESIGN AND TECHNOLOGY 0445/32
Paper 3 Resistant Materials October/November 2018
MARK SCHEME
Maximum Mark: 50

Published

This mark scheme is published as an aid to teachers and candidates, to indicate the requirements of the examination. It shows the basis on which Examiners were instructed to award marks. It does not indicate the details of the discussions that took place at an Examiners' meeting before marking began, which would have considered the acceptability of alternative answers.

Mark schemes should be read in conjunction with the question paper and the Principal Examiner Report for Teachers.

Cambridge International will not enter into discussions about these mark schemes.

Cambridge International is publishing the mark schemes for the October/November 2018 series for most Cambridge IGCSE™, Cambridge International A and AS Level components and some Cambridge O Level components.

Generic Marking Principles

These general marking principles must be applied by all examiners when marking candidate answers. They should be applied alongside the specific content of the mark scheme or generic level descriptors for a question. Each question paper and mark scheme will also comply with these marking principles.

GENERIC MARKING PRINCIPLE 1: Marks must be awarded in line with: • the specific content of the mark scheme or the generic level descriptors for the question • the specific skills defined in the mark scheme or in the generic level descriptors for the question • the standard of response required by a candidate as exemplified by the standardisation scripts.
GENERIC MARKING PRINCIPLE 2: Marks awarded are always **whole marks** (not half marks, or other fractions).
GENERIC MARKING PRINCIPLE 3: Marks must be awarded **positively**: • marks are awarded for correct/valid answers, as defined in the mark scheme. However, credit is given for valid answers which go beyond the scope of the syllabus and mark scheme, referring to your Team Leader as appropriate • marks are awarded when candidates clearly demonstrate what they know and can do • marks are not deducted for errors • marks are not deducted for omissions • answers should only be judged on the quality of spelling, punctuation and grammar when these features are specifically assessed by the question as indicated by the mark scheme. The meaning, however, should be unambiguous.
GENERIC MARKING PRINCIPLE 4: Rules must be applied consistently e.g. in situations where candidates have not followed instructions or in the application of generic level descriptors.
GENERIC MARKING PRINCIPLE 5: Marks should be awarded using the full range of marks defined in the mark scheme for the question (however; the use of the full mark range may be limited according to the quality of the candidate responses seen).
GENERIC MARKING PRINCIPLE 6: Marks awarded are based solely on the requirements as defined in the mark scheme. Marks should not be awarded with grade thresholds or grade descriptors in mind.

0445/32 — Cambridge IGCSE – Mark Scheme PUBLISHED — October/November 2018

Question	Answer	Marks
1(a)	Marking gauge	1
1(b)	Jack, smoothing, block	1

Question	Answer	Marks
2	Extrusion	1

Question	Answer	Marks
3	**Dividers** = 1, used to mark arcs/circles [on plastic/metal] = 1 **Centre/dot punch** = 1, make an indentation in metal before drilling = 1	4

Question	Answer	Marks
4	2 slots drawn in **A** = 1, 2 slots drawn in **B** = 1, 2 biscuits drawn = 1	3

Question	Answer	Marks
5	**A** urea formaldehyde **B** melamine **C** epoxy resin 3 × 1	3

Question	Answer	Marks
6(a)	References to turning: e.g. to hold round or hexagonal shaped metal	1
6(b)	References to turning: e.g. to hold round, square or irregular shaped metal	1

Question	Answer	Marks
7(a)	Carbon fibre reinforced plastic [CFRP]	1
7(b)	Good strength-weight ratio, lightweight, corrosion resistance, stiff, rigid, good tensile strength, low density 2 × 1	2

Question	Answer	Marks
8(a)	Soft	1
8(b)	Hard or silver	1

Question	Answer	Marks
9	Screw thread shown inserted into leg [left-to-right] = 1 Barrel shown inserted into side of rail = 1 Correct positioning/distances = 1	3

Question	Answer	Marks
10(a)	Blow moulding, extrusion blow moulding	1
10(b)	To make flat bottom a flat shape should be drawn on top of bowl shape = 1	1

Question	Answer	Marks
11(a)(i)	4 bend lines drawn 4 × 1	4
11(a)(ii)	Felt marker	1
11(b)	Acrylic shown above strip heater/line bender **or** hot air gun **or** in an oven 0–2 Use of a shaped former or 2 separate blocks 0–2 Technical accuracy of details 0–1	5
11(c)	Waste removed: use of coping saw, Hegner or equivalent, Scroll, band = 1 Acrylic held appropriately: vice or clamped to bench = 1 Rounded corners: use of flat/hand and round/rat tail or half-round files = 1 Technical accuracy of details = 1	4
11(d)(i)	Draw filing	1
11(d)(ii)	Different grades means a finer grade can be used to remove the scratches produced by the previous coarser grade 2 × 1	2
11(e)(i)	Acrylic cement applied to both parts = 1 Clamped using G cramps, sash cramps, vice or weights = 1	2
11(e)(ii)	Fumes given off by acrylic cement can be harmful to user	1
11(f)	Practical idea: additional storage joined to appropriate part of holder 0–2 Details of appropriate processes 0–2 Technical accuracy of named tools and equipment 0–1	5

Question	Answer	Marks
12(a)(i)	Plywood, faced chipboard, MDF, blockboard, laminboard	1
12(a)(ii)	18–20 mm	1
12(a)(iii)	Wide variety available: ash, oak, beech, mahogany, teak	1
12(a)(iv)	anthropometrics	1

Question	Answer		Marks
12(b)(i)	Steel rule, try square, marking gauge, mortise gauge, cutting gauge, marking knife	2 × 1	2
12(b)(ii)	Tenon saw, coping saw, chisel, mallet	2 × 1	2
12(c)	Some form of added strip/blocks/brackets required Processes describing methods of construction Named adhesive	0–2 0–2 0–1	5
12(d)(i)	Sash, bar, F, speed		1
12(d)(ii)	Wide variety available: synthetic resin, PVA. Accept trade names: e.g. Evo-Stik Resin W, Cascamite, Aerolite		1
12(d)(iii)	2 checks: joint pulled together, squareness, not in winding, removal of surplus adhesive, cramps not over-tightened		2
12(e)(i)	Advantage: no need for separate fabricated constructions, quicker Disadvantage: wasteful of material	= 1 = 1	2
12(e)(ii)	Jig saw, router		1
12(e)(iii)	Check overall condition of tool before use, no trailing leads, no loose clothing, work piece secure, hair tied back	2 × 1	2
12(f)	Developments in flat-pack furniture design, self-assembly KD fittings, social/technological trends; eg use of PCs.		3

Question	Answer		Marks
13(a)	Hardwood uprights: wide variety of suitable hardwoods Metal rod: mild steel, stainless steel, aluminium, brass Manufactured board: MDF, chipboard, plywood	= 1 = 1 = 1	3
13(b)(i)	Benefit: gives appearance of solid wood, more attractive Drawback: more easily damaged, veneer could peel off, less hardwearing		1
13(b)(ii)	Drawback: more easily damaged, veneer could peel off, less hardwearing		1
13(c)	Template with 3 holes drilled-no location Template + 1 side located Template + 2 sides located Template + 2 sides + end located Specific named material/s appropriate	= 1 = 2 = 3 = 4 = 1	5
13(d)	Use of vice to support the metal rod Method of force: hammer and scrap wood or mallet Check correct angle of lower bend with former 90° angle checked against vice jaw/wooden former	= 1 = 1 = 1 = 1	4
13(e)	Stages include: degrease metal if necessary. Use steel wool [fine grade] or wet and dry [silicon carbide] paper [2 grades]. Use of polishing mop and appropriate compound to produce quality finish.		3

Question	Answer	Marks
13(f)(i)	Marking and cutting gauges, marking knife, try square	1
13(f)(ii)	Tenon saw, dovetail [tenon] saw	1
13(g)	Threaded rod = 1 Nut screws onto threaded rod = 1 Nut inset into shelf to become hidden = 1 Technical accuracy of method 0–1	4
13(h)	Adjustable height of shelves, good use of relatively few materials, simple design, straightforward to manufacture, easy to adjust height, easy to maintain/clean 2×1	2

Cambridge Assessment International Education
Cambridge International General Certificate of Secondary Education

DESID AND TECHNOLOGY 0445/32
Paper 3 Resistant Materials May/June 2019
MARK SCHEME
Maximum Mark: 50

Published

This mark scheme is published as an aid to teachers and candidates, to indicate the requirements of the examination. It shows the basis on which Examiners were instructed to award marks. It does not indicate the details of the discussions that took place at an Examiners' meeting before marking began, which would have considered the acceptability of alternative answers.

Mark schemes should be read in conjunction with the question paper and the Principal Examiner Report for Teachers.

Cambridge International will not enter into discussions about these mark schemes.

Cambridge International is publishing the mark schemes for the May/June 2019 series for most Cambridge IGCSE™, Cambridge International A and AS Level and Cambridge Pre-U components, and some Cambridge O Level components.

This document consists of **8** printed pages.

0445/32 Cambridge IGCSE – Mark Scheme
PUBLISHED
Generic Marking Principles

These general marking principles must be applied by all examiners when marking candidate answers. They shoul[cut] specific content of the mark scheme or generic level descriptors for a question. Each question paper and mark sch[cut] marking principles.

GENERIC MARKING PRINCIPLE 1:

Marks must be awarded in line with:

- the specific content of the mark scheme or the generic level descriptors for the question
- the specific skills defined in the mark scheme or in the generic level descriptors for the question
- the standard of response required by a candidate as exemplified by the standardisation scripts.

GENERIC MARKING PRINCIPLE 2:

Marks awarded are always **whole marks** (not half marks, or other fractions).

GENERIC MARKING PRINCIPLE 3:

Marks must be awarded **positively**:

- marks are awarded for correct/valid answers, as defined in the mark scheme. However, credit is given for va[cut] scope of the syllabus and mark scheme, referring to your Team Leader as appropriate
- marks are awarded when candidates clearly demonstrate what they know and can do
- marks are not deducted for errors
- marks are not deducted for omissions
- answers should only be judged on the quality of spelling, punctuation and grammar when these features are[cut] question as indicated by the mark scheme. The meaning, however, should be unambiguous.

GENERIC MARKING PRINCIPLE 4:

Rules must be applied consistently e.g. in situations where candidates have not followed instructions or in the ap[cut] descriptors.

0445/32 Cambridge IGCSE – Mark Scheme
PUBLISHED

GENERIC MARKING PRINCIPLE 5:

Marks should be awarded using the full range of marks defined in the mark scheme for the question (however; the use of be limited according to the quality of the candidate responses seen).

GENERIC MARKING PRINCIPLE 6:

Marks awarded are based solely on the requirements as defined in the mark scheme. Marks should not be awarded with grade descriptors in mind.

0445/32 — Cambridge IGCSE – Mark Scheme
PUBLISHED

Question	Answer	Marks
1	Specification points include: must close automatically when foot is removed from pedal, attractive appearance, durable materials, easy to clean, stable in use, large pedal for foot 2 × 1	2

Question	Answer	Marks
2	Metal models: die casting 1 Plastic tubes: extrusion 1 Wooden chair: lamination, steam bending 1	3

Question	Answer	Marks
3(a)	To cut the fibres of the wood to prevent splitting	1
3(b)	To allow for the thickness of saw blade, to leave a small amount to finish square, allow tolerance for sawing, allow margin for error, allows to finish with sanding disc	1

Question	Answer	Marks
4	Angle/angle iron. Round tube. Flat or strip/flat strip. 3 × 1	3

Question	Answer	Marks
5	At least four fingers 1 Equal spacing 1 Accurate drawing of projected lines to show joint 1	3

© UCLES 2019

0445/32 Cambridge IGCSE – Mark Scheme
PUBLISHED

Question	Answer	Marks	
6	CFRP, carbon fibre, GRP, glass fibre, Kevlar, plywood, blockboard, laminboard, MDF, hardboard, chipboard 2 × 1	2	Accept any

Question	Answer	Marks	
7	Facing off 1 Parting off 1	2	

Question	Answer	Marks	
8(a)	Sash	1	
8(b)	To prevent damage to the hardwood strips, to distribute pressure evenly 2 × 1	2	

Question	Answer	Marks	
9	Attractive, hardwearing, does not corrode when in contact with water, easy to clean, does not mark easily, easily bent to shape 2 × 1	2	Accept any Durable mu years, will r

Question	Answer	Marks	
10	Practical idea: some sort of 'hook' or interlocking components 0–2 Added notes to expand on sketch 0–1	3	Pegs, pins, can be pull Technical c

0445/32   Cambridge IGCSE – Mark Scheme
PUBLISHED

Question	Answer		Marks
11(a)(i)	Plywood, MDF, hardboard		1
11(a)(ii)	Aluminium, copper, brass, gilding metal		1
11(b)(i)	Two reasons include: to drill an accurate hole, to prevent the drill from snagging, to prevent distortion, safety issue of board spinning 2 × 1		2
11(b)(ii)	Saw to remove waste; use of coping, jig, Hegner, scroll, band saws Use of files Use of glasspaper	1 1 1	3
11(c)	Method: use of 5 mm wide mortises/added block or bracket behind clock face Use of PVA/adhesive	0–2 1	3
11(d)	More even application, quicker, better finish, no brush strokes 2 × 1		2
11(e)	Legs made from sheet metal cut to shape Bending metal to shape Method of joining: use of rivets, solder or epoxy resin adhesive	1 0–2 0–2	5
11(f)	Self-finished means no applied finish is added The surface is cleaned and then buffed/polished	1 1	2
11(g)	CAD: used to design the numbers on screen, change font, size, on-screen modelling, data transferred/downloaded to CNC machine. 0–2 CAM: numbers engraved into surface or applied to surface; use of specific machine such as CAMM 1 vinyl cutter or CNC router, laser cutter set up, tool parameters. 0–2		4
11(h)	Movement, sound, lights, theme linked to TV, cinema or book character 2 × 1		2

0445/32 Cambridge IGCSE – Mark Scheme
PUBLISHED

Question	Answer	Marks	
12(a)	Reasons include: easy to bend, variety of colours available, attractive, easy to clean, self-finishing.	2	**Not** cheap,
12(b)	Pre-drilled hole 1 Cut out using coping, Hegner, scroll saw 1 Removal of waste to produce shape 1 Finishing: use of wet and dry, scraper, acrylic polish 1	4	
12(c)	Processes/details include: design drawings transferred/downloaded to CNC machine type of CNC machine used setting up of acrylic workpiece setting of machine parameters 4 × 1	4	The transfe rewarded a operation. Reward any overall expl Types of C engraver, la
12(d)	Use of strip heater, line bender, oven 1 Use of former or machine setting [line bender] to obtain required angle 1 Method of retention 1	3	
12(e)(i)	Method of clamping: G cramps or applied weights. 1 Use of scrap wood to prevent damage, distribute pressure evenly 1	2	
12(e)(ii)	Disposable gloves: because acrylic cement is an irritant 1 Face mask: to prevent inhaling toxic fumes/splashes 1	2	Do not acc qualified
12(f)	Sketches showing: layers of wood veneers glued 1 Use of a former/formers 0–2 Method of clamping laminate to retain shape, including vacuum bag 1	4	
12(g)	Evaluation carried out: insert tablet, phone and remote and test accessibility, stability, seek third party opinion re appearance	2	Accept any procedures
12(h)	Consumer demand due to: advances in technology, use of tablets, phones, ease of accessibility essential, fashion trends.	2	Reward we demonstrat issues.

0445/32 Cambridge IGCSE – Mark Scheme
PUBLISHED

Question	Answer	Marks	
13(a)	4 main stages should include : Mark out shape 1 Cut off waste using a saw 1 Make flat and smooth by means of plane/glasspaper/disc sander, linisher 1 Rounded edge could be planed, glasspapered, filed, use of router + cutter 1 Tools/equipment named 1	5	Allow only
13(b)	Safety **features** include: rounded edges/corners, strong materials, strong constructions, anthropometric considerations of height off ground, reach from seat to handlebars, backrest to prevent falling backwards, no sharp/dangerous protrusions, stability of four wheels 2 × 1	2	Acc the
13(c)(i)	To make it easier to start turning 1 Prevent the wood from splitting 1	2	Cor
13(c)(ii)	Two tools include: scraper, gouge, outside calipers, glasspaper 2 × 1	2	Acc tool
13(c)(iii)	Two advantages: plywood more stable, no grain considerations, less likely to split/break 2 × 1	2	No
13(d)(i)	Drilling jig matches shape of end with hole drilled 1 Locates against one side 1 Locates against two sides 1 Locates against three sides 1 Suitable specific material: mild/stainless steel, wide range of non-ferrous metal 1	5	Do
13(d)(ii)	Clearance hole larger than axle shown or stated 1 Free rotation: use of washer, bearing, ball race 1 Method of retention: 'star' washer, 'cap' 1	3	Ax Ax
13(e)(i)	Injection moulding, blow moulding	1	
13(e)(ii)	Soldering, brazing, welding	1	Do
13(e)(iii)	Paint, dip-coated plastic, electroplating. 2 × 1	2	Do

Cambridge IGCSE

Cambridge Assessment International Education
Cambridge International General Certificate of Secondary Education

DESIGN AND TECHNOLOGY 0445/32
Paper 3 Resistant Materials October/November 2019
MARK SCHEME
Maximum Mark: 50

Published

This mark scheme is published as an aid to teachers and candidates, to indicate the requirements of the examination. It shows the basis on which Examiners were instructed to award marks. It does not indicate the details of the discussions that took place at an Examiners' meeting before marking began, which would have considered the acceptability of alternative answers.

Mark schemes should be read in conjunction with the question paper and the Principal Examiner Report for Teachers.

Cambridge International will not enter into discussions about these mark schemes.

Cambridge International is publishing the mark schemes for the October/November 2019 series for most Cambridge IGCSE™, Cambridge International A and AS Level components and some Cambridge O Level components.

Generic Marking Principles

These general marking principles must be applied by all examiners when marking candidate answers. They should be applied alongside the specific content of the mark scheme or generic level descriptors for a question. Each question paper and mark scheme will also comply with these marking principles.

GENERIC MARKING PRINCIPLE 1:

Marks must be awarded in line with:

- the specific content of the mark scheme or the generic level descriptors for the question
- the specific skills defined in the mark scheme or in the generic level descriptors for the question
- the standard of response required by a candidate as exemplified by the standardisation scripts.

GENERIC MARKING PRINCIPLE 2:

Marks awarded are always **whole marks** (not half marks, or other fractions).

GENERIC MARKING PRINCIPLE 3:

Marks must be awarded **positively**:

- marks are awarded for correct/valid answers, as defined in the mark scheme. However, credit is given for valid answers which go beyond the scope of the syllabus and mark scheme, referring to your Team Leader as appropriate
- marks are awarded when candidates clearly demonstrate what they know and can do
- marks are not deducted for errors
- marks are not deducted for omissions
- answers should only be judged on the quality of spelling, punctuation and grammar when these features are specifically assessed by the question as indicated by the mark scheme. The meaning, however, should be unambiguous.

GENERIC MARKING PRINCIPLE 4:

Rules must be applied consistently e.g. in situations where candidates have not followed instructions or in the application of generic level descriptors.

GENERIC MARKING PRINCIPLE 5:

Marks should be awarded using the full range of marks defined in the mark scheme for the question (however; the use of the full mark range may be limited according to the quality of the candidate responses seen).

GENERIC MARKING PRINCIPLE 6:

Marks awarded are based solely on the requirements as defined in the mark scheme. Marks should not be awarded with grade thresholds or grade descriptors in mind.

Question	Answer		Marks
1	Electrical plug: injection or compression moulding Guttering: extrusion Sandwich container: vacuum forming, blow moulding	1 1 1	3

Question	Answer		Marks
2	**A** scriber, marker pen, oddleg calipers	1	3
	B centre or dot punch	1	
	C dividers	1	

Question	Answer		Marks
3	Wall-mounted saves space, can be operated with one hand, cannot be moved about 2×1		2

Question	Answer		Marks
4(a)	To remove the majority of moisture in a board To minimise future problems relating to shrinkage and expansion	1 1	2
4(b)	Open air or natural seasoning		1

Question	Answer		Marks
5	Clamping device shown gripping above and below machine table Use of sacrificial board **under** and on **top** of acrylic	1 2×1	3

Question	Answer		Marks
6	Use of scrap wood clamped to the edge/s to provide support so that the plane can travel across the entire end grain without splitting occurring		2

Question	Answer	Marks
7(a)	oak	1
7(b)	pine	1

Question	Answer		Marks
8	Strengthening requires: use of a single brace [flat strip] joined to the tube, or a triangular shaped gusset joined to the tube Method of joining: soldering, brazing, welding Technical accuracy	1 1 1	3

Question	Answer	Marks
9(a)	Knurling	1
9(b)	To provide additional grip	1

Question	Answer		Marks
10	Laminated table cheaper: fewer constructions, quicker manufacture Fabricated table: less material used, expensive moulds not required, simple constructions	2×1 2×1	2

Question	Answer		Marks
11(a)	Stable, hardwearing, water resistant	2×1	2
11(b)	Tough, attractive, range of colours, fairly quick process, even application resists corrosion	2×1	2
11(c)	Use of dowels, screws or corner blocks to join **sides** together Use of screws to join **base** to underneath sides	0–2 0–2	4
11(d)(i)	Join at **X**: by means of **either** an 'insert' **or** an additional tube over existing tube Practical method shown Added details	 0–2 0–2	4
11(d)(ii)	Join at **Y**: by means of disc insert in [right hand] tube with threaded hole Screw or bolt through [left hand] tube into threaded hole	0–2 0–2	4
11(e)	Use of screws, nuts and bolts for quick removal Use of small 'bracket' or 'clips' shaped over round tube, joined permanently to tube or temporarily Technical accuracy	1 0–2 0–1	4
11(f)	650–700 length × 325–350 width × 70–80 depth	3×1	3
11(g)	Answers should relate to the reusable property of manufactured board or that some are made from waste or recycled materials Mild steel can be disassembled, melted down and reused	1 1	2

Question	Answer	Marks
12(a)	Stable, stronger than 6 mm solid wood, can be worked without danger of splitting, fairly lightweight 2×1	2
12(b)	Stage 1: pencil, compass, template 1 Stage 2: drill, variety of suitable hand and machine saws, router 1 Stage 3: files, glasspaper 1	3
12(c)	Does not need clamping for hours, immediate bonding, quick 2×1	2
12(d)	Saw cut: to provide space for the glue otherwise it would be forced out 1 Chamfer: to provide ease of entry 1	2
12(e)	Marking out: chinagraph pencil, marker pen, scriber, steel rule 1 Cutting out: use of coping saw, tenon saw, Hegner, scroll saws 0–2 Curved shape: use of oven, strip heater, hot air gun 1 Use of former and method of retention 1	5
12(f)	Appropriately named specific material 1 Design of rotor blade 1 Method of fitting onto dowel allowing for rotation 0–2 2 important sizes 0–2	6
12(g)	3 ways include: moving parts, curved/rounded edges, appropriate size, easy to hold, safe materials 3×1	3
12(h)	Environmentally friendly: some boards can be recycled or use recycled materials. Boards are made from sustainable materials	2

Question	Answer		Marks
13(a)	Permanent construction: dowel, mortise and tenon, biscuit named Quality of sketch dependent on technical accuracy, proportion, orientation	1 0–3	4
13(b)(i)	At least 2 cramps shown across the 'ladder' Award 1 mark for 1 cramp only		2
13(b)(ii)	Sash, speed, 'F' cramps/clamps		1
13(b)(iii)	Suitable adhesive: PVA, synthetic resin		1
13(b)(iv)	2 checks: squareness using try square or winding strips/diagonals Is the ladder flat on the cramps, removal of surplus glue	2×1	2
13(c)(i)	Polystyrene, acrylic, ABS		1
13(c)(ii)	Former must show the draft angle rounded corners 'mirroring' the plant pot	1 1	2
13(c)(iii)	Award 0–4 for specific stages: Place mould in machine [on platen] Clamp plastic in place Bring heater across to soften plastic Check flexibility of plastic Bring up mould into soft plastic Turn pump on to remove air Lower mould [on platen] and leave to cool Award 0–2 for technical accuracy of sketches	0–4 0–2	6
13(d)	Practical idea: some form of 'hook' or bracket or clip over rung Appropriate material/s Appropriate construction/s	0–2 1 1	4
13(e)	Modification: some form of 'cap' or cover, material with added friction	0–2	2

Cambridge IGCSE™

DESIGN AND TECHNOLOGY **0445/32**

Paper 3 Resistant Materials **May/June 2020**

MARK SCHEME

Maximum Mark: 50

Published

Students did not sit exam papers in the June 2020 series due to the Covid-19 global pandemic.

This mark scheme is published to support teachers and students and should be read together with the question paper. It shows the requirements of the exam. The answer column of the mark scheme shows the proposed basis on which Examiners would award marks for this exam. Where appropriate, this column also provides the most likely acceptable alternative responses expected from students. Examiners usually review the mark scheme after they have seen student responses and update the mark scheme if appropriate. In the June series, Examiners were unable to consider the acceptability of alternative responses, as there were no student responses to consider.

Mark schemes should usually be read together with the Principal Examiner Report for Teachers. However, because students did not sit exam papers, there is no Principal Examiner Report for Teachers for the June 2020 series.

Cambridge International will not enter into discussions about these mark schemes.

Cambridge International is publishing the mark schemes for the June 2020 series for most Cambridge IGCSE™ and Cambridge International A & AS Level components, and some Cambridge O Level components.

This document consists of **6** printed pages.

© UCLES 2020 **[Turn over**

0445/32 Cambridge IGCSE – Mark Scheme May/June 2020
PUBLISHED

Generic Marking Principles

These general marking principles must be applied by all examiners when marking candidate answers. They should be applied alongside the specific content of the mark scheme or generic level descriptors for a question. Each question paper and mark scheme will also comply with these marking principles.

GENERIC MARKING PRINCIPLE 1:

Marks must be awarded in line with:

- the specific content of the mark scheme or the generic level descriptors for the question
- the specific skills defined in the mark scheme or in the generic level descriptors for the question
- the standard of response required by a candidate as exemplified by the standardisation scripts.

GENERIC MARKING PRINCIPLE 2:

Marks awarded are always **whole marks** (not half marks, or other fractions).

GENERIC MARKING PRINCIPLE 3:

Marks must be awarded **positively**:

- marks are awarded for correct/valid answers, as defined in the mark scheme. However, credit is given for valid answers which go beyond the scope of the syllabus and mark scheme, referring to your Team Leader as appropriate
- marks are awarded when candidates clearly demonstrate what they know and can do
- marks are not deducted for errors
- marks are not deducted for omissions
- answers should only be judged on the quality of spelling, punctuation and grammar when these features are specifically assessed by the question as indicated by the mark scheme. The meaning, however, should be unambiguous.

GENERIC MARKING PRINCIPLE 4:

Rules must be applied consistently e.g. in situations where candidates have not followed instructions or in the application of generic level descriptors.

GENERIC MARKING PRINCIPLE 5:

Marks should be awarded using the full range of marks defined in the mark scheme for the question (however; the use of the full mark range may be limited according to the quality of the candidate responses seen).

GENERIC MARKING PRINCIPLE 6:

Marks awarded are based solely on the requirements as defined in the mark scheme. Marks should not be awarded with grade thresholds or grade descriptors in mind.

Question	Answer		Marks
1	Dividers	1	3
	Centre / dot punch	1	
	Odd legs/ odd leg calipers/ Jenny[s] calipers.	1	

Question	Answer		Marks
2	Dovetail, finger [comb], dowel, lapped, half-lapped		3
	Suitable joint recognised	1	
	Correct orientation [as per Fig. 2.1]	1	
	Good proportion/accuracy	1	

Question	Answer		Marks
3	Beech	1	3
	Stainless steel, mild steel, aluminium, brass	1	
	Melamine	1	

Question	Answer		Marks
4	Marking out	1	3
	Cutting to length	1	
	Method of joining	1	

Question	Answer		Marks
5	Method of locating end against underside of table	1	2
	Method of fixing must be removeable	1	

Question	Answer		Marks
6	3 points include: comfortable to hold, easy to operate/open can, safe to use, easy to clean, durable materials, strong constructions 3×1		3

Question	Answer		Marks
7	2 main processes: drill hole	1	2
	file to shape	1	

Question	Answer		Marks
8(a)	Tough, durable, attractive, resists corrosion, evenly applied	1	1
8(b)	When cut/chipped can be difficult to repair		1

Question	Answer	Marks
9	Thermochromic	1

Question	Answer	Marks
10	Use of pegs, dowels 1 Ease of fitting 1 Attractive/practical for product 1	3

Question	Answer	Marks
11(a)	Male former 1 Female former 1 Veneers glued together 1 Clamping method 1	4
11(b)	Modification should retain the keys: use of grooves or 'stopped' end 0–2	2
11(c)	Additional plate/bracket added to front and back 2×1 Method of pivoting, e.g. use of pin or peg 1 Named materials 1	4
11(d)(i)	Teak oil, Danish oil, white/French polish, lacquer, wax 2×1	2
11(d)(ii)	2 stages: glasspaper, damp cloth to wipe off dust, different grades of glasspaper 2×1	2
11(e)(i)	Use of oven to soften acrylic 1 Use of a former 1 Method of retention 1	3
11(e)(ii)	Acrylic [Tensol] cement named 1 Method of application 1	2
11(e)(iii)	Award any 3: use of scraper, wet and dry [silicon carbide] paper, 2 different grades, polishing mop/ buffing wheel polishing compound 3×1	3
11(f)	Explanation: Timber can be 'managed' and trees replanted, low carbon footprint, wood decomposes Plastic is a finite resource	3

Question	Answer	Marks
12(a)	Sketches to show: tube held in vice 1 hacksaw to cut tube 1 use of files to make edges flat 1 correctly named tools and equipment 1	4

Question	Answer		Marks
12(b)	emery cloth used to clean joint tube positioned on firebricks, set up to produce max. heat flux used to prevent oxidisation and allow spelter to flow blow torch used to heat up tube to reqd. temperature brazing rod heated and melted into joint	1 1 1 1 1	5
12(c)	Steel 'plate' inserted into end of tube or additional nut Hole drilled and threaded in 'plate'	1 1	2
12(d)	Square handle made comfortable: Accept any practical modification Details of materials	1 1	2
12(e)	Former shows draft angle/'sloping' sides Rounded edges to match tray shape	1 1	2
12(f)	2 benefits: fast process, reusable former, repetitive accuracy	2 × 1	2
12(g)	Method of support: extra 'rails' and/or modified 'lipping' shape Ease of removal Appropriate materials and constructions used	0–2 1 1	4
12(h)	Metal: product could be disassembled, reused and/or recycled Plastic: is a finite/unsustainable material, difficult to recycle	0–2 0–2	4

Question	Answer		Marks
13(a)(i)	Suitable manufactured board: plywood, chipboard, blockboard, MDF.		1
13(a)(ii)	Reasons for manufactured board: stable, does not shrink, available in wide boards.	2 × 1	2
13(b)	700 long dependent upon the items for which the table is intended 400 high dependent upon anthropometrics, existing furniture	1 1	2
13(c)(i)	Smoothing, jack		1
13(c)(ii)	Leg shown in vice Angled slightly OR Use of bench stop Leg shown clearly against bench stop	1 1 1 1	2
13(d)(i)	Quicker than by hand, even finish possible, removal of stubborn marks easier	2 × 1	2
13(d)(ii)	Portable tool safety: no trailing leads, clear area below tool, set up of tool correctly before use, electrical safety in use [e.g. unplugging when changing blades etc.]	2 × 1	2

Question	Answer		Marks
13(d)(iii)	2 benefits: tough, heat, stain and water resistant, attractive	2 × 1	2
13(e)(i)	Accurate drawing of hinge Correct position	0–2 1	3
13(e)(ii)	Suitable hinge: butt, back flap, flush named	1	1
13(e)(iii)	Suitable material: steel or brass	1	1
13(f)	'Locking' method: some form of 'stay', rods and holes. Appropriate materials Details of fittings used	0–3 1 0–2	6

Printed in Great Britain
by Amazon